CONTENTS

CONTENTS

The *Right* CHEMISTRY

What it's all for!

Jeffrey Hancock

Hodder & Stoughton

A MEMBER OF THE HODDER HEADLINE GROUP

Acknowledgements

I should like to thank the following, who readily responded to requests for information, often taking much time and trouble to do so:

Ms Caroline Birrane	Cussons (International) Ltd, Stockport
Dr R K Bramley	Forensic Science Service, Birmingham
Dr Paul Davie	Oxford Molecular, Oxford Science Park
Mr D S Josty	Lion Laboratories plc, Barry, South Glamorgan
Dr W J King	Dart Sensors Ltd, Totnes, Devon
Ms Julia Milner	Boots, Nottingham
Mr Colin Waldron	Mopps Hairdressers, Pershore

In addition I should like to thank

Hugh Wright, Chief Master, King Edward's School, Birmingham, for the award of a sabbatical term, during which part of this was written.

The staff of the libraries of the University of Birmingham, the Barnes Medical School and the Department of Chemical Engineering at Birmingham University, for their willing help.

Ted Lister who read much of it and made many helpful suggestions.

The staff at Hodder, especially Julia Morris and Charlotte Litt, for their forebearance and advice.

Most of all I would like to thank Miriam, who put up with my crabbiness and absences, and encouraged me all the time.

Jeff Hancock, 1999

Orders: please contact Bookpoint Ltd, 78 Milton Park, Abingdon, Oxon OX14 4TD. Telephone: (44) 01235 827720, Fax: (44) 01235 400454. Lines are open from 9.00–6.00, Monday to Saturday, with a 24 hour message answering service. Email address: orders@bookpoint.co.uk

British Library Cataloguing in Publication Data
A catalogue record for this title is available from The British Library

ISBN 0 340 70194 3

First published 1999
Impression number 10 9 8 7 6 5 4 3 2 1
Year   2005 2004 2003 2002 2001 2000 1999

Cover illustration from Sarah Jones, Debut Art.
Typeset by Wearset, Boldon, Tyne and Wear.
Printed in Great Britain for Hodder & Stoughton Educational, a division of Hodder Headline Plc, 338 Euston Road, London NW1 3BH by JW Arrowsmith Ltd, Bristol.

Preface

Well, what *is* it for? As chemistry is much more hidden, there is a tendency to think that science is physics, biology and medicine. We hear about gene therapy, we see the little robot trundling about on the surface of Mars, we meet people who have had life-saving keyhole surgery and nowhere, it seems, can we see what chemistry is about or what its contribution is to life and knowledge. But science is a seamless whole and each advance rests on a thousand others, many of them chemical. And much of the current exciting and *revolutionary* work is being done by chemists.

So what is chemistry about? It seems to me that like every scientific endeavour, chemistry is about two things. To start with, it is part of the unique system called science by which we come to understand this wonderful universe and everything in it, from archaeology to other planets, from the effect of drugs to the colour of precious stones. And secondly, it enables us to make life better and more interesting: to grow food, prevent or cure disease, develop new materials, explore space.

That's what this little book is about. I have tried to take the chemistry that we meet at school and link it to the chemistry that surrounds us. So you will find sections on current research, sections on industrial chemistry, sections on the development of drugs, even one or two sections on odd little things you might not have thought were chemistry at all. Some of them discuss work done in the last year or two and they will necessarily be incomplete.

I have tried to place each section in the context of the most relevant piece of basic theory. So, for example, I have placed the discussion of morphine in the context of shapes of molecules, since morphine only works because it is of the right shape to fit a particular receptor in the brain. But it also depends critically on the interactions with the receptor, so I could equally well have put it in the section on forces between molecules. For this reason there is an index.

Who will read the book? I started on it because I wanted extra material to spice up my teaching, so I assumed at first that teachers would use it. But as I have written it I have come to hope that students might read it too. To be sure, I have not explained the sorts of things that are met in standard chemistry courses: I haven't explained what a phase diagram is, for example, or basic equilibrium theory. But if you want to know about that, you can go to any standard chemistry text and look it up there. And since this isn't a textbook, it doesn't matter if you only dip into it, or glance at it, so long as you find it interesting.

I have listed some sources of further information, with an indication of how difficult it is likely to be: 1) for the general reader, 2) for someone studying A level, perhaps and 3) for advanced research material. But don't be put off! You can dip into any book, just get the basic idea and skip the hard bits. (I did!) Some of the books may be difficult to get hold of, though big libraries will have them, and your local library will be able to get them on loan. The Internet will also be a useful place to look for information, especially for the current stuff, and rather than give specific addresses (which may change) I have suggested possible words to use for a search.

ALCOHOLS

Alcohols contain the polar −OH group, which means that they can hydrogen bond. Those with shorter chains are soluble in water. The hydrocarbon chain, however, helps them dissolve in non-polar solvents. Primary alcohols are readily oxidised, first to the corresponding aldehyde, then to the acid.

Drinking ethanol

The absorption of ethanol from the stomach and gut is affected by the presence of food. If the alcohol is drunk with a meal, it is absorbed more slowly and 10–20% of it will not be absorbed at all. And the presence of the alcohol affects the rate of stomach emptying – 12% alcohol (wine, for example) accelerates it, whereas 40% alcohol solutions (such as whisky) slow it down.

The alcohol dissolves in the blood and is carried around the body, crossing rapidly into the brain. Figure 1.1 shows the nmr spectrum of ethanol and of the grey matter of the brains of volunteers 12 and 61 minutes after drinking the equivalent of three or four pints of beer. (Obtaining a spectrum of the brain is quite tricky; it involves difficult nmr techniques, in particular to remove the absorption due to water. As the spectrum shows, the results are quite complex. The letters stand for various brain chemicals: Glu is glutamic acid, Cr, creatine and so on.) Interestingly, the triplet from the CH_3- group of the ethanol is clearly visible at about 1.2 ppm, although the quartet at about 3.7 is lost in general noise.

This enables us to determine the concentration of ethanol in the brain. In this volunteer, at least, when his blood alcohol level had reached around 0.02 mol dm^{-3}, the concentration in the brain was about 0.007 mol dm^{-3}.

Determination of the amount of ethanol someone has drunk is now a routine procedure, done at the roadside to an accuracy of better than 10%. There are various machines on the market for doing this. They all measure the amount of ethanol in the breath, working on the principle that the ratio of the ethanol concentrations in blood and breath is 2300 at body temperature, so that a blood concentration of 80 mg/100 cm^3 of blood is equivalent to 35 μg per 100 cm^3 of breath. They work by utilising the ready oxidation of an alcohol, carried out in a small fuel cell. The breath sample is passed over a platinum anode and atmospheric

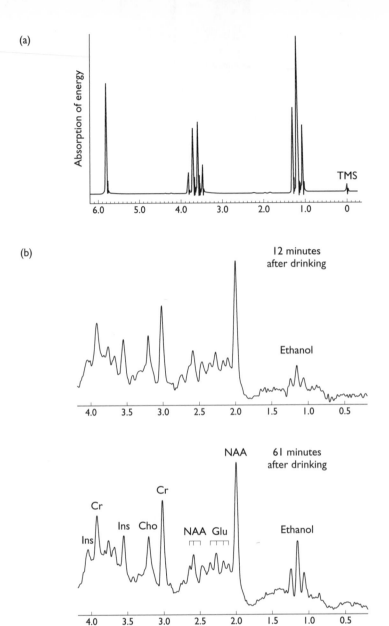

Figure 1.1 Proton nmr spectra of a) ethanol containing a trace of acid and b) brain grey matter

oxygen is supplied to the cathode. Oxidation of the ethanol at the anode produces an EMF proportional to the alcohol concentration. Much work has been done on the effects of other substances: carbon monoxide in the breath of smokers, or inhaled solvents if the person had been spraying paint, perhaps. It is clear that there are a few substances which can interfere with the test (and therefore invalidate the results); if there is any doubt, a more sophisticated machine is available, which also checks the infra red absorption due to the ethanol $C-H$ stretch at 2890 cm^{-1}.

The peak ethanol concentration in the blood and the brain is reached after 1–2 hours, and thereafter begins to decline, in a zero order process (see page 130). It seems that there are at least two, possibly three, routes of metabolism in the body, but the major one occurs in the liver, catalysed by the enzyme alcohol dehydrogenase (ADH). This enzyme oxidises ethanol to ethanal, at the same time reducing the cofactor NAD to reduced NAD, given the symbol NADH.

This NADH is an important molecule, required by other metabolic processes in the liver. It is usually made in the liver by oxidation of fatty acids; this is coupled to NAD reduction, so as the acids are oxidised, the NADH is produced. If there is ethanol present, NADH can be made available by ethanol oxidation instead. As a result, the fatty acids are not oxidised so they build up in the liver. This causes inflammation and is ultimately followed by irreversible liver damage.

There are two different types of alcohol dehydrogenase, one much faster than the other; the fast type is more common in Orientals. Consequently, there is a sudden build-up of ethanal in the body as the enzyme oxidises the alcohol faster than the aldehyde dehydrogenase can cope with the ethanal produced (see Figure 1.2). Individuals with this particular inheritance find themselves flushing after drinking quite a small amount of alcohol.

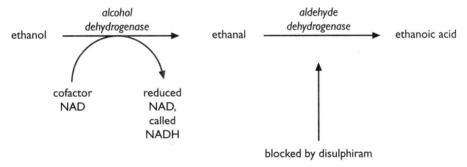

Figure 1.2 Alcohol breakdown

These two enzymes form the basis for a drug treatment for people with an alcohol problem. The drug disulphiram blocks the aldehyde dehydrogenase. Taken by itself the drug has no noticeable effect, but alcohol consumption produces a rapid build-up of large amounts of ethanal, because its breakdown has been stopped by the disulphiram. Ethanal in quantity has some nasty effects: flushing, a racing pulse, hyperventilation, nausea and even panic. This tends to discourage the patient from drinking alcohol. (Or they might just forget to take the disulphiram.)

There is another alcohol dehydrogenase in the retina of the eye, whose function is to convert retinol to retinal (see page 117) as part of the visual process. Unfortunately, this system will also cope with other alcohols, including ethanol and methanol. The latter is a disaster, because the oxidation product, methanal, is *extremely* damaging. Drinking methanol causes methanal to be formed in the retina. As little as 10 g of methanol can result in blindness. Methanol is used as a solvent and is added to methylated spirits to make them undrinkable, but accidental poisoning is quite common. Treatment involves administration of large doses of ethanol, which competes for the alcohol dehydrogenases and thus slows down oxidation of the methanol. Being water soluble, the methanol is eventually eliminated in the urine, a process helped by the well-known diuretic properties of ethanol. Then you have to treat the hangover!

It is now known that ethanol exerts its intoxicating and sedative effects by interfering with GABA receptors in the brain. GABA – γ-aminobutyric acid, or more correctly, 4-aminobutanoic acid, $H_2NCH_2CH_2CH_2COOH$ – is a neurotransmitter, acting to reduce the firing of brain neurones. All the tranquilliser and antianxiety drugs, such as the diazepines Librium and Valium, and sedatives like the barbiturates, act on the GABA receptor. This is a protein which alters its shape when stimulated by raised levels of GABA, opening a channel and allowing chloride ions to flood into the nerve cell and make it less ready to fire (Figure 1.3).

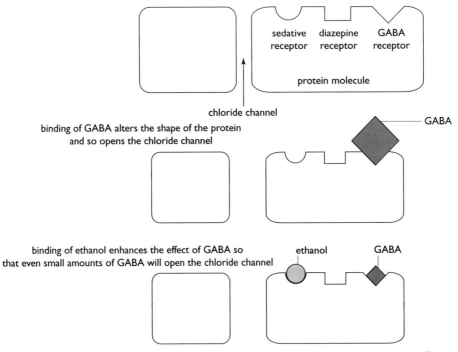

Figure 1.3

Also on this protein, close to but not identical to the GABA binding site, is a site where the benzodiazepines can bind, and another for the sedatives like the barbiturates and alcohol. Binding of either of these classes of compound causes the protein to become more sensitive to GABA, so that lower levels of GABA can open the chloride channel and have the same inhibitory effect on the cell. Alcohol seems also to bind to the sedative site, but very weakly. This is why we need to take such huge quantities of it to achieve an effect: whereas barbiturates are effective at 10^{-5} or 10^{-6} moles per kg of body weight, 3 pints corresponds to about 10^{-2} moles of ethanol per kg in an adult man – at least a thousand times as much. This also explains why it is dangerous to take alcohol with barbiturates or tranquillisers; they either act on the same receptors or on sites close by, and the effect of the one may increase that of the other.

Further reading

Buzz, Stephen Braun, Oxford University Press, 1996 (1) is a delightful account of the effects of alcohol and caffeine.

Drugs and the Brain, S H Snyder, Scientific American Books, 1986 (1)

Any pharmacology textbook will discuss this: that by H P Rang and M M Dale, Churchill Livingstone, 2nd edn 1991, is good (2)

Antifreeze

The density of liquid water at 0°C is 0.999 g cm^{-3}; that of ice is 0.917 g cm^{-3}, so when water freezes, it expands by about 9%. This expansion will break open any container holding it. If the container is the cylinder block of a car engine, expansion is disastrous, so it is customary to add a liquid which will lower the freezing point of the water and thus keep it liquid.

The depression of the freezing point of any liquid by an added solute is known as a colligative property, one which depends on the concentration of solute. It is found that one mole of any solute in one kg of water lowers its freezing point by 1.86°C. To lower the freezing point to, say, -15°C, about $\frac{15}{1.86}$ or 8.06 moles of solute per kg of water would be required. Although the theory is less accurate for a solution so concentrated, this answer is about right. Early antifreezes used methanol, which would need 257.9 g in 1 kg of water. Antifreezes have an additional bonus: because their molecular shape disrupts the ice lattice, any ice that does form tends to be slushy and soft, and so is unlikely to break radiators or engine blocks. Unfortunately, methanol boils at 65°C, so at the running temperature of the engine it tends to evaporate. One of the higher alcohols would have a greater boiling point, of course, but would not be soluble enough in water (and would be very much more costly). Ethane-1,2-diol is cheap (it is readily made from ethene), has a boiling point of 198°C and because of the two $-$OH groups is completely soluble in water. Unfortunately (every silver lining has a cloud), to reach a concentration of 8.06 mol per kg, a much higher mass is needed: 8.06×62.1 g or 500.5 g.

There is a more serious problem still, however. Ethane-1,2-diol tastes sweet (see page 182), so it is sometimes drunk by mistake, especially by children or animals. In addition, ethane-1,2-diol is acted upon by the same enzyme systems that oxidise ethanol (especially liver alcohol dehydrogenase, LADH), first to the aldehyde, then to the acid:

$$CH_2OH-CH_2OH \rightarrow CHO-CHO \rightarrow COOH-COOH$$

The product, ethanedioic acid, is very toxic indeed, because it reacts with calcium ions in the body to form insoluble calcium ethanedioate. Not only does this remove calcium ions from solution in body fluids (calcium ions play a vital role in many body processes), but it also produces crystals of calcium ethanedioate in the blood stream, interrupting the blood supply to brain, heart, lungs and – worst of all – the kidneys. If this cannot be prevented, the victim dies of kidney failure. As little as 1 g of ethanedioic acid can be fatal. Poisoning by ethane-1,2-diol is treated in the same way as methanol poisoning, by administering ethanol to prevent oxidation to the acid. Ethanol binds to LADH about 100 times more strongly than ethane-1,2-diol, so if the patient can be kept gently drunk, the ethanol will block the LADH. As a result, the ethane-1,2-diol is not oxidised and is eliminated from the body unchanged.

Safer antifreezes have been developed recently, using propane-1,2-diol. Not only is a larger mass of this required to get the same concentration in mole per kg, however, but it is also more expensive.

ALUMINIUM

Aluminium's position in the periodic table is intriguing: it sits on the boundary between metals and non-metals. For that reason, its chemistry is quite complex. A few of the main features are listed below.

- The cation has a high charge and small radius so is highly polarising which results in the aqueous cation being strongly hydrolysed. Solutions are therefore acidic.

- The various species formed in the hydrolysis reactions have differing charges, so the solubility of the element varies according to the pH of the solution.

- It is a 'hard' Lewis acid, so will form complexes with O- and N-containing ligands, especially polydentate ligands.

- It is one of the relatively few elements of the first 30 not to have a biological role and indeed is seriously toxic.

Aluminium poisoning

In the early days of dialysis treatment for kidney failure, it was found that numbers of patients were developing a fatal dementia. This was eventually traced back to the presence of aluminium in the dialysis solution; the patients absorbed some of the aluminium from the fluid and because their kidneys weren't working, they were then unable to excrete it. The problem was solved when aluminium levels in the dialysis liquids were reduced to zero, but it focused attention on an element which up until then had been assumed to be entirely harmless.

Second only to oxygen and silicon, aluminium is the most abundant metal in the Earth's crust, so its complete absence of any biological function is intriguing (see page 166). The main reason for this must surely be its solubility behaviour. The Al^{3+} cation undergoes hydrolysis in aqueous solution, involving equilibria such as:

$$[Al(H_2O)_6]^{3+} \rightleftharpoons [Al(H_2O)_5(OH)]^{2+} + H^+$$

and

$$[Al(H_2O)_5(OH)]^{2+} \rightleftharpoons [Al(H_2O)_4(OH)_2]^+ + H^+$$

with the result that the solution of an aluminium salt is markedly acidic. If the solution is made less acidic, these equilibria are shifted to the right, and eventually $Al(H_2O)_3(OH)_3$ is formed; because it is uncharged, it is much less soluble. Increase

7

of the pH still further produces species such as $[Al(H_2O)_2(OH)_4]^-$, which is soluble, and further replacement of the water ligands by OH^- leads ultimately to $[Al(OH)_6]^{3-}$. The solubility of the aluminium therefore varies with pH as shown in Figure 2.1.

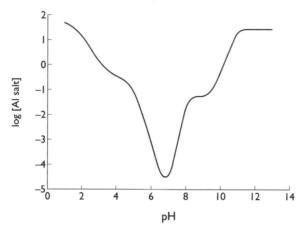

Figure 2.1 The variation in solubility of aluminium salts with pH

At the physiological pH of 7.4, therefore, aluminium salts are as insoluble as possible. This is presumably the reason why they have no biological role, and the organism uses other ions instead.

Unfortunately, the aluminium ion can replace these other ions, often being absorbed more strongly than the original. For example, their higher charge and smaller size mean that aluminium ions complex 10^5 times more strongly with the three phosphate groups of ATP than magnesium does. Since Mg^{2+} is implicated in many enzymes catalysing the reactions of ATP, this is potentially very serious. And although Al^{3+} is a little smaller than Fe^{3+} (radius 0.053 nm compared with 0.064 nm) the two ions are similar enough for mistakes to be made. In particular, Al^{3+} may become bound to transferrin, the Fe^{3+} transport protein in the body. Since the Al^{3+} ion is smaller than Fe^{3+}, we should expect it to complex with transferrin more strongly. This looks potentially disastrous. Fortunately two factors work in our favour: ligand exchange reactions (with other chelating ligands, such as citrate, for example) are faster for Al^{3+} than Fe^{3+}, so aluminium can be excreted more readily. Secondly, the sheer business of absorbing the ions from food in the first place (in other words, getting it across the stomach wall) seems to be harder for Al^{3+} than for Fe^{3+}. Because it is so serious if Al^{3+} ions get in, the body takes great care to keep them out.

Hot upon the heels of the dialysis dementias mentioned previously came the observation that the brains of people who had died with Alzheimer's disease – also a dementia – contained characteristic structures, called neurofibrillary tangles, and that these structures contained aluminium. Indeed, injection of experimental animals with aluminium solutions induced the formation of these tangles, and it seemed that people living in regions with more aluminium in the water supply had a slightly higher incidence of the disease. Could Alzheimer's disease be directly caused by aluminium? Dopamine (Figure 2.2) and other neurotransmitters have

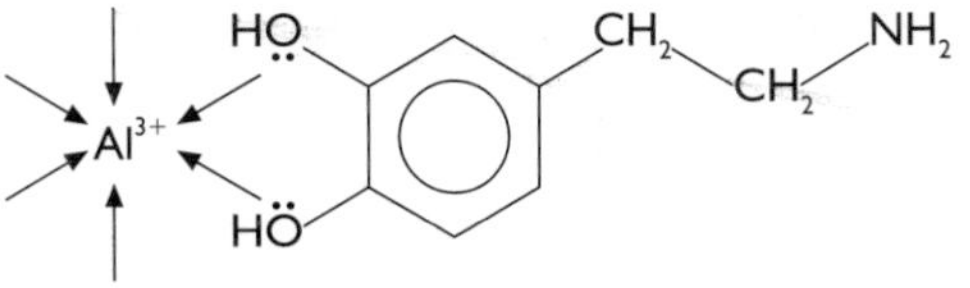

Figure 2.2 Dopamine, showing how it may complex with an aluminium ion

exactly the right structure to function as bidentate ligands to a cation such as aluminium: do the aluminium ions form complexes with dopamine in the brain? In addition, Alzheimer's patients have lower transferrin activity, perhaps caused by co-ordination by Al^{3+}. More to the point, prolonged treatment with desferrioxamine (see page 210) has been shown to slow down or even reverse the progress of the disease. Desferrioxamine is the treatment for iron poisoning, which acts by chelating the Fe^{3+} ions: perhaps it also acts to remove Al^{3+} from the body.

Current opinion holds that aluminium is probably not a direct cause of dementia. Nor, it is said, is there any need for us to replace our aluminium cookware with stainless steel. After all, tea leaves concentrate aluminium, there is quite a lot in beer, and some indigestion remedies contain grams of the stuff. It seems that although aluminium is damaging once it gets into the brain, our defences are generally adequate to prevent this.

The effects of Al^{3+} in the rest of the natural world, however, are unambiguous and serious. Aluminium occurs everywhere as aluminosilicates and these are very vulnerable to acidity. For example, kaolinite can react as shown below:

$$Al_2Si_2O_5(OH)_4(s) + 6H^+(aq) \rightleftharpoons 2Al^{3+}(aq) + 2SiO_2(s) + 5H_2O(l)$$

If we neglect the various hydrolysis equilibria of the aqueous Al^{3+} ion, the equilibrium constant, K, is given by

$$K = \frac{[Al^{3+}]^2}{[H^+]^6}$$

Because the hydrogen ion concentration is raised to the sixth power, this equilibrium is *very* sensitive to acidity. At pH 6, the concentration of Al^{3+} ions is about 10^{-10} mol dm^{-3}, but if the pH drops to 4, the Al^{3+} concentration rises to about 10^{-3} mol dm^{-3}. This is just one sample aluminosilicate, but it is clear that rain which has a pH much below 5 may cause the release of aluminium ions. Sulphur dioxide and nitrogen oxides cause rainfall over south-east England to have an average pH of around 4.5, and in December 1982, Los Angeles recorded a fog with pH *1.7*.

The effects of aqueous Al^{3+} ions are serious. Fish are particularly vulnerable. Their gills are buffered to around pH 7, so any aluminium in solution will tend to precipitate out (see Figure 2.1). This will result in clogging of the gill surfaces and the fish suffocates. The ill effects of aluminium ions on plants arise because they take the place of Mg^{2+} or Ca^{2+} ions and as a result of the higher charge and smaller size of the aluminium ion, it will be more stable. In particular, Al^{3+} will inhibit Mg^{2+}-dependent enzymes very effectively.

There are only two remedies. The best is to reduce acidic emissions, a process requiring much subtle chemistry, and one under way in every developed country. A quicker but less satisfactory alternative for aquatic systems is to raise their pH. This has been done in Sweden by controlled addition of crushed limestone.

Further reading

For a discussion of acid rain, see any textbook on environmental chemistry, such as that by Colin Baird (2)

The biological effects of aluminium will be mentioned in most textbooks of bioinorganic chemistry; try **Bioinorganic Chemistry: Inorganic Elements in the Chemistry of Life**, Wolfgang Kaim and Brigitte Schwederski, John Wiley, 1991 (2)

There is an Alzheimer's disease research forum web site; search on 'alzheimer'.

3

AMINES

It might seem perverse that I have put the section on surfactants here, under amines. After all, amines have a thousand other uses, and many surfactants are not amine derivatives. But quaternary nitrogen compounds have a massive use, not only in cleansing products and fabric softeners, but also in heavy industry, for example as emulsifiers of drilling mud in oilfield exploration.

Shampoos

Hair is extraordinary stuff. The human head may have as many as 150 000 hair follicles, the hair growing at a rate of about 1 cm a month. This growing phase lasts for some three to four years in men and up to six years in women, at the end of which the follicle rests for about six months, then sheds the hair and starts all over again. Each hair can support about 80 g, so to pick up a 70 kg man by his hair would need only 875 hairs (provided they didn't pull out!).

The follicles are deep pits in the skin which are well supplied with nutrients, enabling rapid cell multiplication to occur. These cells are then pushed upwards by those following on behind, and as they go they gradually fill up with the protein keratin, harden and die. By the time they emerge from the skin, the keratin chains have been aligned within a protein matrix and tangled together to form thin threads which are in turn twisted together. All these twisted fibres are embedded in a matrix of protein, and the whole thing is surrounded by multiple overlapping layers of flattened cells, rather like the tiles on a house roof. This circular sheath of 'tiles', the cuticle, is pressed against the core of the fibre as the hair emerges from the skin, forming a tight layer of protective plates around it.

There seem to be two main classes of keratins in hair. The central fibres are low in sulphur and have a mainly helical structure, held together by hydrogen bonding. Both the keratins of the cuticle, the outer covering of the hair, and those of the matrix surrounding the fibres in the central region are high in sulphur and their structure is controlled by $-S-S-$ bridges in cystine residues. There are more than twice as many acidic amino acids as basic ones, so at pH values close to neutrality, hair fibres will carry an excess negative charge.

Hair gets dirty in two ways. First by accumulation of body substances: the sebaceous glands of the scalp secrete an oily substance called sebum, skin cells die and cuticle cells become detached from hair fibres. To these must be added those substances we deliberately apply to the hair – sprays, conditioners and so on – and the dirt that floats in from the outside world. This accumulation of muck may eventually add up to 5% of the total hair mass. It makes the hair feel sticky and uncomfortable and it will ultimately begin to smell as the sebum is oxidised in air. So it has to be removed.

Washing hair requires the cleaning of around 10^5 hair fibres, and if the hair is 10–20 cm long, this means that a total area of 4–8 m^2 must be cleaned. Some task! Cleaning agents belong to the class of compounds called surfactants, the molecules of which have two parts: a non-polar part, which is essentially insoluble in water but which will mix well with grease or oil; and a charged or polar part, which will be water soluble. The non-polar part of the molecule dissolves into the grease, leaving the charged or polar portion on the outside, in contact with the water. Working up the lather with the fingers will tend to lift the grease off the hair, and more surfactant molecules will cluster round it, the polar heads helping to suspend it in the water (see Figure 3.1).

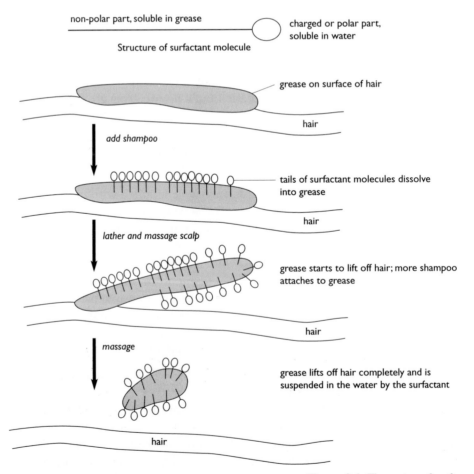

non-polar part, soluble in grease

charged or polar part, soluble in water

Structure of surfactant molecule

grease on surface of hair

hair

add shampoo

tails of surfactant molecules dissolve into grease

hair

lather and massage scalp

grease starts to lift off hair; more shampoo attaches to grease

hair

massage

grease lifts off hair completely and is suspended in the water by the surfactant

hair

Figure 3.1 The action of surfactants

The efficiency of the cleaning process will depend on the nature of the long non-polar chain and of the polar group at the head of the surfactant molecule. The cleaning strength or mildness of the shampoo will then depend on the precise mix of surfactants used.

The earliest surfactants were soaps, made by heating plant or animal fats with sodium hydroxide or carbonate: they are salts of long-chain carboxylic acids (see Figure 3.2a).

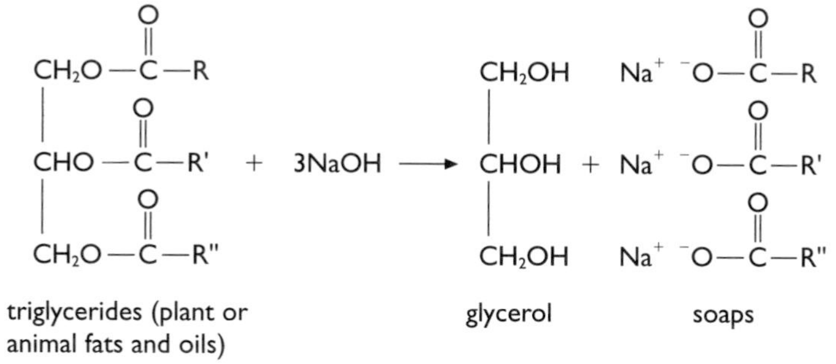

(a) Soap

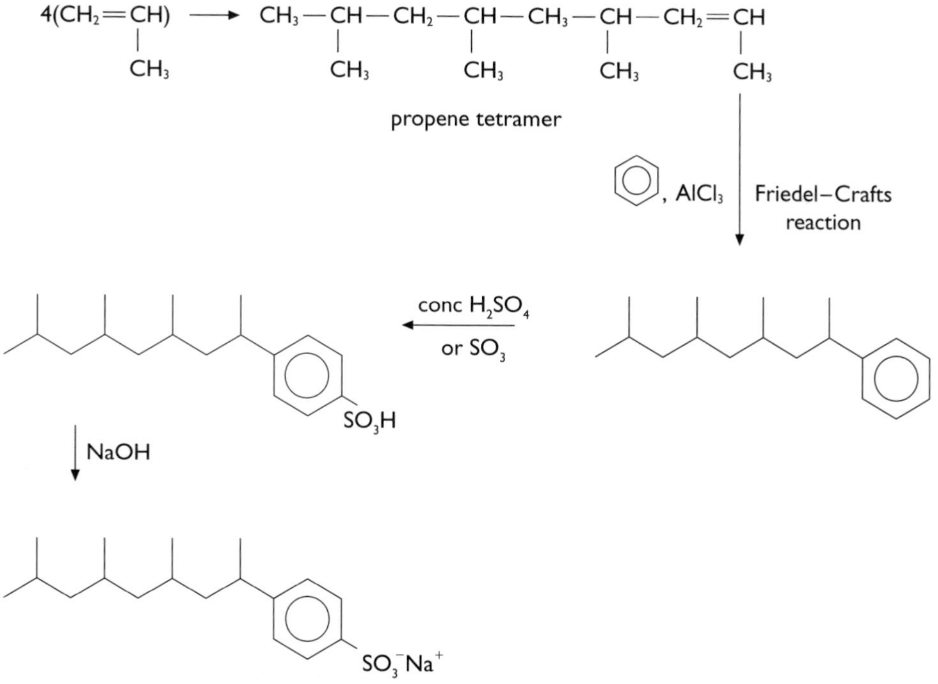

(b) Detergents

Figure 3.2 The structures of some surfactants

Unfortunately, the corresponding calcium and magnesium salts are insoluble in water, so in hard water areas, soaps react to form insoluble scum, wasting soap and making it more difficult to rinse articles clean. So soaps were replaced by detergents, such as the alkylbenzene sulphonates. The original molecules started from a propene tetramer, which was joined to a benzene ring by a Friedel–Crafts' reaction. Sulphonation and neutralisation of the sulphonic acid gave alkylbenzene sulphonates, or ABS, which were very effective detergents. Unfortunately, the branching in the side chain made it resistant to bacterial breakdown, so that the ABS left sewage treatment works almost completely unaffected, resulting in frothy rivers. Modern alkylbenzene sulphonates have linear chains and biodegrade much faster.

(a) Anionic

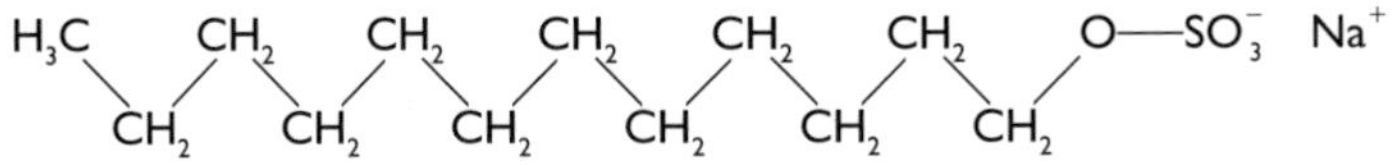

sodium lauryl sulphate

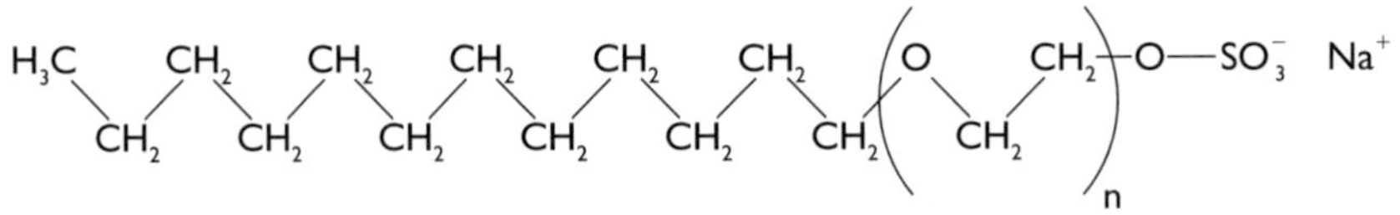

sodium laureth sulphate (n is between 1 and 4)

(b) Cationic

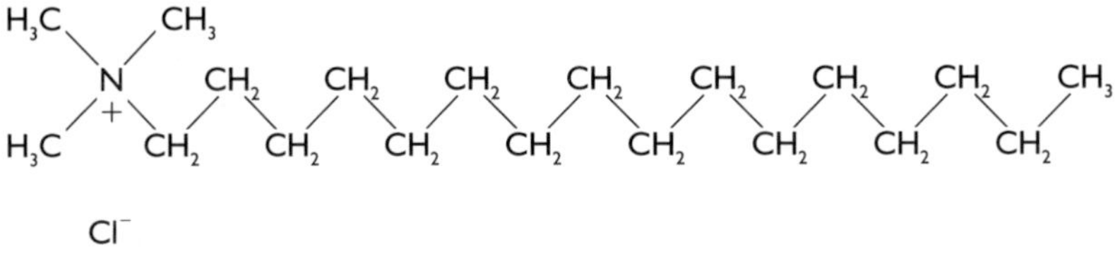

cetrimonium chloride

(c) Amphoteric

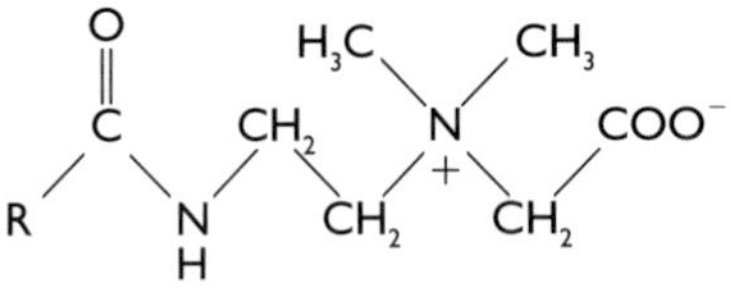

cocamidopropyl betaine

(R—CO—represents fatty acids derived from coconut oil)

(d) Non-ionic

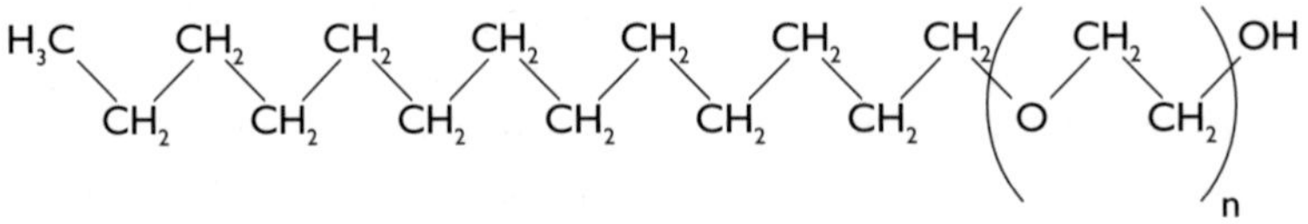

trideceth-12 (n averages 12)

Figure 3.3 Some surfactants used in shampoos

These very effective detergents are generally too fierce for use in shampoos. On the other hand, it may occasionally be necessary to use a strong shampoo to remove build-up. This sort of strong cleaner may contain surfactants similar in structure to the alkylbenzene sulphonates above (see Figure 3.3a). These are sulphates of long-chain alcohols, neutralised to form the salts. The alcohol concerned is most commonly lauryl alcohol, $C_{12}H_{25}OH$ (more correctly called dodecan-1-ol) as the sodium or ammonium salts. Along with the lauryl sulphates, the so-called lauryl ether sulphates (or laureth sulphates: see Figure 3.3a) are widely used. They are made by reacting dodecan-1-ol with epoxyethane prior to formation of the sulphate, and are less irritating than the simple lauryl sulphates, presumably because they have bigger molecules and are therefore less able to penetrate the skin. On the other hand, the extra chain contains oxygen atoms which will result in some polarity and will therefore increase the water solubility.

The anionic surfactants are the work-horses of most shampoos, but other surfactants have a role to play. The main class of cationic surfactants is based on quaternary ammonium salts (Figure 3.3b). These are less soluble in water than the anionics (the interaction of the $-NR_3^+$ end group with water is weaker than that of the $-OSO_3^-$) so they are less effective cleaning agents. They are, however, more soluble in lipids, so they cross biological membranes more readily. Perhaps for this reason, they are more irritating to the eyes. Because they are positively charged, they tend to form insoluble compounds with the negatively charged anionics. This is why soap sometimes causes bubble bath foam to collapse: if the foam is made by a cationic surfactant, the soap anions will react with it. If these quaternary ammonium compounds are incorporated into shampoos with an anionic cleanser, some means must be found to prevent their reaction. They do, however, have the great advantage that because hair fibres are negatively charged, unless the pH is very low (and shampoos are buffered to have pH values in the range 5–7), cationics tend to adhere to the fibres, making them smooth and silky. These surfactants are also used in fabric conditioners for the same reason. Their ready penetration of bacterial membranes leads to their use as mild antiseptics: they damage the membranes so that the contents leak out and the bacteria die. Domiphen bromide, used to impregnate the lint pad in the middle of adhesive wound dressings, and cetrimide are two common examples (Figure 3.4).

The so-called amphoteric surfactants are actually internal salts, the most common of which, called cocamidopropyl betaine by manufacturers, is shown in Figure 3.3c. They have the advantage that they do not sting the eyes, and are pretty effective cleansers. They are thus the basis of baby shampoos.

Finally there are the non-ionic surfactants, perhaps the most common of which is made by extensive reaction of tridecan-1-ol with epoxyethane (see Figure 3.3d). This class of molecule is a much less effective cleanser because the polar part of the molecule is uncharged, so its interaction with water molecules will be weaker still. These non-ionics find their major use in shampoos as foam stabilisers and thickening agents. Arguably the most important non-ionic surfactant is nonoxynol-9 (Figure 3.4), used as a spermicide – most condoms are coated in it. Like the bactericidal cationics mentioned above, it acts by penetrating the sperm

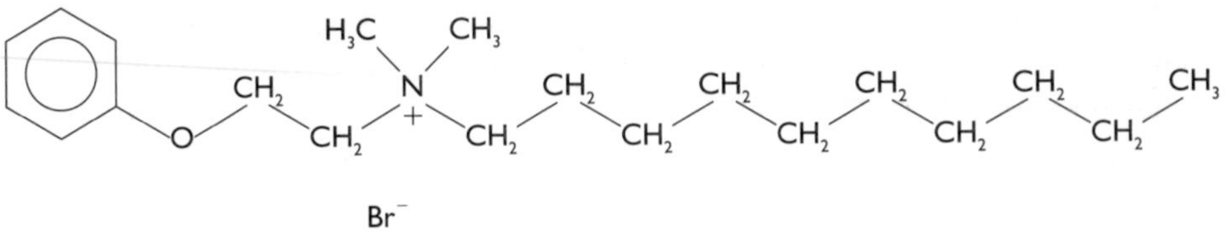

domiphen bromide

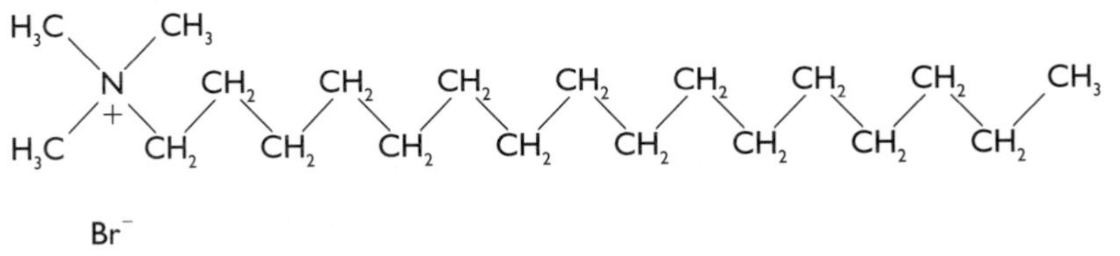

cetrimide

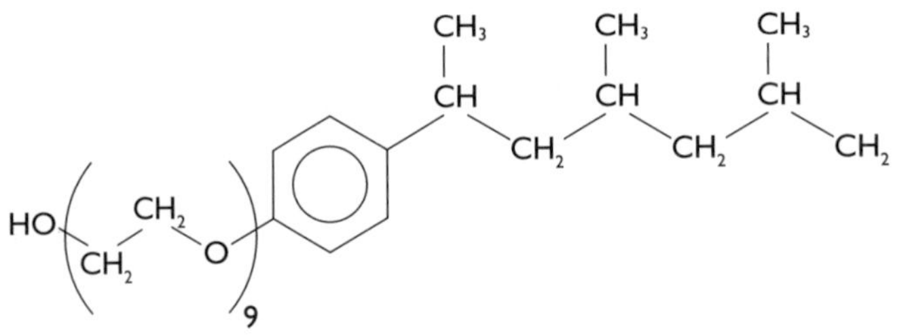

nonoxynol-9

Figure 3.4 Domiphen bromide, cetrimide and nonoxynol-9

membranes and making them leak. It should have the same effect on other membranes too, including those of the bacteria and viruses responsible for sexually transmitted diseases like syphilis and even HIV. Some early research has shown that use of nonoxynol-9 is associated with a lower incidence of STDs. On the other hand, it may also attack the vaginal membrane, leading to irritation.

Look at a bottle of shampoo and you will see a list of 20 or 30 ingredients. What do all the other components do? Here are some possibilities, in approximate order:

1. *Conditioners.* As well as cationic detergents, there may be other conditioning agents, among them silicone derivatives, which will probably have names like dimethiconol. These compounds are absorbed onto the hair, coating it with a water-resistant layer. The tendency of an individual hair fibre to hydrogen bond with another will thus be reduced, so the hair becomes more manageable.

2. *Viscosity modifiers.* We have come to expect our shampoos to be thick and viscous, and various molecules will be added to achieve this. Usually they will have an abundance of $-OH$ groups to promote hydrogen bonding: look for glycols (1,2-diols) and their derivatives.

3. *Buffers.* It is important to keep the pH of the shampoo constant, because acidic or alkaline conditions may result in its decomposition, and also to control the charge carried by the hair. Typically weak acids or their salts will be added to achieve this: look for citric acid for example.

4. *Preservatives.* These will stop bacteria decomposing the mixture: the so-called parabens have this function, as do hydantoins.

Further reading

Encyclopedia of Chemical Technology, 4th edn, Kirk–Othmer, Wiley Interscience, 1994 (2)

Chemistry in the Market Place, 4th edn, Ben Selinger, Harcourt Brace Jovanovich, 1989 (1)

The names of constituents are obscure so if you want to find out what a given compound is and what it does, contact the manufacturers. Some of them are very helpful; others less so.

ATMOSPHERE

There are three sections here: one dealing with the origins of the atmosphere of the Earth, another discussing the filth that civilised nations throw into it, and the third considering the future: the effect of that inevitable by-product of life and energy use, carbon dioxide.

The origin of the Earth's atmosphere

Radioactive dating of lunar samples tells us that our solar system is 4.6×10^9 years (4.6 Gyr) old. Current theories suggest that dust and gas became concentrated in the arms of spiral galaxies, and that these collapsed under the influence of gravity to form a solar nebula, the potential energy released by this process raising the temperature. Eventually the temperature and the pressure of the hydrogen at the centre of this became so great that fusion began and a sun was born. What happened next, leading to the creation of planets, is still the subject of heated debate. One theory is that the dust grains scattered through space became stuck together by gravity, forming metre-sized 'planetesimals'. Collisions between planetesimals might fragment them again, or knock them into different orbits, so that some might even have escaped into space, but other collisions could result in smaller ones sticking together. As the lumps of matter grew larger, their gravitational forces grew, so they would increasingly have swept up the smaller planetesimals. About 100 Myr (million years) after the Big Bang, this process was essentially, although not totally, complete. Even today the Earth is bombarded by meteorites.

The atmosphere of the planet could have arisen by capture of the gases of the solar nebula before it dispersed; in other words, as the planet formed, it trapped its atmosphere from the original mix that formed the solar nebula. This seems to be the case for the outer planets – for example the atmosphere of Jupiter is 80% hydrogen and 20% helium (see page 194) – but the atmospheres of Venus, Earth and Mars are very different from this and from each other. The table at the top of page 19 gives the composition of each as a percentage.

Gas	Venus	Earth	Mars
CO_2	96	0.03	95.3
N_2	3.4	78	2.7
O_2	6.9×10^{-3}	21	0.13
H_2O	0.1–0.3	0–4	0.03
Ar	$\sim 5 \times 10^{-3}$	1	0.016

It is now accepted that these three atmospheres arose from outgassing of the planetary material – the gases of the atmosphere were given off by volcanoes which, in the early hot days of the infant planet, must have been furiously active.

The best evidence for this might seem rather bizarre. Essentially it involves looking at all the atmospheric components and adding up all the contributions of possible sources. For example, the total mass of CO_2 present in the Earth's atmosphere is 2.5×10^{15} kg, together with another 1.4×10^{17} kg as compounds (carbonates, hydrogencarbonates) in the hydrosphere and 2.3×10^{20} kg in sedimentary rocks. This makes a grand total of 2.3×10^{20} kg of CO_2 either as the gas in air or as compounds in seas and rocks. Where did all this come from? One possibility is the weathering of igneous rocks, but it seems that only about 2.5×10^{18} kg could have arisen in this way, leaving around 2.2×10^{20} kg unaccounted for. Similar calculations can be done for water, nitrogen, chlorine, sulphur and so on. So we end up with a list of 'missing' atmospheric components. The bulk of this – 93.6% – is actually water, 4.6% is CO_2 and so on. Could this all have come from volcanoes? The data below compare this missing mass with the composition of some volcano gases (again, given as percentages).

Location	H_2O	CO_2	N_2	Cl	S	H_2	CO
Hawaii	79.3	11.6	1.3	0.05	6.7	0.6	0.4
Surtsey, Iceland	86.0	6.0	0.07	0.4	2.5	4.7	0.4
Lassen, California	93.7	2.1	0.6	0.3	0.9	0.4	0.6
Missing components	93.6	4.6	0.2	1.2	0.4	–	–

The correlation is pretty good. It seems, therefore, that the early atmosphere did arise through being blown out in volcanic eruptions and consisted mainly of CO_2 and N_2 with significant amounts of HCl, H_2S, SO_2 and maybe H_2. There was no free O_2, and since H_2, H_2S and SO_2 are all reducing agents, the atmosphere was quite strongly reducing.

As the temperature fell, the water condensed to form the oceans, and the CO_2, H_2, HCl and SO_2 dissolved. Confirmation of the nature of this pre-life atmosphere is found from metamorphosised sediments dating from 3.8 Gyr BP (before present) found in Greenland.

Then came life, at first very primitive single-celled organisms, then eventually plants. As plants photosynthesised, CO_2 was absorbed and, for the first time, oxygen was released into the atmosphere. (This explains why the atmospheres of Venus and Mars are so different from that of Earth – Earth alone supports life.)

The famous experiments of Miller and Urey showed how biologically significant molecules – amino acids and so on – could arise if electrical discharges were passed through mixtures of methane, ammonia, hydrogen and water. [Although there was probably almost no methane or ammonia in the primordial atmosphere – there are no known chemical processes that produce either of them, and both would disappear quickly – this does not invalidate the Miller–Urey experiments. Recent work has shown that similar results can be obtained if mixtures of carbon oxides, nitrogen and water are used.]

How the organic molecules gave rise to living systems is still not yet clear. What is clear is that the early organisms were anaerobic, and records of these bacteria have been found in rocks dating from 3.5 Gyr BP. Larger celled organisms, possessing a nucleus and requiring oxygen, are found in the fossil record from around 2 Gyr BP.

The fascinating thing is that the development of more complex organisms can only occur as the atmospheric oxygen builds up. The oxygen is necessary so that significant amounts of ozone can form and absorb the harmful ultra-violet radiation from the Sun. Until ozone levels were high enough, the only way that living materials could be protected against ultra-violet damage was for them to form *underwater*, so that the ultra-violet radiation could be absorbed by the column of water above them. This explains why life first developed in the sea; until the oxygen levels had risen to about 10% of present day values, several metres of water were needed. It has been calculated that this magic figure was passed around 600 million years ago, and this may have been the trigger allowing the migration of plants onto dry land.

And so the oxygen levels went on rising. Indeed, it is possible that the oxygen level rose *above* present day values because of the lush vegetation growth occurring during the carboniferous period (340 Myr BP). But as CO_2 levels fell, the reduced greenhouse effect caused lowering of the planetary temperature and slower photosynthesis. Indeed, the lowered CO_2 levels may have been responsible for the temperature drop which led to the Ice Age. During this time the temperature became so low that photosynthesis was severely reduced, CO_2 was not used up, atmospheric levels rose, and the temperature climbed again. So the various factors – levels of O_2 and CO_2, temperature of the planet and rate of photosynthesis – are all interlinked and circle slowly about each other. It may be that this stately dance is still going on, with O_2 and CO_2 levels oscillating over a period of about 100 million years.

Further reading

Chemistry of Atmospheres, Richard P Wayne, Oxford University Press, 1991 (2)
Chemistry of the Natural Atmospheres, Peter Warneck, Academic Press, 1988 (2)
Global Environmental Change, Jonathan Graves, Duncan Reavey, Longman, 1996 (2)

Mucky air

We may think that the automobile is responsible for more pollution than any other invention, but it is as well to recall that when it was introduced into New York, the car looked like the answer to a cleaner environment. Every day nearly 2000 tons of horse muck had to be cleared off the city's streets and the stench of urine from the stables was enough to blister paint.

How things change! Already some cities – those with particular combinations of traffic and climate – are seriously polluted, and all cities have bad days or weeks. Cases of asthma continue to rise. Fortunately, at last it seems that politicians are beginning to realise that control measures will not only be necessary, but also acceptable to the electorate.

What are the major problems and what can we do about them? The main pollutants emitted by road vehicles and by industry are: unburnt hydrocarbons (HC), nitrogen oxides (mainly NO and NO_2, called NO_x), sulphur dioxide (SO_2), carbon oxides (CO and CO_2) and particulates. To these must be added the methane emitted in quantity by agriculture, for example in flatus from cows. Let's look at the consequences and possible remedies for some of these.

The reagent that takes the main role in the transformations of these pollutants is the hydroxyl radical, ·OH. This is produced from trace amounts of atmospheric ozone (and given suitable conditions will give rise to lots more ozone). Under the influence of ultra-violet light, ozone is split into oxygen molecules and excited (i.e. energetic) oxygen atoms:

$$O_3 \rightarrow O_2 + O^* \qquad\qquad [1]$$

These excited oxygen atoms can then attack atmospheric water, producing hydroxyl radicals:

$$O^* + H_2O \rightarrow 2 \cdot OH \qquad\qquad [2]$$

Hydroxyl radicals are furiously reactive, and will attack almost anything. One possible reaction is with the double bond of SO_2, to begin the process of oxidation that will ultimately lead to dilute sulphuric acid rain.

$$SO_2 + \cdot OH \rightarrow HSO_3 \cdot \qquad\qquad [3]$$

Alternatively, the ·OH radical may attack methane to abstract a hydrogen atom:

$$CH_4 + \cdot OH \rightarrow CH_3 \cdot + H_2O \qquad [4]$$

The $CH_3 \cdot$ can react with oxygen:

$$CH_3 \cdot + O_2 \rightarrow CH_3-O-O \cdot \qquad [5]$$

This peroxy radical may do all sorts of things, such as breaking the weak O–O bond:

$$CH_3-O-O \cdot \rightarrow CH_3-O \cdot + O \cdot \qquad [6]$$

or reacting with another molecule or radical, such as NO:

$$NO + CH_3O_2 \cdot \rightarrow NO_2 + CH_3O \cdot \qquad [7]$$

This is the main route of oxidation of NO in air.

But unsaturated or branched saturated hydrocarbons are particularly vulnerable to attack by ·OH radicals. This path produces a high concentration of peroxy radicals, leading to much oxidation of NO, and thus high concentrations of NO_2. In bright sunlight, the NO_2 decomposes:

$$NO_2 \rightarrow NO + O \qquad [8]$$

$$\text{then} \quad O + O_2 \rightarrow O_3 \qquad [9]$$

resulting in the production of ozone at street level. Alternatively, the peroxy radicals may break down to aldehydes in the atmosphere, which are in turn attacked by ·OH:

$$R-CH{=}O + \cdot OH \rightarrow R-C \cdot {=}O + H_2O \qquad [10]$$

and the acyl radical, $R-C \cdot {=}O$, can add to oxygen to form the peroxyacyl species, which with NO_2 forms the peroxyacyl nitrate, or PAN for short:

$$R-C \cdot {=}O + O_2 \rightarrow R(CO)-O-O \cdot \qquad [11]$$

$$R(CO)-O-O \cdot + NO_2 \rightarrow R(CO)-O-O-NO_2 \qquad [12]$$

PAN is a horrid irritant and leads to photochemical smog. Los Angeles is famous for it, of course, but this sort of thing is familiar wherever cars and sunlight come together. Even cities in Britain are now seeing daytime levels of ozone sufficient to cause concern. Figure 4.1 shows how the levels of some of the nastier constituents of Los Angeles air varied during one 24-hour period.

This is familiar stuff, known for 30 years or more. Less familiar, beginning only now to be understood, is the impact of particulate emissions from combustion. These may be liquids, such as small water droplets, or solids, for example tiny particles of soot or dust. We know these as mists or as smoke from a chimney or a lorry exhaust. Basic physics, called Stokes' Law, shows that a piece of soot about 1 μm in diameter will settle slowly, at the rate of around 10 m a day. Add in the effect of air currents, and it is easy to see that such particles will hang around in the air for a long time. The larger the particle, the quicker it settles (and the more easily it is removed by filters, for example), but

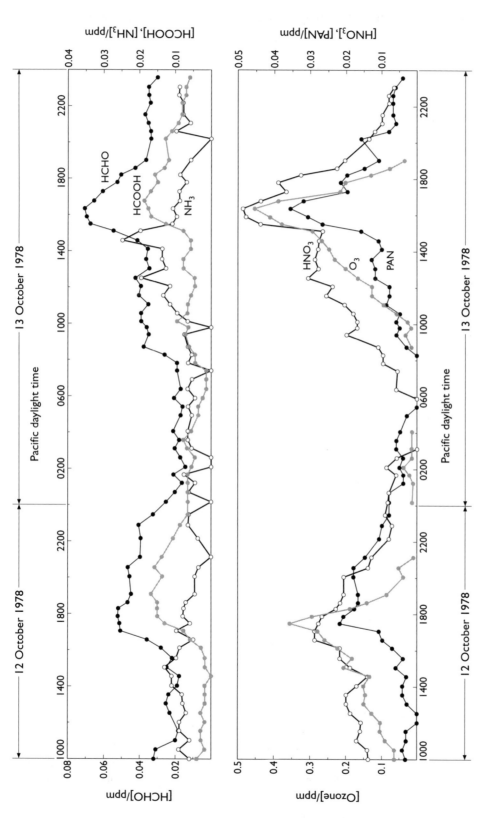

Figure 4.1 The build-up and decay of ozone, peroxyacyl nitrate (PAN) and other species during two successive days in Los Angeles

unfortunately it is the smaller ones that cause the most concern, because not only do these travel deeper into the lungs, they also have a relatively greater surface area.

These particles cause concern because of the substances that are adsorbed onto their surface. These adsorbed species may include acidic HSO_4^- ions (from oxidation of SO_2) and organic molecules such as unburnt hydrocarbons from fuels, more complex aromatic species and other organic molecules formed during combustion in a vehicle engine or in other industrial processes. Almost all of these are toxic or carcinogenic. Standards are now being introduced, especially for the smaller particles. The current standard in the US for particles of diameter less than 10 μm (the so-called PM_{10}) is 150 μg per cubic metre of air.

What are the consequences to us of this multitude of chemicals that now bathes us? Is there evidence that it is harmful? The famous London smog of December 1952 was caused by a combination of cold weather (so more sulphur-laden coal was burnt), fog and a thermal inversion, trapping the pollutants. Visibility dropped in places to 1 metre, cinemas had to close because only the front couple of rows could see the screen, an aircraft got lost on the ground at Heathrow after an instrument landing – as did the search party that went to look for it – and 4000 people died. Sulphur-linked problems are still with us, particularly in the countries of the former Soviet bloc. SO_2 levels in Prague have reached 3000 μg/m^3 (set against a US maximum of 80 μg/m^3) and 80% of children admitted to hospital in some areas of the Czech Republic in the early 1990s were suffering from respiratory problems. Even in areas where the air is cleaner, it is possible to show that airborne sulphur and/or nitrogen oxides, aerosols and ozone are all linked to ill health, particularly respiratory problems. There is increasing evidence that the particulates are more damaging still. Studies have shown that a rise in the PM_{10} levels of a city by 100 μg/m^3 will raise the mortality rate by up to 17%; that as many as 9% of all deaths in the US may be linked to sulphate aerosols; and that the American cities with the highest PM_{10} figures have premature death rates 25% higher than those of the cleanest cities.

Air pollution kills. Not dramatically, not spectacularly, not in a way that would cause the ignorant to sit up and take action, but by a slow suffocation, by an insidious poisoning.

What can we do about all this? There's no *simple* means of preventing it, of course. In the complicated modern world there never could be. We cannot suppose that we could sweep civilisation away – abandon our cars, close factories and go back to ancient agriculture. All these activities must pollute; zero pollution, like perpetual motion, is not possible. The only way forward is to use some very subtle, very complicated science to minimise our impact.

Sulphur is being tackled by being removed during the processing of liquid or gaseous fuels. The faint cabbagey smell of a car with a catalyst is due to H_2S, detectable at 0.02 ppm; this shows how little sulphur has been left in the petrol. Coal is more of a problem, although flue gas desulphurisation can remove about 90% of the SO_2. In this process, the waste gases are passed through powdered limestone, forming $CaSO_3$ which is oxidised to $CaSO_4$; the resulting gypsum is either buried in landfill sites or used to make plasterboard.

Reduction of street-level ozone is a more intractable problem. Since one route of ozone (and PAN) production involves reaction of unburnt hydrocarbons, one stratagem involves limiting the amount of hydrocarbons released to the atmosphere by:

- redesigning fuel pumps on garage forecourts. Californian pumps now have a rubber seal which fits over the opening to the fuel tank and fuel vapour is sucked out and recycled as the fuel is pumped in.

- reformulating fuels to reduce the volatile components (though this is tricky as the fuel has to evaporate in the engine!)

- imposing limits on the use of other volatile organic compounds: oil-based paints, for example, cleaning fluids or even starter liquids for barbecues – all these have been controlled.

These measures are quite successful: although the number of miles driven by Los Angeles drivers rose by 65% in the period 1970–1990, the levels of ozone fell by 43%.

Measures for control of nitrogen oxides have either involved control of flame temperature in the engine (higher flame temperatures give rise to more NO_x) or removal of NO_x from the exhaust gases. Since over 60% of the NO_x produced in the Los Angeles area, for example, came from vehicles, some means had to be found of tackling this.

The composition of the exhaust gases emitted by gasoline-fuelled vehicles depends upon many factors, the major one of which is the fuel:air ratio. The stoichiometric ratio is about 1:14.6 by mass. Figure 4.2 shows the effect of this ratio on the levels of various pollutants.

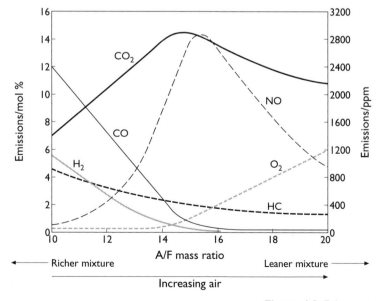

Figure 4.2 Exhaust gas composition

It is noticeable that the amounts of hydrocarbons and CO fall as the mixture becomes leaner, but the levels of NO fall significantly only if the mixture is very lean. Above an air to fuel mass ratio of 20:1, levels of all the pollutants are very low, but it is difficult to keep the combustion stable, and any instability results in high levels of hydrocarbons. This problem might be soluble by advanced engineering, but faced by immediate falls in emission standards, vehicle manufacturers decided to invest in exhaust catalysts. Since 1975, all new American cars have had to have a catalyst fitted. Catalysts for diesel engines became available in 1995, and work is going on to fit filters to remove a significant proportion of the PM_{10} particles.

The catalytic unit consists of a stainless steel box containing the actual catalyst. This consists of a honeycomb, usually of a ceramic material called cordierite (which is especially shock resistant). The exhaust temperature may exceed 1000°C, so metal supports are difficult to devise, but an iron/chromium/aluminium alloy with small amounts of cerium or yttrium has been used. (The walls of the metal honeycomb can be thinner and the gas pores larger, so there is a lower pressure drop, leading to better engine performance. Porsche, for example, use these.) Onto the support material are deposited small ($\sim 10\ \mu$m) particles of aluminium oxide (with oxides of other metals incorporated to improve stability). The total surface area of the honeycomb of a 1.6 dm^3 catalyst might be about 4.6 m^2, but the total area of the aluminium oxide could be as much as 7000 m^2. The catalyst is applied as a solution of a compound of palladium, platinum or rhodium (see below). This is adsorbed into the pores of the Al_2O_3 and then reduced to the metal or an oxide; both will work. The size of the catalytic particle varies because different sized crystals are effective for different reactions. For example, larger platinum crystals are needed for hydrocarbon oxidation than for conversion of CO to CO_2.

A huge range of reactions are catalysed, depending on the amount of oxygen in the exhaust gases. If the exhaust is richer in oxygen, reactions of hydrogen, CO and hydrocarbons with the remaining oxygen predominate. At other times, NO and water are the oxidising agents for reactions like:

$$2CO + 2NO \rightarrow N_2 + CO_2$$

$$\text{or} \quad CO + H_2O \rightarrow H_2 + CO_2$$

Similar reactions can be written for hydrocarbons. Other reactions include:

$$2NO + 5H_2 \rightarrow 2NH_3 + 2H_2O$$

At temperatures of around 200°C, quite substantial amounts of N_2O can result:

$$2NO + H_2 \rightarrow N_2O + H_2O$$

If the fuel contains sulphur this will enter the catalyst box as SO_2, where it may be oxidised to SO_3 (catalysed well by platinum but less by the other metals used) or be reduced by hydrogen to H_2S. (The SO_3 will show some tendency to react with the Al_2O_3, converting it to the sulphate and thus degrading the support material. Minimising this has required much work.)

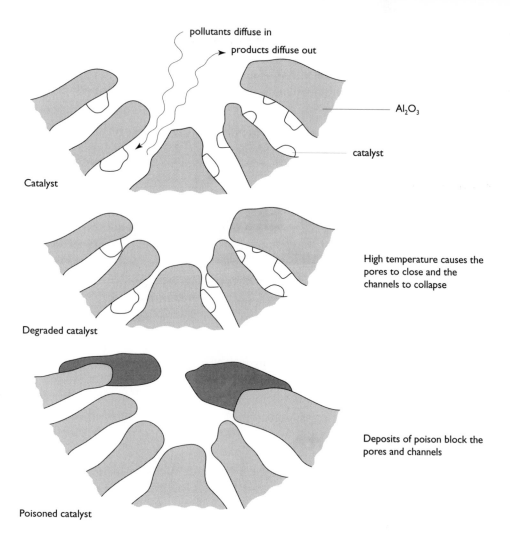

Figure 4.3 Picture of a catalyst surface

As always, choice of catalyst involves consideration of effectiveness and cost. Platinum reaches an effective operating temperature quickly from cold, is the best catalyst for CO and hydrocarbons and is least susceptible to poisoning, but is poor for NO_x. Palladium is pretty good for all three gases, but is slow from cold. Rhodium is excellent for NO_x but is expensive.

The invention and engineering of the exhaust catalyst was a major achievement, and hugely successful. There are three areas where work goes on to improve performance. First, there is the observation that 75–85% of the pollutants that the car will emit in its lifetime are given out in the first 100 seconds or so of each journey while the catalyst is reaching its lowest operating temperature of about 300°C. Solutions to this include putting the catalyst box close to the exhaust manifold so that it is closer to the hot engine, or providing electrical preheaters to warm it up faster. Secondly there is the problem of high temperature degradation of the catalyst. If, for example, the engine is poorly maintained and large quantities of unburnt hydrocarbons reach the catalyst, the very exothermic oxidation reactions may raise the catalyst temperature too much, resulting in collapse of the aluminium oxide pores and loss of efficiency. Finally there is the problem of chemical poisoning of the catalyst. Avoidance of leaded fuels is well known. Sulphur compounds (as always) will also tend to act as poisons although platinum is less susceptible.

US catalysts also have trace amounts of NiO present, which catalyses oxidation of H_2S to SO_2; UK catalysts do not, hence the eggy smell. We can live with that; but why should we have to?

Further reading

Environmental Chemistry, Colin Baird, W H Freeman and Co, New York, 1995 (2)
The Chemistry of Atmospheres, R P Wayne, Oxford University Press (2)
Encyclopedia of Industrial Chemistry, 4th edn, Kirk–Othmer, Wiley Interscience, 1994 (2)

Internet: search on 'air pollution' and 'catalytic converter'

Greenhouse Earth

Warnings about global warming have been with us for 20 years. In 1988 the World Meteorological Organisation and the United Nations Environment Programme jointly set up a committee, the Intergovernmental Panel on Climate Change (IPCC), to assess the scientific evidence for climate change and suggest strategies of response. The IPCC has produced three documents, culminating in the latest full report in 1995.

So what does this say? The *average* amount of radiation arriving on any square metre of the Earth's surface is about 342 joules per second (i.e. 342 watts). Of course, the Earth must radiate exactly the same amount of heat back into space as it receives; if it emits less than this the excess heat will raise its temperature. It does this by a combination of reflection from the clouds and the surface, and radiation of long wavelength light. Figure 4.4 is taken from the IPCC report and shows that the 342 W m^{-2} arriving from the Sun is exactly balanced by 107 W m^{-2} reflected and 235 W m^{-2} radiated from the upper atmosphere.

It can easily be calculated (see the book by Wayne, for example) that in the absence of an absorbing atmosphere, the average temperature of the planet would be about 256 K, or −17°C, some 32°C colder than it is now. Florida would have a mean summer temperature around freezing point and the Thames in London would be solid all year round. We owe this crucial extra 32°C to the presence of gases in the atmosphere that can absorb some of the heat that the planet would otherwise

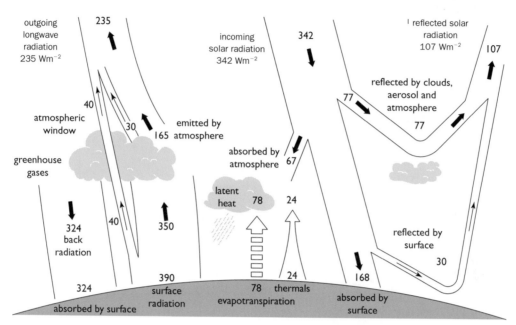

Figure 4.4 The Earth's energy balance

re-emit into space, so that 235 W m^{-2} are emitted instead of 390 (see Figure 4.4). (Venus has a CO_2 pressure 25 000 times higher than Earth and a temperature of 459°C rather than the calculated -46°C.)

The greenhouse effect, then, is not a disputed theory but a fact accepted by the entire scientific community. The only question is how much it has been enhanced by the effect of human activities.

Not all the gases in the atmosphere can absorb infra red. In order for a molecule to be able to interact with and absorb radiation, it must have a dipole. This may be an overall molecular dipole, as in N_2O or H_2O, or it may be an individual bond dipole in a molecule which, because of symmetry, has no overall dipole (as is the case with CH_4 or CO_2). And there is no doubt that the concentration of all the main greenhouse gases is increasing. Figure 4.5 gives recent data for CO_2 from the IPCC report.

The IPCC report makes clear that the concentrations of all the other gases are rising, too. The theory is quite clear: there should have been a rise in the Earth's temperature as a result. But this is the first point of dispute. *Has the Earth got warmer?*

This is difficult to establish. For one thing, there have been so many fluctuations of the Earth's temperature since records began. Think of the ice ages, the last of which ended about 15 000 years ago. There was a cold spell in the late 18th century; many winters saw skating on the Thames. Can we spot an upwards trend (if there is one) against this background of frequent wide variation?

Perhaps the most famous piece of evidence is from Antarctic ice cores. The polar ice caps contain ice that has been laid down over hundreds of thousands of years,

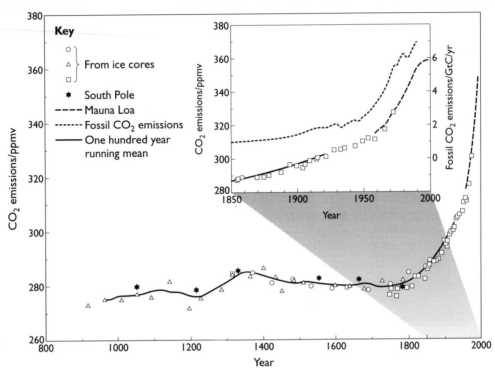

Figure 4.5 Global CO_2 levels for the last thousand years

and cores up to *2 km* long have been drilled. Now when snow falls and becomes compacted into ice, air is trapped, and the CO_2 content of this can be determined. It is also possible to determine the Earth's temperature when the snow fell, by analysis of the $^{18}O/^{16}O$ ratios of the water. (The lower the proportion of the heavy isotope, the lower the Earth's temperature; the theory can be found in the references below.) The diagram shows plots of temperature and concentration of CO_2 over the past 160 000 years, obtained from ice cores taken from the Russians' Vostok base in East Antarctica. The correlation is extraordinary.

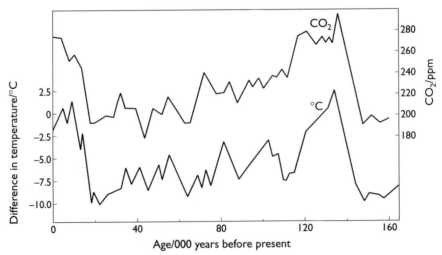

Figure 4.6 Changes in the concentration of CO_2 and temperature over the past 160 000 years

Or take more recent times. While one cannot look at data from just one weather station – there may be special local factors – it is possible to collect data from large numbers of stations, make allowances for factors such as changes in instrumentation, location or time of reading, and determine a mean temperature for the globe. These data are shown in Figure 4.7 expressed as a temperature difference compared to the average of 1961–90. The upward trend is obvious.

After the earlier reports of the IPCC, there was general agreement among the

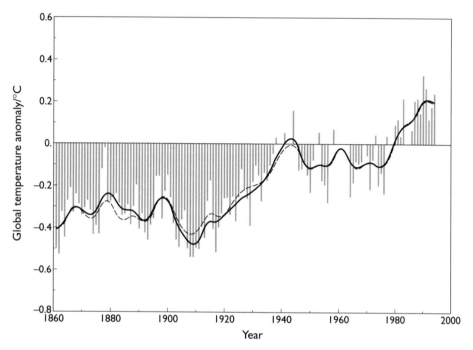

Figure 4.7 Combined land, surface air and sea surface temperatures from 1861 to 1994, relative to 1961 to 1990. The solid curve represents smoothing of the annual values shown by the bars

scientific community that the rise in levels of greenhouse gases must eventually produce some effect on the Earth's climate, but it was not yet detectable. In 1995 for the first time it was: 'The balance of evidence suggests a discernible human influence on global climate' they said, and added: 'While there is already initial evidence . . . , it is likely . . . that the signal will emerge more and more convincingly with time'. In other words, it is clear that the Earth is heating up, and we must expect the picture to become clearer as time passes.

This is worth stressing. Whatever the newspapers say, whatever industrialists concerned about their profits may pretend, however the few dissident scientists may argue, the IPCC report is unambiguous: the enhanced greenhouse effect is a reality. The list of people involved in the IPCC report fills *45 pages*. We have to believe it!

But what are the consequences going to be? Do we need to do anything about it?

The future greenhouse Earth

How can we discover what is going to happen if global temperatures carry on rising? There are two ways. One is just to wait; our children will find out. The only other method is to try to construct computer models of the world climate and make predictions. To sneer that these predictions are 'only based on computer simulations' sounds a bit like the tobacco executives of the 1960s who kept saying that the link between smoking and cancer was 'only statistical'. *Of course* these models (global circulation models or GCMs) must be computer based, and of course they will be inaccurate at first. (The first weather forecasts weren't too good, either, but nowadays you don't leave your umbrella at home if they say it's going to rain.)

The GCMs attempt to describe all the physical processes of the planet in terms of mathematical equations. Some of this is relatively straightforward: for example, it is easy to compute the extent of evaporation from a sea of known temperature. But this evaporation puts more water vapour into the atmosphere, and since water is a potent greenhouse gas, it results in more energy being absorbed by the atmosphere, which in turn raises the surface temperature of the sea, producing more evaporation still. It is this sort of coupling of phenomena which is so critical to the models, and which is so difficult to take accurate account of.

There are other changes which are even more difficult to model. For example, how does the nature of the vegetation on an area of land affect the absorption of sunlight by the land, the rate of moisture evaporation or the extent of water run-off into rivers? If we are to create computer models of sufficient accuracy we have to consider and understand the whole range of processes, from the microscopic – for example the behaviour of plant stomata under different conditions of Sun, moisture and CO_2 levels – to some of the biggest on the planet – such as the circulation of the oceans. As Dr Johnson said (in another context) it's '. . . like a dog walking on his hinder legs. It is not done well; but you are surprised to find it done at all.'

But just how well is it done? If we were to look back into the past and compare the theoretical results with the actual measurements of winds, rainfall, temperatures, pressures, sunshine, cloud cover, sea level and so on taken over the last 50 years, we would get a pretty good test of the theory. The IPCC report of 1995 did just this: it examined 16 different models to test how well they performed.

Figure 4.8 gives the average levels of infra red radiation emitted by the planet from December to February, plotted from pole to pole. The black line gives the actual observed values and the white the average obtained from all the available models.

No dogs' back legs here! This is *remarkable* agreement. As the IPCC authors said: '. . . current models are now able to simulate many aspects of the observed climate with a useful level of skill.' Not all variables are modelled equally well, and while prediction of global values is pretty good, the models are less reliable for local parameters: the rainfall in London, say, or temperatures in New York. But there is a high level of confidence in the general picture. Moreover, the 10 years since the

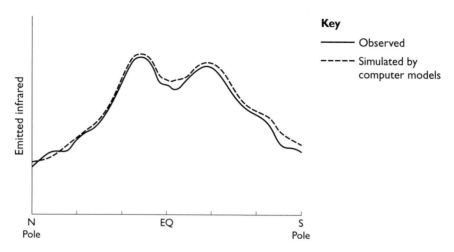

Figure 4.8 Infra red radiation emitted by the planet

founding of the IPCC have seen a refining of the models and a growing confidence in the predictions. The picture has not changed: it has just become clearer.

But the problems multiply now. In addition to the uncertainties in the models, we cannot predict what political decisions will be taken. How will the population grow? How will fossil fuel usage change in the future? How will land use vary (for forest clearance has its own effect on CO_2 levels, of course)? The IPCC developed different scenarios and used them to estimate the growth of atmospheric CO_2 and the climate models to make predictions about the likely outcome. It makes the following points:

- most ecosystems are vulnerable to climate change
- successful adaptation to change depends partly on technological advance
- less developed countries will be more vulnerable to change
- the effects of the change on any given ecosystem will initially be difficult to detect
- unexpected changes cannot be ruled out.

The report then goes on to consider some possible consequences. High confidence predictions include:

- changes to forests, with a loss of biodiversity

- deserts becoming hotter and drier, with desertification more likely

- the disappearance of between a third and a half of mountain glaciers; this may have significant effects on water resources

- a rise in sea levels 2–5 times more than over the last 100 years; this will have serious effects on water supplies, fisheries, agriculture and so on. Protection of low-lying islands (such as the Maldives) or countries with large deltas (including China and Bangladesh) may be impossible

- a change in the availability of fresh water, possibly increasing the number of countries whose supplies are inadequate

- a significant impact on agriculture, although the effect on food supplies is difficult to determine. For example, the rice crop of China or the maize yield in Africa may increase or decrease. We just cannot predict precisely enough yet. But we might ponder what the consequence will be for China if – as one model suggests – its rice yield falls by over three quarters.

What about extreme events? What about floods, cyclones or hurricanes: will they be more frequent or more violent? The total insurance bill for the world's natural disasters for the whole of the 1980s was $50 bn. The total for 1990–98 is $300 bn. Things *are* getting worse.

Some policy-makers – most notably the United States – have argued that there is insufficient evidence for a greenhouse effect, and we should wait until there is; there will be time enough then to start to implement changes to deal with the problems. I hope that it is clear that this is nonsense: unambiguous evidence of human influence on the climate is now available. But can we wait until the problems get more acute? Making changes to the world climate has been likened to turning an oil tanker at sea: it takes a long time. The IPCC report makes clear that measures taken now might not have any detectable effect for tens or hundreds of years *or even longer*.

What sorts of measures could we take? Are they all of the belt-tightening variety, likely to hurt the rich and damage the poor? Interestingly, they aren't, as the second report of the IPCC makes clear, and as a moment's thought will convince you.

Just under 40% of the total global energy budget was used for commercial and domestic purposes in 1990. Some of this was for domestic heating, and there is plenty of scope for reduction of greenhouse emissions here. Much of this is familiar everywhere, and is routine in some countries.

Does your house have double glazing? Scandinavian homes have *quadruple* glazing. Do your windows have draughts? Scandinavian windows are pressure tested. So how is the house ventilated? By a purpose-built system that pumps the stale air out, using its heat to warm up the incoming air. No condensation, no draughts and permanent fresh air.

How do we actually heat our houses? Many homes use some sort of furnace burning a fuel such as oil or gas and heating up water which is pumped through radiators. Much of the energy is lost in the hot waste gases, so the efficiency is only about 70%. Modern condensing boilers have a second heat exchanger which allows the hot steam to condense to liquid water. This extracts more heat from the fuel, so efficiencies rise to over 95%. Of course, these condensing boilers are a little more expensive, but the fuel savings pay for this in under 7 years.

Why don't we adopt the best technology we can? Why don't we build low energy houses and use condensing boilers? Because we don't have to! New houses are built to meet the requirements of the building regulations, and in Britain, they are not as good as they could be. We build houses that give out more greenhouse gases than they need to *and they cost more to heat*!

It might seem that many of the proposals to reduce fuel use in transport would be unpleasant, but this is not so. Some of the measures the IPCC report suggests include more regular maintenance of vehicles, reduction of rolling friction and air resistance by improved design or use of advanced materials, producing a 35–80% fuel saving by 2010. Improved gasoline engine design will probably save an extra 15–30%, and using engines with direct injection of the gasoline will save another 20%. All these proposed measures will improve fuel consumption and reduce bills. Why don't we do it?

One reason, of course, is that in many parts of the world, fuel is still pretty cheap. It's cheaper to burn the fuel than to spend money on developing measures to conserve it. In 1990 the price in the USA (the biggest user) was less than 40% of that in Italy. Higher fuel prices encourage people to use more efficient or smaller cars, or even other means of transport: bicycles, public transport and so on. They will have to come.

Singapore has 2.8 million people crammed into a small island and has no fuel reserves of her own, and has thus been forced to meet her transport problems head-on. Since the early 1970s an integrated transport policy has evolved. Measures include computerised traffic signals, electronic road pricing, high import duties (*twice* the value of the car), high fuel tax, road taxes linked to engine size to encourage small cars, tax rebates if cars are used only at weekends, and from 1990 a vehicle quota system. The trade-off is efficient public transport: a rapid-transit system providing a 20 km/h service. (The London average is at present about 7 km/h.) Imagine how much nicer the city is to live in – and fuel consumption has been reduced by about 40%. *What are we waiting for?*

Further reading

Climate Change 1995: the Report of the IPCC, edited by J T Houghton *et al.*,
Cambridge University Press, 1996 (2)
Global Environmental Change, Jonathan Graves and Duncan Reavey, Longman, 1966
(2)

BONDING

There is little here, because this is a theory topic well covered in any textbook of physical chemistry. I have restricted myself to two small sections that will be needed if we are to understand later sections on the behaviour of oxygen and nitrogen monoxide.

Bonding in oxygen

The electron configuration of oxygen atoms is $1s^2\,2s^2\,2p_x^2\,2p_y^1\,2p_z^1$, and at A level it is usual to treat the bonding in dioxygen as a σ bond, formed by overlap of the $2p_y$ orbital, then a π orbital formed by sideways overlap of the $2p_z$ orbital, like ethene, for example. In reality, the bonding is more complex. We still assume that the 1s and 2s orbitals are not involved in the bonding. The $2p_x$ orbitals interact to produce a σ (and σ^*) orbital, and the other two 2p orbitals ($2p_y$ and $2p_z$) overlap sideways to produce two π orbitals (and two π^* orbitals) whose energies can be represented as in Figure 5.1.

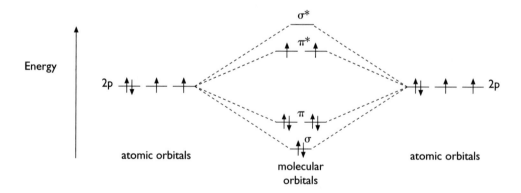

Figure 5.1 Bonding in oxygen

The orbitals are now filled up from the bottom, two electrons per orbital. This results in the filling of three bonding orbitals and the half filling of two antibonding orbitals, as shown in the diagram. This still results in a net bond order of two. Much more significantly, though, it means that we are left with *two unpaired electrons.* Molecular oxygen is therefore a diradical. We are familiar with the high reactivity of free radicals, so it should be no surprise that oxygen is very reactive, and readily initiates free radical chain reactions.

Indeed, it was the first initiator of the free radical polymerisation of ethene, leading to the early low density polythene, and in the addition of HBr to propene it causes a free radical mechanism which gives addition *the opposite way round* to that predicted by Markovnikov. One of Markovnikov's achievements was to realise that this competing mechanism was occurring. And perhaps most significantly of all, the fact that we breathe in a diradical every moment of our lives has huge implications (see page 93).

Oxygen can be reduced in a variety of ways. If one electron is added, forming the superoxide (or hyperoxide) ion, the extra electron goes into one of the π^* orbitals. Note that this O_2^- is actually a radical as well as an anion – it has an unpaired electron, and should perhaps be written $\cdot O_2^-$. Gain of another electron forms the peroxide ion, O_2^{2-} with two extra electrons, one in each π^* orbital. The overall bond order is now one, and there are no unpaired electrons, so the O_2^{2-} ion is not a radical.

Further reading

Any advanced textbook on bonding or physical chemistry; perhaps the best is **Physical Chemistry** by P W Atkins, Oxford University Press.

Bonding in NO

NO is similar to oxygen in that the same atomic orbitals interact to produce the same molecular orbitals. But nitrogen has one less electron than oxygen, so only one antibonding π^* orbital is occupied. This means that the bond is effectively a 2.5-bond and, in keeping with this, it is found that the bond length is 0.115 nm, compared to 0.106 nm in the triply bonded NO^+ or ~0.120 nm in double bonded $-N=O$ species. Loss of this one π^* electron will convert the molecule into NO^+, and because NO^+ has a triple bond and is therefore rather stable, the ionisation energy of NO is relatively low (about 890 kJ mol^{-1}, compared to 1500 for N_2 or 1350 for CO).

The lone antibonding π^* electron seems to be delocalised on both atoms, so the molecule is not very polar (dipole moment of 0.5×10^{-30} C m, 0.15 D; compare this with, say, 6.2×10^{-30} C m, 1.84 D for water). The presence of an unpaired electron means that NO is a free radical, but the delocalisation makes it less likely to dimerise than, say, NO_2, where the lone electron seems to be localised on the N atom to a much greater extent (although there is some dimerisation in liquid or solid NO).

NO has recently (1987) been identified as a biological messenger of widespread occurrence and huge importance (see page 155).

Further reading

Any advanced textbook on inorganic chemistry.

Chemistry of the Elements by N N Greenwood and A Earnshaw, Pergamon, 1989 is excellent (2)

CARBONYL COMPOUNDS

The Pauling electronegativity of carbon is 2.5, that of oxygen, 3.5, so the carbonyl group is polar, with the carbon carrying a small positive charge. The results of the calculation of the charges on the atoms of propanone using Nemesis (see page 179) are shown in Figure 6.1.

Because of this $\delta+$ charge on the carbon atom, it is susceptible to attack by a nucleophile, a species containing an atom with a lone pair which it will use to form a bond to the carbon.

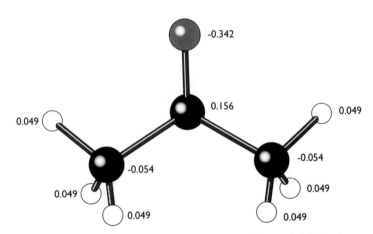

Figure 6.1 The charges on propanone

Beer and barbecue, toast and cataract

Alone among mammals we eat our food cooked rather than raw. If it were not so, think how different our diet would be. No staples: no bread or potatoes, no coffee or tea, no chips, no fish, no sticky toffee pudding. Fruit, raw vegetables and water would form the backbone of our eating. Why is this? There are some very subtle reasons why we cook our food but one reason is certainly to help us to digest it, to break down big complex molecules into smaller ones that our guts can cope with. But a big part of it is to develop flavour. And colour – think how much food (and drink) is brown or brownish in colour. All this starts from the Maillard reaction – discovered in 1912, but only now starting to reveal its full complexity.

This all stems from the fact that sugars contain the carbonyl group, C=O. Because of the polarity of this group, it is susceptible to nucleophiles, such as the cyanide ion, CN^-, or ammonia and its derivatives. Water is the most common nucleophile, of course, but in foods of low water content, other nucleophiles become important. (This is why these browning reactions tend to occur in the later stages of cooking, when much of the water has been evaporated.) Chief among these is the $-NH_2$ group, most often found in the side chains of basic amino acids as part of proteins. Particularly susceptible to this sort of reaction is the terminal $-NH_2$ group in the side chain of the amino acid lysine. As a result, sugars can become linked to amino acids or proteins by an attack of the sort shown in Figure 6.2.

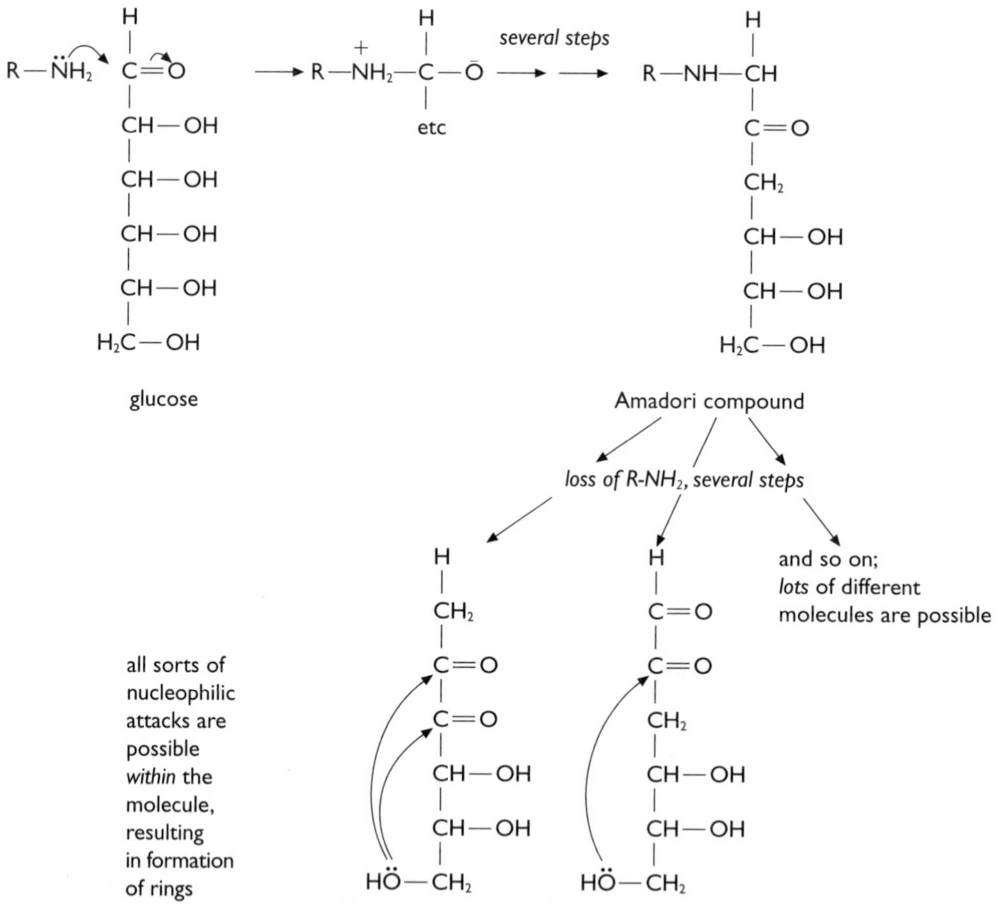

Figure 6.2 The Maillard reaction scheme

The first attack by the $-NH_2$ group is rapidly followed by loss of water and formation of the so-called Amadori compound. This can undergo many more reactions, most of which lead to loss of the amine (which therefore seems to function as a catalyst), and produce a whole variety of new carbonyl compounds (see Figure 6.2). Now the $-OH$ groups of these new compounds also possess lone pairs and can therefore react as nucleophiles. If they attack the C=O group *in the same molecule*, cyclic compounds containing five- and six-membered rings can be formed. (I have shown just three possibilities in Figure 6.2.) If the R−NH− group is not lost from the Amadori compound, it can undergo ring-forming reactions, too. Some of the rings that can be formed are shown in Figure 6.3.

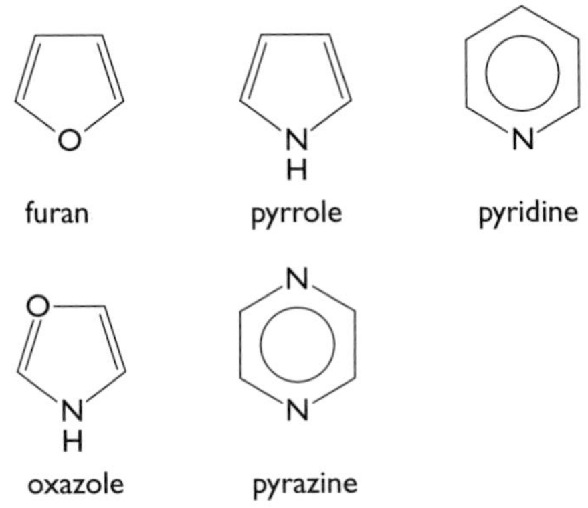

furan

pyrrole

pyridine

oxazole

pyrazine

Some types of rings produced in Maillard reactions

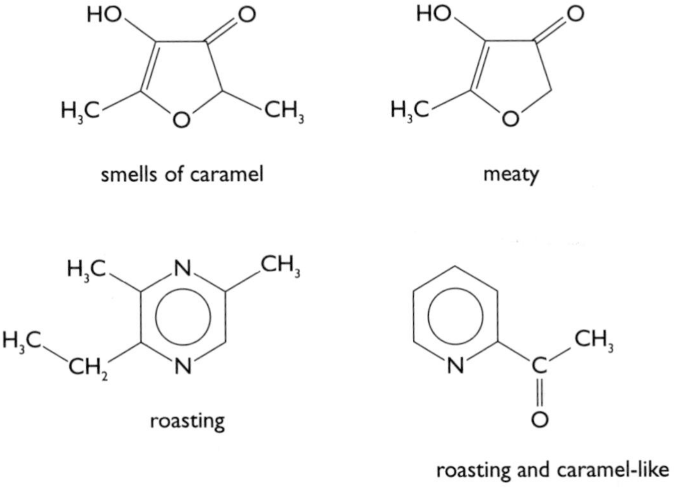

smells of caramel

meaty

roasting

roasting and caramel-like

Some Maillard products that actually contribute to the smell and flavour of foods

Figure 6.3 Some cyclic Maillard products

The details of the Maillard reactions are important only to food chemists, but this outline should show that *thousands* of Maillard products can be formed. Many of them contribute to the aroma of the food. For example, some furanones, such as the 3-methyl derivative given in Figure 6.3, have sweet, caramel-like odours, while others are meaty. Substituted pyridines and pyrroles are part of the smell of baked bread.

Reaction does not stop here, though, with these relatively small molecules. Further reactions can occur giving rise to large polymers. These are all brownish in colour.

41

Thus we get the dark crust on bread, the gold of lager and the brown of beer, the deep notes of roasted meat, the honeyed colours of toasted cheese, and so on. Gorgeous! Evolution has apparently ensured that however tiresome it may have been to have to cook stuff before we ate it – and on an open fire in poor weather it is anything but pleasant – there were strong incentives to persuade us to do so.

Why was this? Why was it vital that human beings learned to cook? One reason I have mentioned: it is to use heat to break down big molecules in food into smaller ones that our guts can cope with. But there are other reasons. Think of the energy stored in various foods. During the millennia when humans were evolving, plants formed by far the greatest part of their diet. Now it is the seeds that are the energy-rich part of the plant. (They might provide 800–2800 kJ per 100 g of food, whereas the other parts of the plant would give no more than 400 kJ per 100 g, at most.) Human beings need some 10 000 kJ every day (or 2500 kcal or Calories, in the jargon of weightwatchers), so to avoid spending most of their time foraging and feeding – as all other herbivores do – they had to eat seeds. But it is the seeds that are the most important parts of the plant – they represent survival, after all – and plants have developed mechanisms to protect them. In particular they may contain toxic chemicals that would kill anyone who ate them. Heating these seeds and cooking them destroyed many of these chemicals and made them safe to eat. But overcooking produces burnt flavours, as well as cancer-causing chemicals, so the early humans had to learn when to stop the cooking and eat. Maybe it was the Maillard aromas that taught them when to do this. Thus cooking made these energy-rich foods safe, and also made available the time to do other things besides hunting for food and eating it. (Such as farming, for example.)

There are down-sides to these reactions, however. The reactions of protein side chains or free amino acids to create large polymers might actually render them *less* available to the digestive enzymes. This is hardly likely to be of significance for people on a Western diet vastly overloaded with protein, but for the developing world, where protein supplies are more limited, it may be important. If food has been stored for long periods in case of emergency, a very large proportion of the essential protein may have been locked up in this way.

Maillard reactions are also implicated in ageing. One of the theories of ageing is that errors accumulate in body chemicals until one day it is all too much for us and we die. These errors may arise through free radical reactions – see *Getting ill, growing old*, page 95 – but another possibility is that Maillard-type reactions lock up body proteins in useless adducts, which the researchers called advanced glycosylation endproducts, or AGEs. This may not be a problem if the proteins are recycled throughout the life of the person, but some proteins, most notably the crystalline proteins of the lens of the eye, have a long lifetime and may never be replaced. This area of research has been active for only 10 years or so, but already AGEs have been identified in the lens, accumulating with age and at a greater rate in diabetics. They might even be a cause of cataracts.

Although almost all the browning that we see on cooking food is a consequence of Maillard reactions, tanning – the brownness produced by 'cooking' skin in sunlight – is not. Sunless tanning preparations do, however, involve this reaction. They contain 1,3-dihydroxypropanone (whose old name was dihydroxyacetone), usually dissolved in 50% aqueous propan-2-ol. When you apply it to your skin, brown Maillard products arise from the attack of $-NH_2$ groups in skin protein on the carbonyl group of the reagent. It is different from the tanning produced by sunlight, of course, but it may be less harmful to the skin and the product affords some protection against ultra-violet radiation, with a Sun protection factor of about 3–4.

Further reading

Food, the Chemistry of its Components, 3rd edn, T P Coultate, Royal Society of Chemistry, 1996 (2)

Maillard Reactions in Chemistry, Food and Health, T P Labuza *et al.* (eds), Royal Society of Chemistry, 1991 (3)

CARBOXYLIC ACID DERIVATIVES

We might represent acid derivatives by the general formula RCO–X, where –X might be –Cl (acid chloride) or –O–COR (acid anhydride), for example. The reaction discussed here involves transfer of this RCO– group.

Acylation

Acylation is the transfer of an RCO– group. In the laboratory this is usually carried out by an acyl halide or an acid anhydride. Commercial ethanoylation (acetylation in the old terminology) is done using ethanoic anhydride, a cheaper and more controllable agent than the acid chloride, as in the final stage of aspirin synthesis (Figure 7.1).

$$\text{OH} \quad \text{COOH} \quad + \quad (CH_3CO)_2O \quad \longrightarrow \quad OCOCH_3 \quad COOH \quad + \quad CH_3COOH$$

Figure 7.1 Manufacture of aspirin

But acylating agents – the source of the RCO– group – can belong to a range of other molecules.

In the body, aspirin functions as a painkiller, an anti-inflammatory and an antipyretic (tending to lower the temperature), and it turns out that it does this by acting as an acetylating agent, transferring its CH_3CO– group to the active site of an enzyme. All these problems – pain, inflammation and high temperature – are linked with a family of molecules called prostaglandins. If you can interfere with the synthesis of these prostaglandins, you can reduce or prevent these adverse results. All the prostaglandins are synthesised from a carboxylic acid called arachidonic acid (the C_{20} carboxylic acid, with four C=C groups, all of them *cis*), which is converted into the prostaglandins by a complex sequence of reactions. An early step in this sequence is catalysed by the enzyme cyclo-oxygenase, and aspirin reacts with this enzyme, acetylating the active site. When the active site has a CH_3CO- group covalently bonded to it in this fashion, it is irreversibly blocked, prostaglandin synthesis is reduced and with it, the pain, inflammation and high temperature.

Unfortunately, aspirin can cause stomach bleeding in some people – another consequence of its interference in prostaglandin synthesis. There is a range of effective substitutes, perhaps the most common of which is ibuprofen (Figure 7.2). It works by binding to the active site of cyclo-oxygenase (reversibly, by hydrophobic interactions) and thus stopping the enzyme working, although, unlike aspirin, ibuprofen has no $RCO-$ group, so cannot also acylate it. Nevertheless, ibuprofen is as effective as aspirin, or better.

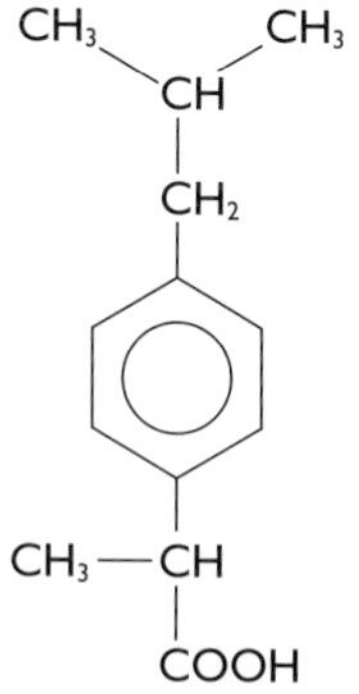

Figure 7.2 The structure of ibuprofen

Prostaglandins synthesised in the blood platelets are involved in blood clotting. Patients who have suffered a heart attack are vulnerable to further blockage of their blood vessels, so any treatment which will tend to reduce blood clotting is beneficial. A 75 mg dose of aspirin (about a quarter of a normal tablet) is now an immediate and routine treatment for heart attack patients. Long-term aspirin therapy reduces the risk of further attacks by 30%. (Unfortunately, there is no evidence that long-term aspirin use in healthy people will reduce the risk of future heart problems.)

Penicillins also act by acylation, but in this case the acyl group is the whole molecule (see Figure 7.3).

The first key to their action is in the difference between the wall surrounding a bacterium and the membranes of animal cells. Bacteria have a high internal osmotic pressure and have particularly strong walls to stop them exploding. The penicillins bind strongly to bacterial cell walls (but not to the membranes of animal cells). The four-membered β-lactam ring of penicillins (a cyclic N-substituted amide) is very strained, with bond angles of about 90° instead of about 109° as you would expect. This makes the ring very reactive. There is a crucial enzyme involved in synthesis of the cell wall, and it seems that a nucleophilic group (perhaps an $-NH_2$ group) at the active site of this enzyme reacts with the reactive

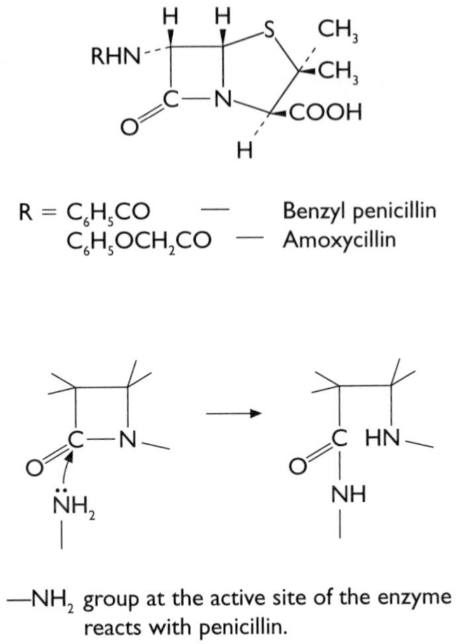

R = C_6H_5CO — Benzyl penicillin
$C_6H_5OCH_2CO$ — Amoxycillin

—NH_2 group at the active site of the enzyme reacts with penicillin.

Figure 7.3 The structure of some penicillins

β-lactam ring of the penicillin. This blocks the enzyme, cell wall synthesis is stopped and the growing bacterial cell bursts under its own pressure.

The effectiveness of some drugs is improved by acetylation. For example, when the two HO– groups of morphine (one phenolic, in an aromatic ring, the other in a saturated ring) are converted to CH_3CO–, heroin is obtained, which is some 2–3 times more effective. HO– groups can hydrogen bond well, and will hydrogen bond to water molecules – a fact which makes morphine a little less soluble in the non-polar lipids of cell membranes. Conversion of the HO– into CH_3CO– groups makes heroin less soluble in water and more soluble in lipids, so it crosses cell membranes faster and therefore gets to the brain more quickly.

Conversely, many drugs are broken down in the body by having other groups attached to them, often the CH_3CO– group. Drugs of this type will have a nucleophilic group, such as –OH or –NH_2. A case in point is isoniazid, a very effective (and cheap) anti-tuberculosis drug which is metabolised as in Figure 7.4.

Reactions of this type involve transfer of the CH_3CO– group from a coenzyme, acetyl-CoA, catalysed by an enzyme called an acetyltransferase. This is a nuisance in that the drug is now inactive, but allowance can be made for this by repeating the dose. Approximately 40% of a black or white population (but about 90% of Chinese and Japanese people) acetylate rapidly, while the rest are slow acetylators. Fast acetylators will metabolise and eliminate a drug like isoniazid rapidly (and so need more frequent doses to keep the concentration of the drug in their bodies high enough) whereas the remainder will not, and they run the risk of building up toxic amounts of the drug unless they take it less frequently.

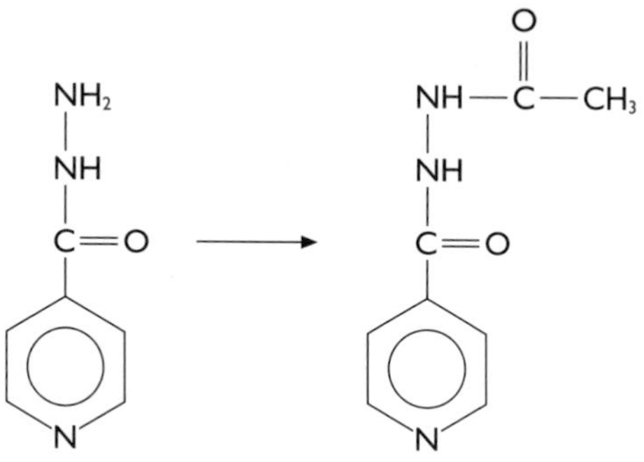

isoniazid

Figure 7.4 The reaction of isoniazid

For the same reason, slow acetylators are at greater risk of developing bladder cancer after exposure to aromatic amines, while fast acetylators react to them more quickly and so avoid the ill effects.

further reading

Any pharmacology text will have the information about penicillins and other related antibiotics (but details of their mode of action may be limited). That by H P Rang and M M Dale, published by Churchill Livingstone (many editions), is good (2)

Selective Toxicity, Adrien Albert, Chapman and Hall (many editions), is fascinating but quite complex – try dipping into it (2)

Internet: search on 'aspirin'

CATALYSIS

Catalysts accelerate reactions without being used up by providing an alternative pathway of lower activation energy. Almost all the industrial catalysts of history have been (and still are) heterogeneous, with the catalyst in a different phase from the reaction. This is good, in that separation of catalyst from products after the reaction is easy, but is less satisfactory in that solid catalysts have fewer atoms available for catalytic action (only those on the surface) than a catalyst in solution.

Nutrasweet™

Nutrasweet™, or aspartame, was discovered by accident in 1965. The patent expired in 1987 and sales world-wide are now worth billions. It is the methyl ester of a dipeptide, and is made by linking the methyl ester of phenylalanine with aspartic acid (Figure 8.1).

aspartic acid   phenylalanine   aspartame

Figure 8.1 The formation of aspartame

It is 200 times sweeter than sucrose, so it can be used in tiny quantities, and is entirely safe (except for sufferers of the genetic disorder phenylketonuria). The big disadvantage is its instability. Chemically it is an N-substituted amide, and like all acid derivatives (amides, esters, acid chlorides, and so on) it is hydrolysed in water (or in the body) back to the original amino acids and methanol. (This formation of methanol in the body might be thought to be a problem because methanol is so toxic but because aspartame is used in such small amounts, the quantity of methanol produced is less than occurs naturally in some fruit juices.)

All amide hydrolyses are subject to acid and base catalysis. These involve attack by H^+ and OH^-, respectively (see Figure 8.2). Subsequent steps regenerate the catalyst.

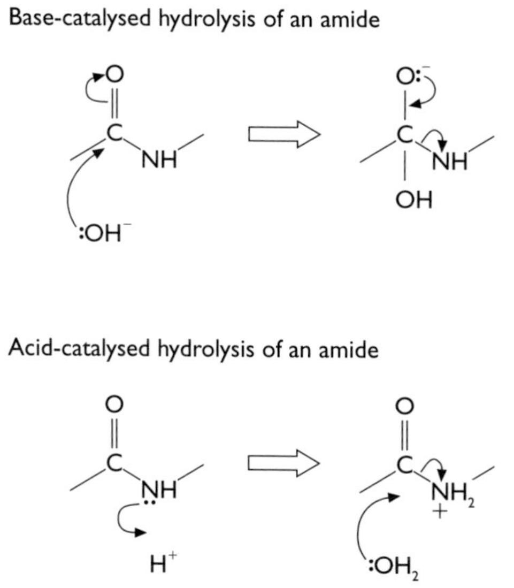

Base-catalysed hydrolysis of an amide

Acid-catalysed hydrolysis of an amide

Figure 8.2 Acid- and base-catalysed hydrolysis of amides

Because of this we should expect that the hydrolysis will be slowest at pH 7, when the concentrations of both H^+ and OH^- are at a minimum, and will get faster as the pH falls below 7 or rises above it. But aspartame undergoes an additional decomposition reaction, involving attack by the free $-NH_2$ group on the $-CO-$ of the ester, resulting in the formation of a diketopiperazine (Figure 8.3).

a diketopiperazine

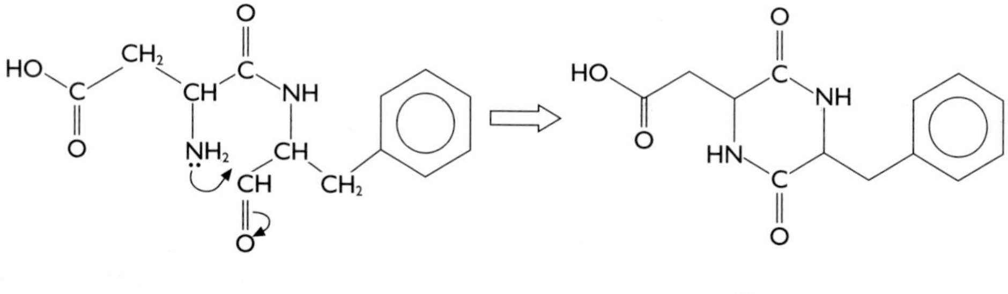

Figure 8.3 Formation of diketopiperazine

The precise details of this cyclisation reaction are unimportant; what matters is that in order for it to occur, there must be a free $-NH_2$ group. As the pH falls, this basic group will tend to be protonated and form $-NH_3^+$. This now has no lone pair, is therefore no longer a nucleophile, and so cannot attack the $-CO-$ group of the ester and carry out the cyclisation. The rate of the cyclisation will therefore drop as the pH is reduced. The effect of pH on these various decomposition reactions is summarised in Figure 8.4.

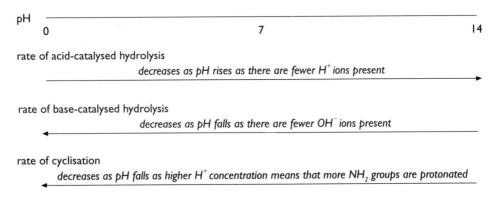

pH

0   7   14

rate of acid-catalysed hydrolysis
decreases as pH rises as there are fewer H^+ ions present

rate of base-catalysed hydrolysis
decreases as pH falls as there are fewer OH^- ions present

rate of cyclisation
decreases as pH falls as higher H^+ concentration means that more NH_2 groups are protonated

Figure 8.4 Aspartame decompositions

The effect of these three different breakdown mechanisms means that the rate of decomposition in solution is at a minimum at about pH 4.3. This is shown in Figure 8.5, which gives the half life of the sweetener in solution at 25°C. Even under the best conditions, the half life of a solution of aspartame is less than a year, and in neutral solution it is days or less. And of course, if you heat the solution, decomposition is faster still, so aspartame cannot be used in cooking. This restricts its use to sweeteners you add to your food or drink immediately before consumption, or to products with a rapid turnover, such as soft drinks. And whereas most fizzy and fruit-flavoured drinks would have a pH in the range of 3.0–4.5, it would obviously be better if they could be adjusted to as near 4.3 as possible.

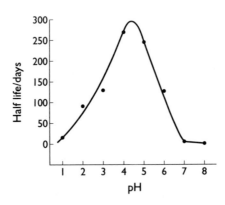

Figure 8.5 The half life of aspartame in water at 25°C

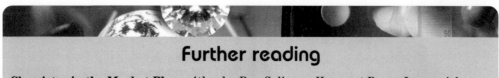

Further reading

Chemistry in the Market Place, 4th edn, Ben Selinger, Harcourt Brace Jovanovich, 1988

Heterogeneous catalysts

If a clean metal surface is exposed to a gas, it rapidly becomes coated with a layer of the gas molecules. This surface *ad*sorption (as opposed to *ab*sorption which occurs if the molecules can penetrate into the interior of the metal) will happen with any gas, and is slightly exothermic, with an enthalpy change of less than -10 kJ mol^{-1} of gas adsorbed. Presumably the interaction involves van der Waals' (transient dipole–induced dipole) forces. Most gases then undergo a much more exothermic process, involving some sort of chemical bonding to the surface. Early direct evidence of this came from the observation of the infra red spectra of adsorbed species. Whereas gaseous ethyne has a $\equiv$C–H stretch at 3300 cm^{-1}, this disappears when it is adsorbed on palladium, to be replaced by several infra red peaks, among them one at about 3030 cm^{-1}, precisely the same place as that of the C–H stretch in the $=$CH$_2$ group of an alkene. The implication, therefore, is that the triple bond of the ethyne becomes a double bond and that the electrons thus made available are used to form a bond with the surface metal atoms, as in Figure 8.6.

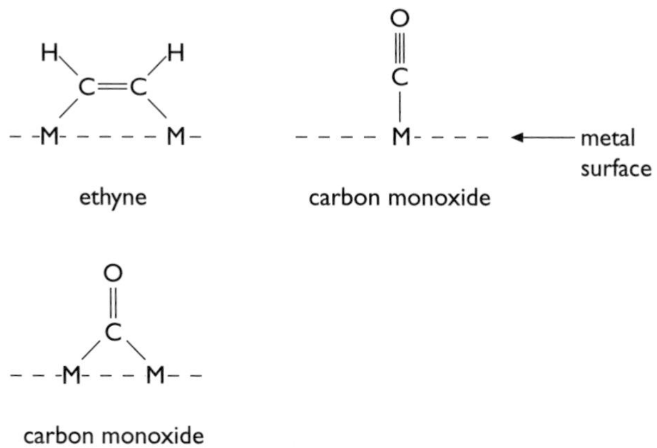

ethyne

carbon monoxide

metal surface

carbon monoxide

Figure 8.6 Some possible adsorbed species

The bonding to the metal surface may occur in different ways, as with carbon monoxide in Figure 8.6.

Even if perfect metal crystals could be used as catalysts, their surfaces would not all be identical. Figure 8.7 shows that even in a perfect lattice (in this case, cubic close packed), different planes of atoms may be exposed at the surface, leading to different separations between the atoms.

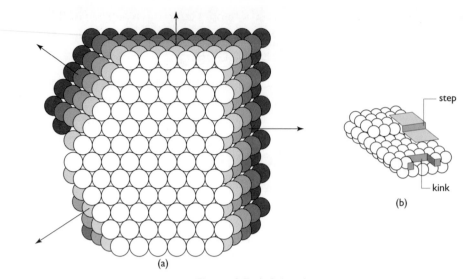

Figure 8.7 a) Cubic close packed lattice showing the different planes (marked with arrows); b) possible imperfections on the surface of a crystal

So the enthalpy of binding to a metal surface varies depending on which surface is exposed and which metal is used. For example, the adsorption of CO onto the surface of palladium metal releases 142, 151 or 161 kJ mol^{-1} depending on which surface the CO bonds to, whereas binding to nickel gives out only 109–125 kJ mol^{-1}.

This is not surprising. The strength of the bond formed will depend on the effectiveness of overlap between the orbitals of the gas molecule and those of the metal, and that will depend on the energy and symmetry of the metal orbitals (presumably d orbitals in these cases). If the interaction of the gas is with more than one metal atom (as with ethyne or the bridged carbon monoxide in Figure 8.6), then the separation of the two metal atoms – which will vary from face to face – is also critical. Indeed, it is quite conceivable that imperfections, such as steps or gaps, might be crucial in that they will provide several metal atoms in the right position to interact with the adsorbed molecule (see Figure 8.7). There may, then, be relatively few 'active sites' on the surface, where faults or gaps give rise to fortuitous arrangements of atoms.

But what does the catalyst do? And does this have any bearing on the strength of the bonding of the adsorbed species to the surface? To some extent, heterogeneous catalysis is a little like homogeneous catalysis in that exactly what is going on in each reaction depends on what the reaction is. But since the catalyst has speeded up the reaction, it must have made the reaction of the adsorbed species easier, and this in turn must be related to their binding to the surface. If the reacting molecules bind too strongly to the metal surface, there is no catalysis; the reactant molecule just gets stuck tightly on the surface of the catalyst, which is rapidly filled up, so that no more reactant molecules can be adsorbed. This is what happens when a catalyst is poisoned. On the other hand, if the adsorbed molecule interacts only very weakly with the catalyst surface, perhaps by not much more than a van der

Waals' interaction, nothing much will have happened to the electrons of the adsorbed species, so it won't be more reactive. We thus come to the idea that an effective catalyst has a bond strength to the adsorbed species which is intermediate: not so strong that the catalyst is poisoned and not so weak that the reactant is essentially unaffected. We should therefore expect that a plot of the rate of the catalysed reaction against the enthalpy of adsorption should show a maximum in the middle – a so-called 'volcano diagram'. Figure 8.8 shows such a diagram.

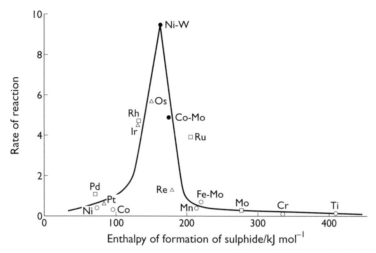

Figure 8.8 Rate of hydrodesulphurisation of crude oil on various catalysts

Crude oil contains up to 4% sulphur, as thiols (RSH) and cyclic compounds, and if these are not removed, not only will they poison the metal catalysts used in the production of high octane fuels, but the fuels will give rise to serious quantities of SO_2 when they are burnt. Catalytic hydro-desulphurisation is therefore used to convert the sulphur compounds into hydrocarbons. Figure 8.8 gives the rate of this sort of reaction, plotted against the enthalpy of formation of the metal sulphides (which is related to the enthalpy of adsorption of sulphides onto the catalyst). For many years the catalyst used was a cobalt–molybdenum alloy, supported on aluminium oxide, but recently a nickel–tungsten mixture has been investigated (see the filled circles in Figure 8.8).

The kinetics of surface-catalysed reactions are not simple. Figure 8.9 shows an outline of the processes involved. If – as usually happens – the rate determining step is the actual reaction on the catalyst surface, the rate is given by

$$\text{Rate} = k\theta_R$$

where θ_R = fraction of catalyst surface covered by reactant molecules. Since θ_R depends on the pressure of R in the gas phase, the rate of reaction will depend on the pressure of R so it will be first order in R. On the other hand, if adsorption of R on the catalyst is very strong, the whole catalyst surface will be covered, and θ_R will be 1. In other words, as soon as a space becomes available on the catalyst surface, it will be filled (so long as there is any R in the gas phase to do it). This

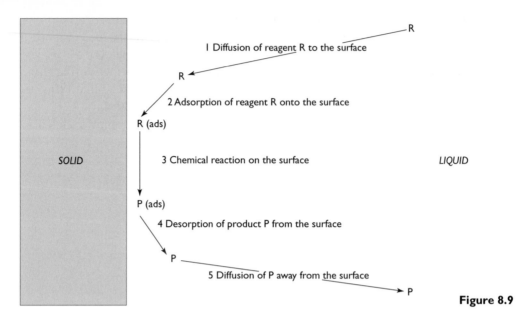

1 Diffusion of reagent R to the surface

2 Adsorption of reagent R onto the surface

3 Chemical reaction on the surface

4 Desorption of product P from the surface

5 Diffusion of P away from the surface

Figure 8.9

means that the rate of the reaction will be a constant, determined only by the speed of diffusion of R to the catalyst surface. The reaction will be zero order. The hydrogenation of unsaturated oils to make margarine is zero order with respect to alkene, because the surface is saturated with alkene molecules as a consequence of its strong adsorption. Hydrogen is much less strongly adsorbed, however, so the rate is first order in hydrogen.

In the dehydration of ethanol or propan-2-ol to the alkene over a calcium phosphate catalyst, on the other hand, the rate determining step is loss of the product water from the catalyst surface. The surface is therefore virtually completely filled with water molecules and only when one leaves can another alcohol molecule be adsorbed and dehydrated; the reaction is therefore also zero order, the rate independent of alcohol concentration. The breakdown of alcohol in the body is similar (see *Drink driving*, page 130).

Further reading

Heterogeneous Catalysis, 2nd edn, G C Bond, Oxford University Press, 1987 (2)

Fats and oils

Saturated fats are linked to coronary heart disease, so current dietary advice is that we should reduce our consumption of all fat, especially the saturated variety. If we want to continue to eat some fat, therefore – and what is toast without butter, what are strawberries without cream or salad without mayonnaise? – we should attempt to reduce the intake of *saturated* fats by changing to unsaturated ones. There are two particular problems associated with unsaturated fats, however: firstly they go 'off' rather rapidly and start to taste horrid, and secondly they are liquids – spread them on your toast and they trickle through the holes and end up in a puddle on your plate. Fortunately we can get round both of these difficulties by hydrogenating them.

Vegetable oils are triesters of glycerol (systematic name propan-1,2,3-triol), esterified with various long-chain carboxylic acids (see Figure 8.10).

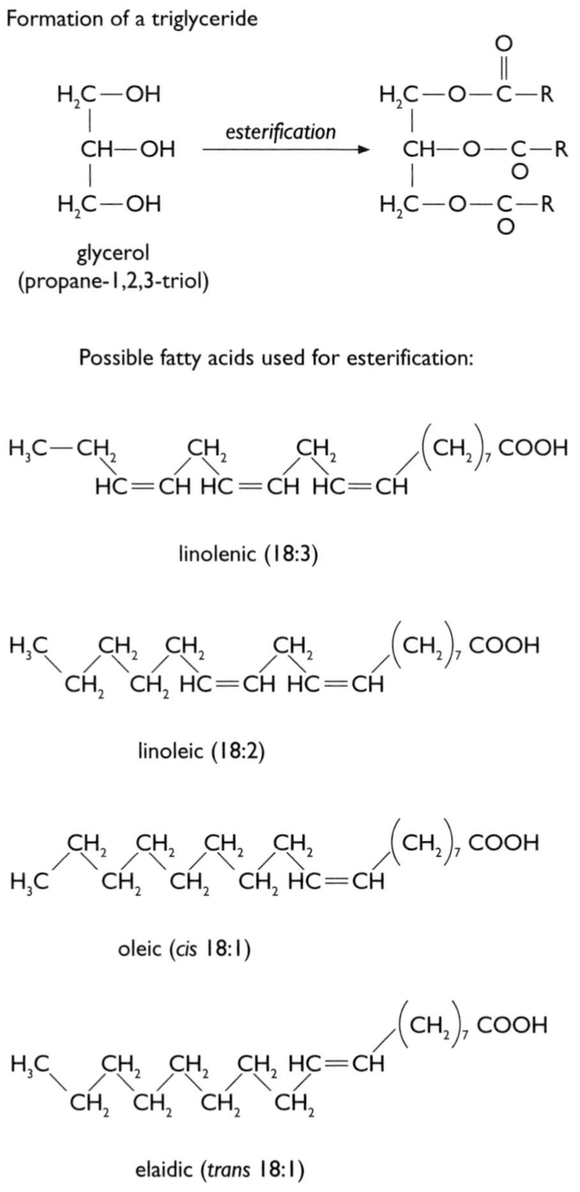

Formation of a triglyceride

glycerol
(propane-1,2,3-triol)

Possible fatty acids used for esterification:

linolenic (18:3)

linoleic (18:2)

oleic (*cis* 18:1)

elaidic (*trans* 18:1)

Figure 8.10 The structures of glycerol and various fatty acids

(Food chemists will often refer to the fatty acids by the abbreviations given in Figure 8.10, where the first number signifies the total number of carbon atoms and the second, the number of double bonds.) Note that the triesters present in vegetable oils will be mixtures, with the three −OH groups of glycerol esterified by various acids, but for simplicity we can consider the acids separately.

It is the presence of unsaturation in the acid that lowers the melting point of the resulting fat. Naturally occurring −CH=CH− groups are virtually always *cis* with the result that the acid chain has a kink in the middle (see Figure 8.10) and the molecules cannot pack together so well in the solid. Consequently, unsaturated acids will have weaker intermolecular forces and lower melting points and will be liquids rather than solids at room temperature. So if we can reduce the extent of unsaturation we should expect the melting point to rise. Of course, we don't want to remove the unsaturation totally, after all the whole point is that we are trying to reduce our saturated fat intake.

If there are two −CH=CH− groups in an oil molecule, almost invariably they are 1,4-dienes – in other words they occur in a grouping of the type −CH=CH−CH$_2$−CH=CH−, and it is the middle −CH$_2$− group that is so susceptible to oxidation (see page 96). Reduction of the occurrence of this grouping will reduce air oxidation and hence increase the shelf-life of the oil. On the other hand the 18:2 acid, linoleic (*cis, cis*-9,12-octadecadienoic) acid, which is of precisely this type, is also the only fatty acid that is essential in our diet; we therefore want to retain some of it in the finished fat.

Fortunately the catalytic hydrogenation of alkenes has been well studied ever since the first discovery by Paul Sabatier in 1900. The mechanism is now thought to be as shown in Figure 8.11.

The reactant molecules diffuse to the surface (A) where they first interact by van der Waals' forces (B). This is followed by formation of chemical bonds to the surface (C); this results in the loss of the π-bond between the carbons of the alkene, and breakage of the H−H bond (so that the adsorbed hydrogen is essentially atomic). These hydrogen atoms can then react with the adsorbed alkene (step C to D), forming the alkane (E). The alkane has no spare electrons with which to bond to the catalyst surface, so it can only interact by van der Waals' forces. Since these forces are so weak, the alkane rapidly leaves the surface.

It is interesting that the first hydrogenation step (C–D) is reversible. If D$_2$ is used instead of H$_2$, the complete range of possible deuterated alkanes *and alkenes* is formed, in amounts that depend on the catalyst used. This reversibility also allows the position of the double bond to alter, and the *cis* isomer to be converted into the *trans*.

But *trans* fatty acids do not occur naturally, and recent work suggests that they are perhaps as harmful as saturated fats. We therefore want a catalyst that will not give much *trans* isomer – although we must have some *trans* isomer or saturated fat if we are to raise the melting point.

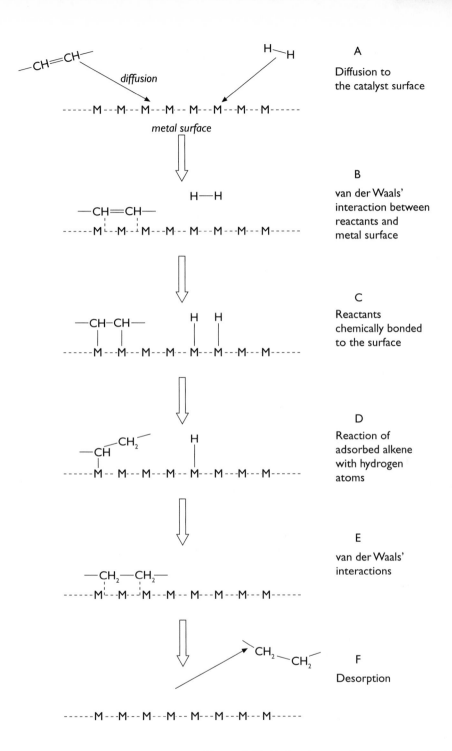

Figure 8.11 Hydrogenation of an alkene on a metal surface

A
Diffusion to
the catalyst surface

B
van der Waals'
interaction between
reactants and
metal surface

C
Reactants
chemically bonded
to the surface

D
Reaction of
adsorbed alkene
with hydrogen
atoms

E
van der Waals'
interactions

F
Desorption

Another factor in our choice of catalyst will inevitably be the rate of reaction, and the dependence of rate on catalyst is given by a volcano diagram (Figure 8.12; see also page 51).

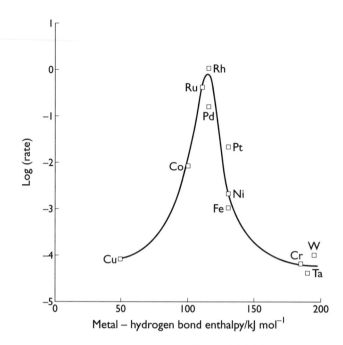

Figure 8.12 Volcano diagram for hydrogenation

And finally we have to think about how selective the catalyst will be. When we hydrogenate our polyunsaturated oil, we want to reduce the extent of unsaturation (so as to produce a solid fat) but without forming large amounts of the saturated product. In other words, we want to add hydrogen first to the polyunsaturated molecules without, if possible, adding any to the monounsaturated ones. This we can examine with, say, the butadienes, where we can find the rate of reaction of hydrogen with the diene as compared to the rate with butenes. Again this varies with the catalyst: for example, in the presence of palladium, hydrogen reacts with all the diene before it reacts with any of the butenes, whereas iridium gives very poor selectivity.

In the choice of our catalyst, we therefore have to weigh up three factors: extent of isomerisation, rate of reaction and degree of selectivity, together, perhaps, with capital cost. As always, there is no perfect answer. Rhodium is a very effective catalyst (see Figure 8.12) but is not very selective and gives a great deal of isomerisation. Nickel is universally used: it is very selective and although the reaction is slow, this can be overcome by heating. Unfortunately there is also quite a lot of isomerisation.

A batch process is used, done at 470–480 K in the presence of 0.3 MPa (about 3 atmospheres) of hydrogen. The finely powdered nickel catalyst is supported on silica, and the reaction is stopped (by cooling to about 370 K) when there is an average of about one −CH=CH− group left per molecule. At this point virtually no increase in the amount of the fully saturated acid has occurred (see Figure 8.13). Probably the most common vegetable oil is soya bean oil. The following table gives the approximate percentage composition of the starting oil and the margarine produced by partial hydrogenation of it.

Fatty acid	Soya bean oil	Margarine
linolenic (18:3)	7	0
linoleic (18:2)	52	12
oleic (*cis*-18:1)	28	57
elaidic (*trans*-18:1)	0	16
stearic (18:0)	6	7
palmitic (16:0)	7	8

Figure 8.13 shows how this change is brought about by showing the change in amounts of each component as the hydrogenation proceeds.

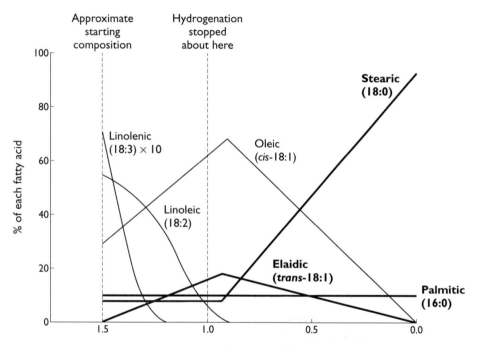

Figure 8.13 The process of hydrogenation of soya bean oil (undesirable components are given in bold)

Further reading

Heterogeneous Catalysis, 2nd edn, G C Bond, Oxford University Press, 1987 (2)

CHANGES OF STATE

Solids, liquids, gases, solutions, melting and boiling – these all are familiar ideas. This section first examines the peculiar fact that small bubbles of gas or small crystals of solid are much more difficult to form from a solution than big ones. The other two passages look at two different consequences of changes of state.

Fizzy drinks

If you take the top off a can of drink, there is a fizz as the pressure is released. Because the pressure of carbon dioxide above the drink is now so much lower, there is much more CO_2 dissolved in the drink than there should be, and this excess CO_2 will leave the solution. But after this initial fizz, it will do so very slowly over several hours. If you drop a spoonful of salt (or sugar) into the drink, however, all the gas comes out of solution in a rush, and the drink foams up. This is a direct illustration of a widespread phenomenon.

To blow up a balloon, or a bubble, you have to force gas into it. In other words, an excess pressure of gas inside the bubble is required, because the tension in the rubber of the balloon or the surface of the liquid is tending to make the bubble collapse. The Laplace equation expresses this in numerical terms:

$$\text{Excess pressure} = 2\gamma/r$$

where r is the radius of the bubble or the balloon and γ is the surface tension of the liquid being used to make the bubble or the tension in the rubber of the balloon. Let us use this equation to calculate the excess pressure inside the gas bubble, knowing that the surface tension of water (assuming that the drink isn't very different from water) is 7.28×10^{-2} N m^{-2}:

Radius of bubble/m	10^{-9}	10^{-6}	10^{-3}
Excess pressure/Pa	1.5×10^8	1.5×10^5	150

As the bubble of CO_2 gas starts to grow, huge pressures are required inside it just to stop it getting squashed out of existence. Even when it has reached a diameter of 10^{-6} m, the extra pressure is 1.5×10^5 Pa – over an atmosphere. Of course, as it grows, the pressure needed inside gets smaller and smaller, until the bubble is 1 mm across, when the excess pressure is only 150 Pa, about 0.15% of an atmosphere – nothing. But in the first moments of its birth, the pressures are so big that it will be very difficult for more CO_2 molecules to come out of solution to join it. The smaller the bubble, the bigger the pressure needed to stop it collapsing.

So how is a bubble ever to start off? There are just two ways. The first relies on randomness. A bubble 10^{-9} m across, with an extra pressure inside it of 1.5×10^8 Pa would have around 150 molecules in it. On this sort of scale, chance fluctuations, allowing CO_2 molecules to escape into this growing bubble, just might happen, even against such a pressure difference. It's very unlikely, though, so the bubbles form very slowly and the CO_2 gas takes many hours to escape.

The second comes back to the salt or sugar crystals. A crystal already takes up quite a space – of the order of 0.1 mm, or 10^{-4} m, perhaps – so if a bubble forms around this, the excess pressure required is much smaller. This is perfectly possible, so the bubbles form rapidly and the gas rushes out. This sort of phenomenon is surprisingly widespread.

The bubble chamber, used to detect nuclear radiation, is similar. When the chamber is operated, the temperature is raised suddenly and the liquid becomes superheated and ready to boil. But exactly as with the drink bubbles, the formation of tiny droplets of vapour from the liquid is especially difficult. The charged particles resulting from the passage of the radiation through the liquid come to the rescue – they attract the vapour molecules and start the bubbles off.

Crazy though it seems, small particles of a solid are more soluble in a liquid than big ones, so it's very difficult to grow tiny crystals. This makes for real problems in the formation of bone from solutions of calcium and phosphate ions (see page 65).

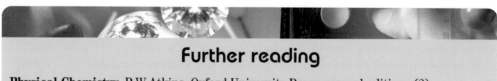

Further reading

Physical Chemistry, P W Atkins, Oxford University Press, several editions (2)

Decaffeinated coffee

The methyl-substituted xanthines (Figure 9.1) include theobromine, theophylline – used to treat asthma – and caffeine. A cup of tea or a can of cola might contain 50 mg of caffeine, instant coffee a little more, and filtered or percolated coffee as much as 200 mg.

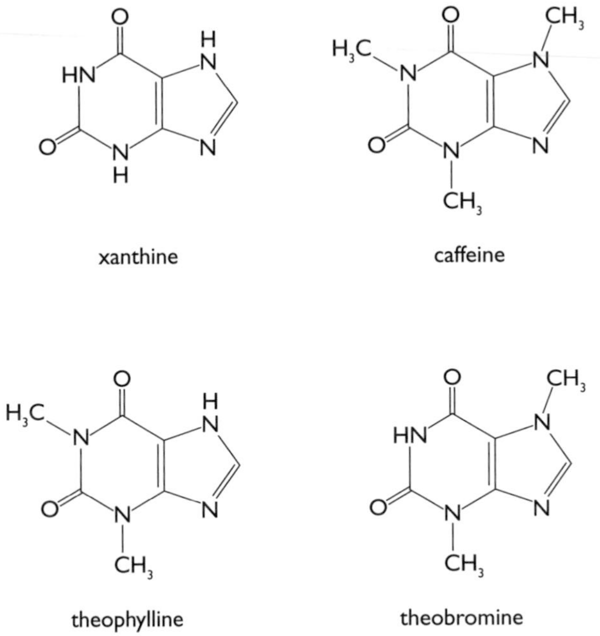

xanthine

caffeine

theophylline

theobromine

Figure 9.1 Xanthines

It has been alleged that caffeine improves the performance of a huge range of activities, from putting the shot to revising for exams. Certainly it excites the central nervous system, with effects such as restlessness, irritability, anxiety and, in high doses, tremor and interference with sleep. It is a mild diuretic (makes you urinate) and can produce effects on the heart, including a faster pulse and palpitations. Very high doses lead to convulsions and death, but since the amount required in humans would be of the order of 10 g (at least 50 cups of strong coffee), deaths are rare.

The half life in the body is between 2.5 and 12 hours, and dependence develops, so some 12–18 hours after the last dose, withdrawal symptoms are seen: headache, lethargy, nervousness and inefficiency. Perhaps because people are reluctant to submit to this sort of dependence or possibly because they fear as yet undiscovered ill-effects, there is a growing market for tea and coffee from which most of the caffeine has been removed. At first this was accomplished by treating the beans with dichloromethane to dissolve the caffeine, but of course it was not possible to remove all traces of the solvent from the final product, and these minute amounts of dichloromethane were possibly more harmful than the original caffeine. So the use of supercritical carbon dioxide was a step forward.

Figure 9.2 shows the phase diagram for CO_2. The critical point marks the conditions above which a liquid does not exist. The system denoted by the shaded region, bounded by the dashed lines, is a supercritical fluid. It is not a liquid nor is it a gas, but it has properties of both. Supercritical fluids are much better solvents than the normal liquid, and if mixed solvents are used, the solubilities can be higher still. For example, supercritical water (above a temperature of 374°C and a pressure of 22 MPa, nearly 218 atmospheres) *will dissolve petrol.*

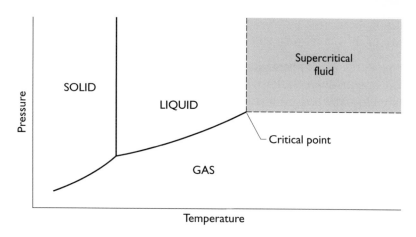

Figure 9.2 The phase diagram for carbon dioxide

Carbon dioxide is a particularly useful supercritical fluid. Not only does it have a conveniently low critical point (31.1°C and 7.38 MPa – about 73 atmospheres), but it is cheap, easily removed after the process and completely non-toxic. The process for extracting caffeine from the green unroasted coffee beans was patented in the United States in 1974 and the first commercial plant went on-line in Germany in 1978. The process uses supercritical CO_2 saturated with water, and can reduce the caffeine content from about 3% to around 0.2%.

Supercritical carbon dioxide has also been used to extract fats and oils from a range of food materials, and flavours and fragrances from spices and flowers. Think of the range of solvents that could be used. Supercritical pentane, for example, is used to separate the components of the heaviest fractions of crude oil. This is only the beginning.

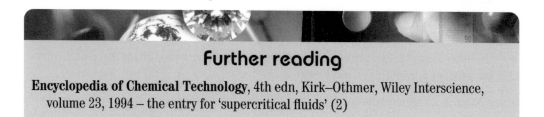

Further reading

Encyclopedia of Chemical Technology, 4th edn, Kirk–Othmer, Wiley Interscience, volume 23, 1994 – the entry for 'supercritical fluids' (2)

Planetary atmospheres

The planets of the solar system were formed as dust particles whirling around the Sun came together under the influence of gravity. The loss of potential energy as these solids collapsed together caused temperature rises, and as a result, the volatile components of the planetary rocks boiled out and were captured to form the beginnings of an atmosphere. One of the major components of this primitive atmosphere for each of the three planets Venus, Earth and Mars was water. But water is a potent greenhouse gas (see page 28), so as the amount of water in the planet's atmosphere rose, more escaping infra red radiation was captured and the temperature of the planet rose still further.

Figure 9.3 plots the usual phase diagram for water showing the regions of temperature and pressure under which each phase is stable, but – unusually – plotted with a *logarithmic* pressure scale (so the diagram is a different shape from the more familiar plot). The dotted lines show the effect of increasing amounts of water vapour on the temperature of each planet. The surface temperature of the infant Earth is reckoned to have been about 265 K. Then as water was boiled off from the core of the planet, the temperature rose, slowly at first then as more water was given off, faster and faster. But then when the vapour pressure of the water in the atmosphere reached about 10^3 Pa and the temperature of the Earth had risen to about 288 K, the water reached the point of condensation, and any more water vapour produced from the inside of the Earth immediately condensed to liquid.

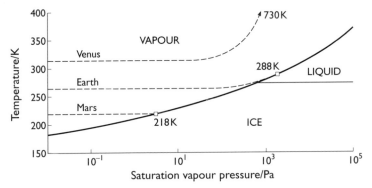

Figure 9.3 Phase diagram of water

This had two hugely important consequences:

- since the amount of water vapour in the atmosphere had reached a limit, its greenhouse contribution was also limited and there could be no further rise in temperature

- the developing lakes and seas provided a place protected from the Sun's ultra-violet rays where life could begin.

Since Mars is so much further from the Sun, its initial temperature was lower, so the water vapour started to condense much sooner, when there was very much less water vapour in the atmosphere. As the temperature was lower, it now formed ice, not water. Conversely, Venus is so close to the Sun that its temperature was high to start with, so high that the increasing amounts of water vapour never reach condensation point.

Further reading

Chemistry of the Natural Atmosphere, Peter Warneck, Academic Press (3)

10

EQUILIBRIUM

There is no need for me to summarise basic equilibrium theory here; all that can be found in any textbook. Particularly important in what follows will be an understanding of Le Chatelier's Principle and of the theory of acids and solubility products. Perhaps it is worth reminding ourselves that equilibrium theory takes no account of the speed of any reactions. It may be that a system is far from equilibrium, so therefore a reaction should be occurring, but if the reaction is too slow – because the activation energy is too high – nothing will in fact happen.

Bones and teeth

Although silica and calcium carbonate are used as structural material by other living systems, vertebrates all use some form of calcium phosphate as their main inorganic constituent, with one or more organic components. Although the X-ray diffraction pattern obtained from bone is diffuse – because the mineral comprises small crystals of varying sizes embedded in a matrix of protein (mainly collagen) – the pattern is characteristic of hydroxyapatite, at least in part. Hydroxyapatite is $Ca_{10}(PO_4)_6(OH)_2$, which would have a composition of 39.8% Ca, 18.5% P, 41.4% O and 0.2% H. The composition of human bone is 32–34% Ca and 14–15% P, while tooth enamel seems to approach hydroxyapatite more nearly – typical figures might be 34–39% Ca and 16–19% P. The X-ray work also indicates that there is an amorphous calcium phosphate component to human bone, which might make up as much as 40% in adults, and probably more in young children.

Bones are not fixed blocks of inert matter, formed once and immutable for ever after. They are dynamic and are constantly being renewed. If this were not so, there would be no such thing as osteoporosis and a broken bone could not be mended.

As a physical chemist I must view this as a precipitation from solution, and if possible will have to look at it in terms of the solubility product of the various possible precipitates. There are quite a large number of possible equilibria.

Phosphoric acid undergoes three dissociations:

$$H_3PO_4 \rightleftharpoons H_2PO_4^- + H^+ \qquad pK_1 = 2.1$$

$$H_2PO_4^- \rightleftharpoons HPO_4^{2-} + H^+ \qquad pK_2 = 7.2$$

$$HPO_4^{2-} \rightleftharpoons PO_4^{3-} + H^+ \qquad pK_3 = 12.4$$

The approximate variation in concentration of the three species is shown in Figure 10.1. At pH 7.4, therefore, the major species in solution will be $H_2PO_4^-$ and HPO_4^{2-} with a little more of the latter.

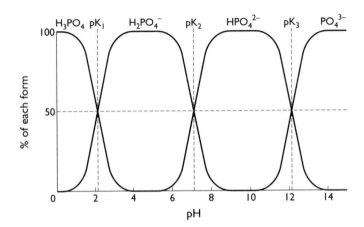

Figure 10.1

There are several possible precipitation equilibria:

$$2Ca^{2+} + 3PO_4^{3-} \rightleftharpoons Ca_2(PO_4)_3 \qquad K_{sp} = {\sim}1 \times 10^{-14}\ mol^5\ dm^{-15}$$

$$Ca^{2+} + HPO_4^{2-} \rightleftharpoons CaHPO_4 \qquad K_{sp} = 2.6 \times 10^{-6}\ mol^2\ dm^{-6}$$

In addition there is the formation of hydroxyapatite:

$$10Ca^{2+} + 6PO_4^{3-} + 2OH^- \rightleftharpoons Ca_{10}(PO_4)_6(OH)_2$$

Fortunately, test tube studies of biological apatite show that its solubility is best described in terms of the simple solubility product of $[Ca^{2+}]$ and $[HPO_4^{2-}]$:

$$K_{sp}\ (\text{biological apatite}) = [Ca^{2+}][HPO_4^{2-}] = 6.9{\times}10^{-7}\ mol^2\ dm^{-6}$$

We are now in a position to think about the formation of bones and teeth.

The concentration of free calcium ions in serum is about 1.3×10^{-3} mol dm^{-3}. The concentration of free phosphate ions, as PO_4^{3-}, is very low, perhaps 5×10^{-9} mol dm^{-3}. The value for the product $[Ca^{2+}]^3[PO_4^{3-}]^2$ is therefore about 6.5×10^{-26} mol^5 dm^{-15}, well *below* the solubility product. There is, therefore, no tendency for calcium phosphate crystals to precipitate out in the blood.

Hydrogenphosphate is another matter. Its concentration is much higher and varies from about 8×10^{-4} mol dm^{-3} in adults, to perhaps 1.5×10^{-3} mol dm^{-3} in babies. The product $[Ca^{2+}][HPO_4^{2-}]$ therefore varies from about 1.0×10^{-6} to 2.0×10^{-6} mol^2 dm^{-6}. The product of the calcium and hydrogenphosphate concentrations therefore *exceeds* the solubility product of hydroxyapatite, so we should expect crystals of it to form. Do they?

Fortunately not. If an aqueous solution of calcium and hydrogenphosphate ions of the same concentration as blood serum is left to stand, nothing happens. But if a crystal of hydroxyapatite is dropped into this solution, the expected crystallisation does occur. (This is exactly the same as the familiar demonstration of supersaturation using sodium thiosulphate, when a crystal of the salt *or even a fragment of dust* initiates wholesale crystallisation.) If new solutions of increasing concentrations of calcium and hydrogenphosphate ions are made up, nothing happens until the ionic product reaches around $3 \times 10^{-6}\,mol^2\,dm^{-6}$ (well *above* the solubility product, you will notice), when crystals of $CaHPO_4.2H_2O$ start to form. This solid is only stable over a relatively narrow range of pH. If the solution is too acidic, it redissolves, and above a pH of 6.2 it transforms slowly into hydroxyapatite:

$$10CaHPO_4 + 4OH^- \rightarrow Ca_{10}(PO_4)_6(OH)_2 + 2H_2O + 4H_2PO_4^-$$

These observations show two things:

1. Crystallisation from a saturated solution, even a supersaturated one, is more difficult to achieve than the growth of an existing crystal. We know this from elsewhere – the thiosulphate demonstration for example – it is a consequence of the bizarre fact that very small crystals *are more soluble than big ones* (see page 60)

2. Hydroxyapatite is especially difficult to crystallise, perhaps because of the additional difficulty of collecting and assembling so many particles in just the right way to make the solid. It is easier (and therefore faster) to form the simpler hydrogenphosphate and allow this to change into it.

But how is bone formation initiated and *in the right place*? Of course, if there are already small crystals of apatite present, it is easy for growth of the crystals to occur (as in supersaturated thiosulphate). But what if absolutely new bone growth is required, as in the infant? What can provide the starting point on which crystallisation occurs, and how can we prevent crystallisation in places where it is not wanted?

There will be more than one mechanism of bone formation. One we have already seen – crystallisation of more-or-less amorphous calcium phosphate from serum. Of course, this requires a high concentration of ions – the ionic product must reach or exceed $2.6 \times 10^{-6}\,mol^2\,dm^{-6}$, remember. How this may be achieved is mentioned below. Then once this amorphous calcium phosphate has formed, it may undergo a solid state transition to form hydroxyapatite. Or it may not; all bone, but especially young bone, contains appreciable amounts of unchanged calcium phosphate.

Alternatively, there may be direct crystallisation of hydroxyapatite. But this will not occur spontaneously, even from supersaturated solutions, without some suitable solid to start the crystallisation off. It seems that it is the protein collagen which provides these nucleation sites. The charged groups attached to the protein backbone attract the crystallising ions, holding them in the right arrangement to allow bone formation to begin. It is no accident that collagen contains a relatively large number of amino acids with polar side chains: this means that there will be an abundance of charged groups to interact with ions. And if the $-COOH$ side chains of aspartic and glutamic acids in collagen are chemically blocked, bone formation does not occur.

But how are we to control the bone growth? How can we prevent it occurring where it is not wanted? One control mechanism seems to be the diphosphate ion, $P_2O_7^{2-}$. If this bulky ion gets incorporated into an apatite lattice, further crystal growth is stopped. In those sites where bone formation is wanted, enzymes called alkaline phosphatases have a dual role – by catalysing the hydrolysis of diphosphates, they remove the inhibitor and also raise the local concentration of phosphate ions, making crystallisation still more likely.

Further reading

This is a difficult topic. I used **Biochemistry and Oral Biology**, 2nd edn, A S Cole and J E Eastoe, Wright, 1988 (3)

Accounts of synthetic bone can be found in **Made to Measure**, Philip Ball, Princeton University Press, 1997 (1)

Tooth decay

Teeth, like bones, are made predominantly of hydroxyapatite, $Ca_{10}(PO_4)_6(OH)_2$ (see page 65), but within moments of their being cleaned, they become covered with a thin layer of protein and carbohydrate called 'pellicle'. This is rapidly colonised by bacteria, and eventually significant quantities of protein are deposited; the whole pellicle–bacteria–protein mass is known as plaque. Not surprisingly, the nature of the plaque depends on the sort of food being eaten. Overnight or during fasting, the plaque is relatively open and loose-textured, but when it is exposed to food it changes. If sugar-free foods are eaten, or even foods containing some sugars, such as glucose, there is still little change in the appearance of the plaque, but when the glucose is replaced by sucrose, the plaque becomes thick and gelatinous. While it may be removed from some areas of the teeth by chewing or brushing, plaque can stay in sheltered areas – between the teeth for example – for long periods.

The bacteria present in plaque can carry out a number of reactions.

1. Streptococci of various types are common among the plaque flora. These contain no cytochromes so they must rely on anaerobic respiration. Analysis of plaque in fasting volunteers showed that its pH was close to neutral or even slightly alkaline but as long ago as 1940, Stephan showed that as soon as the

plaque encountered any sucrose, the pH plummeted as lactic acid (2-hydroxypropanoic acid) was formed. Figure 10.2 shows some typical Stephan curves.

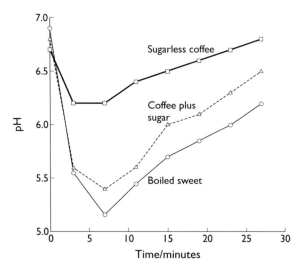

Figure 10.2 Variation of plaque pH with time after intake of food or drink

Studies of the composition of plaque fluid have shown that 5 minutes after contact with sucrose, the levels of lactic acid reach 350–900 mol dm^{-3}. This would have a pH below 2 if it were not for the buffering due to proteins. As it is, values down to around 4 have been recorded.

2. Urea (carbamide) can be absorbed from saliva into the plaque where it is broken down to ammonia by bacterial ureases. This ammonia may in part act to reduce the acidity of the plaque, but it is also used to synthesise amino acids and other structural materials which help to build more plaque.

3. If the pH of plaque falls too far, another group of enzymes, with optimum pHs in the range 4.5–6.0, swing into action. These are the decarboxylases, which react with amino acids to carry out the reactions shown in Figure 10.3.

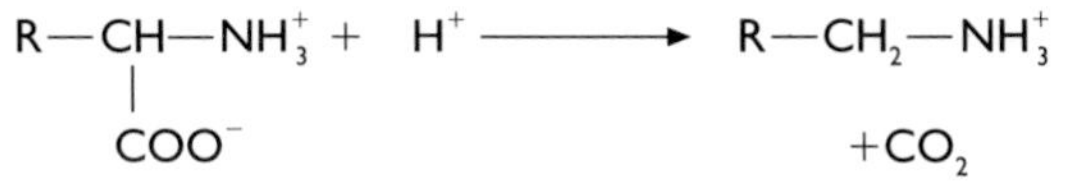

$$R\text{---}CH\text{---}NH_3^+ + H^+ \longrightarrow R\text{---}CH_2\text{---}NH_3^+$$
$$\underset{\displaystyle COO^-}{|} \qquad\qquad\qquad +CO_2$$

Figure 10.3

These form amines and if you start with lysine (R = $H_2N(CH_2)_4$) the product is 1,5-diaminopentane or cadaverine, whereas ornithine (R = $H_2N(CH_2)_3$) will result in 1,4-diaminobutane or putrescine. The names speak for themselves: these diamines are produced when flesh decays, and they smell as bad as you would think.

So metabolism of sucrose in the plaque tends to drive the pH of the plaque down.

What effect might this have on the teeth? The first thing that a chemist would note about hydroxyapatite is that it contains two ions which can be protonated: OH^- and PO_4^{3-}. OH^- is a stronger base than PO_4^{3-} so we should expect it to be protonated preferentially. Whatever happens, the net result is:

$$Ca_{10}(PO_4)_6(OH)_2 + 8H^+ \rightarrow 6CaHPO_4 + 2H_2O + 4Ca^{2+}$$

and calcium ions are lost. $CaHPO_4$ is still very insoluble, however, but if the pH falls still further, HPO_4^{2-} will also get protonated:

$$CaHPO_4(s) + H^+(aq) \rightarrow Ca^{2+}(aq) + H_2PO_4^-(aq)$$

and the net result is that the tooth will dissolve.

All is not lost, however. Teeth are not inert lumps: they are dynamic and the liquids that bathe them are dynamic, too.

Saliva and plaque fluids contain Ca^{2+}, $H_2PO_4^-$ and HPO_4^{2-} ions. As the pH rises, $H_2PO_4^-$ ions tend to be converted into HPO_4^{2-}, and the value for the ionic product may rise to exceed the solubility product. As a result, precipitation of calcium hydrogenphosphate will occur. This may be undesirable; for example, if plaque is not removed from the teeth, it may in time acquire deposits of calcium phosphates and become hard and very difficult to remove. On the other hand, if there has been some calcium loss from tooth material when the pH fell, remineralisation starts to occur as the pH rises. The teeth actually grow! These deposits of $CaHPO_4$ can then slowly change to form hydroxyapatite once more. We can describe this process by equations of the sort:

$$10CaHPO_4 + 8OH^- \rightarrow Ca_{10}(PO_4)_6(OH)_2 + 6H_2O + 4HPO_4^{2-}$$

This is wishful thinking however – hydroxyapatite is too complex a material to form in this neat fashion. Instead it seems that the $CaHPO_4$ undergoes a solid state transition to end up at hydroxyapatite via a series of odd-looking intermediates, among them $Ca_3(PO_4)_2$ and $Ca_9(PO_4)_6$. This process is slow and is favoured by high pH.

But what can we do to prevent teeth dissolving in the first place? One piece of evidence comes from a study carried out on a group of patients at a mental hospital in Vipeholm, Sweden. Four hundred patients were selected for the study and all of them received an identical basic diet. To this was added extra food (the control group) while others received sucrose solution at meal times. Two other groups were given caramels or toffees, either at meal times (dotted lines) or between meals (solid lines) (see Figure 10.4). Everything wears out eventually, including teeth, so everyone got more fillings as they got older, but the startling rise in the number of decayed, missing or filled teeth was for those groups who ate sweet foods *between meals*. The message is clear. Whenever we eat, we expose our teeth to acid, so we should do so as infrequently as possible.

Since saliva has a pH in the range 6.2–7.6 and also has dissolved oxygen, it will tend to raise the pH of the plaque and remove the anaerobic conditions in which the main bacteria thrive. To finish a meal with a food of high pH (such as cheese) or

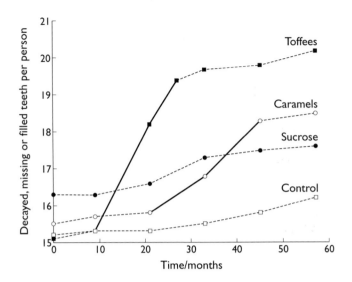

Figure 10.4 Vipeholm data

with some salivary stimulant (such as sucrose-free gum) will reduce the time of low pH still further (see Figure 10.5).

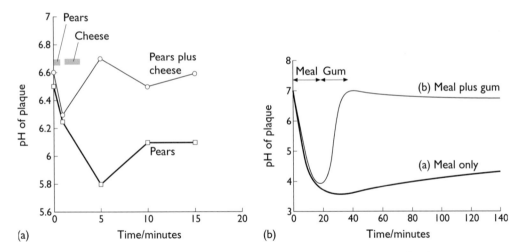

Figure 10.5 Effect of cheese and gum on Stephan curves.
a) Effect on plaque pH of following a pear with a piece of cheese;
b) effect of gum on plaque pH after a meal

But what about fluoride? Fluoride ions have a slightly smaller radius than hydroxide (0.133 nm compared to the calculated 0.137 nm). As a result, ionic fluorides always have a slightly higher lattice enthalpy than the corresponding hydroxides. We should expect the fluorapatite to have a higher lattice enthalpy than hydroxyapatite, therefore, and to be even less soluble. And it is true that incorporation of fluoride ions into teeth makes them more resistant to decay. This is most effectively done while the teeth are forming, and it seems crazy that all water companies do not add safe levels of fluoride to water supplies and end the misery of childhood tooth decay. Surface application of fluoride – by toothpastes or mouthwashes, for example – is of limited effect, although the reaction below can occur, especially if the pH drops:

$$Ca_{10}(PO_4)_6(OH)_2 + 2F^- \rightleftharpoons Ca_{10}(PO_4)_6F_2 + 2OH^-$$

Further reading

Biochemistry and Oral Biology, 2nd edn, A S Cole and J E Eastoe, Wright, 1988 (3)

Prescribing medicines

The first problem is getting the stuff into the patient. There are some eight or 10 ways of doing this, including inhalation (for example salbutamol for asthma), rectally (as with ergotamine for migraine) or various methods of injection. But despite problems of taste, the best method is surely by mouth. In order to be absorbed, the drug has to pass across the wall of the gut, a wall made of lipids, non-polar molecules of various sorts. Of course, even injected drugs will have to cross membranes, such as the so-called blood–brain barrier, if they are to reach their ultimate site of action. There are essentially three ways for any molecule or ion to cross a membrane.

1. It can diffuse through holes or pores in the membrane. A high proportion of ethanol is absorbed in this way.

2. It can fool the body into treating it like a nutrient molecule of a similar shape and size so it is absorbed by the same transport mechanism. The anticancer drug fluorouracil is mistaken for uracil and assimilated in this fashion.

3. The majority of drugs dissolve into the hydrophobic interior of the gut wall and diffuse across the lipid region.

In order for drugs to be able to achieve this last method, the molecules must be able to dissolve in lipids to some extent. Charged species are essentially insoluble in non-polar solvents, so in order to dissolve in the non-polar wall of the stomach or intestine, it is necessary for the molecule to be uncharged. If it carries any acidic or basic groups, the proportion of uncharged molecules in the equilibrium will depend on the pK value of the acidic or basic group and the pH of the medium. For example, for an acid, HA, the equilibrium:

$$HA \rightleftharpoons H^+ + A^- \tag{1}$$

will be set up. The lower the pH, the greater the concentration of H^+ ions and the further to the left (by Le Chatelier's principle) the equilibrium will lie. So in the stomach (pH ~ 1.5), a weakly acidic drug like aspirin will mostly exist as uncharged molecules, so we should expect that absorption from the stomach will be very effective (see Figure 10.6).

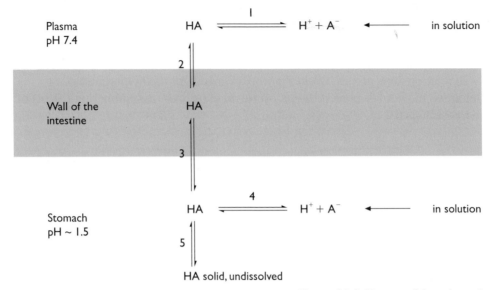

Figure 10.6 Diagram of drug absorption

Two factors tend to work against this. Firstly, the uncharged molecules are rather insoluble so the concentration of aspirin in solution in the stomach contents is pretty low. Secondly, the stomach was designed primarily to initiate digestion, so its wall is thick and relatively little absorption occurs here anyway.

It is, therefore, to the intestine that we must look for most of the absorption of drugs. The intestine is much less acidic, with a pH of between 5 and 7, so what happens to an acidic drug here? Because the concentration of H^+ ions is lower than in the stomach, the equilibrium above lies more to the right, so the concentration of HA is lower. Indeed, if the drug is quite a strong acid, it will be highly dissociated, the concentration of HA will be tiny and there will be very little of it to be absorbed across the membrane. If our drug is acidic, therefore, we want it to be a weak acid so that its K_a is as small as possible, or its pK_a as big as possible. When we are designing the drug, then, we may need to modify its structure to achieve this.

Fortunately the body helps us in another way. The pH of blood plasma and most body fluids is around 7.4. This means that once it has been absorbed, acid HA dissociates more strongly than before: equilibrium (1) in Figure 10.6 lies further to the right. This results in a lowered plasma HA concentration, which pulls equilibrium (2) over, which pulls (3) over, and so on. The slightly alkaline blood plasma helps to pump the drug across the membrane.

What if the drug is basic? In this case we are considering the equilibrium:

$$B + H^+ \rightleftharpoons BH^+ \qquad\qquad [2]$$

and we can describe this in terms of K_b. Chemists usually, however, think about the dissociation constant, K_a, of the conjugate acid, BH^+:

$$BH^+ \rightleftharpoons B + H^+ \qquad\qquad [3]$$

In this case we want the concentration of B in the stomach or intestine to be as high as possible, because the protonated form, BH^+, will not be soluble in membrane lipids. We therefore want the K_a to be large, so that equilibrium (3) lies as far to the right as possible. In other words, for a base, a small pK_a is favourable. These relationships are shown in Figure 10.7, which plots the percentage of uncharged molecules against the pK_a of the acid or base, assuming that the pH of the intestine is 6.0.

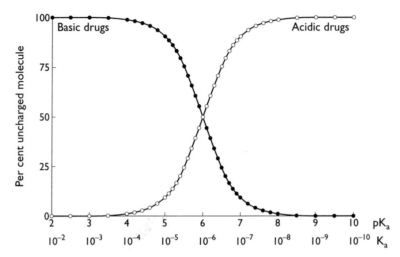

Figure 10.7 Variation in percentage of uncharged molecules

How does this work out in practice? Figure 10.8 plots the percentage absorption of various drugs from the intestine.

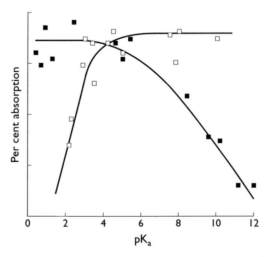

Figure 10.8 Absorption of drugs from the intestine

Although drug absorption will depend on other factors as well as the pK (its solubility, for example, as with aspirin), there is a similarity.

The pH effects also explain the popularity of crack cocaine. As far back as the 16th Century, the Incas discovered that chewing the leaves of the coca tree helped to keep fatigue and hunger at bay. The active agent is cocaine, which is a base (Figure 10.9) and which is extracted as a salt. Because this is charged, it crosses the membranes of the stomach or the nasal cavity (if sniffed) relatively slowly.

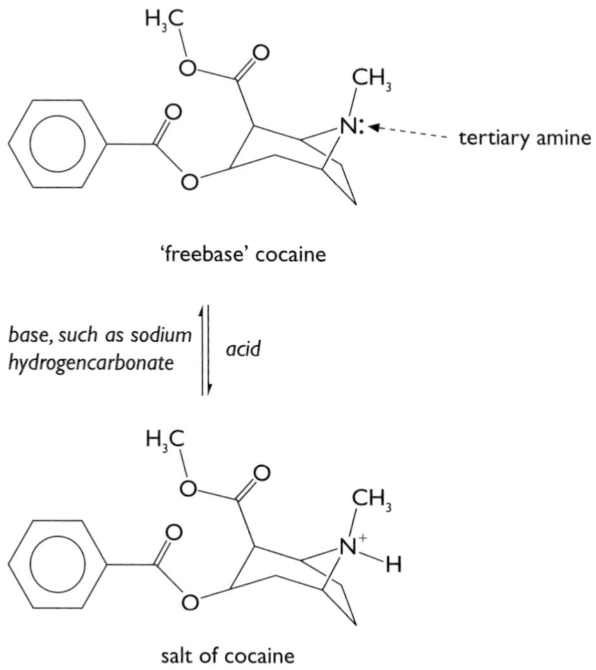

'freebase' cocaine

base, such as sodium hydrogencarbonate ⇅ acid

salt of cocaine

Figure 10.9 The structure of cocaine

When treated with sodium hydrogencarbonate, however, the base is formed (hence one of the street names: 'freebase'). When this is smoked, it crosses the membranes of nose and lungs very fast, leading to a rapid – and extremely addictive – high.

Further reading

There is little about this in textbooks, although some pharmacology texts may have some information.

Drug Design, John Smith and Hywel Williams, Wright PSG, 1983 (2) is interesting.

11

FORCES BETWEEN PARTICLES

This section looks at some of the uses made of the various modes of interaction of chemical particles. These include ionic, ion–dipole (as in hydration of an ion in aqueous solution, for example), dipole–dipole and transient dipole–induced dipole interactions. These last ones are like the very weak forces of attraction between the atoms in liquid neon and are often called van der Waals' forces, although this term should probably also include dipole–dipole forces.

Of course, the whole of chemistry, indeed the whole of existence, makes use of forces between particles, so the contents of this section are a slightly arbitrary selection, and there is much elsewhere in the book.

Glues

They are largely hidden, of course. Screws and bolts, welds and rivets – these we can see, but we can often detect the use of an adhesive only by the smoothness of the surface, the absence of blemishes. Glues are so puzzling: what holds the joined pieces together? Why is sticky tape sticky? Why will it peel easily off wood but off glass with great difficulty? What *is* stickiness?

The range of glue uses would astonish the ignorant. Much of the face material of an aircraft might be glued to the underlying honeycomb strengthener. Chips are glued onto circuit boards; fillings into teeth; heat-shield tiles onto the space shuttle. Indeed, much of modern construction involves structural adhesives: bridges, buildings, cars and even aircraft are held together by glues. And closely related to this is the application of any coating: paint, for example, to a metal surface.

To start with, we should perhaps consider the different sorts of adhesive or coating. Some feel sticky to start with. Sellotape, for example, and the whole family of adhesive tapes, are tacky to the touch. They don't depend on any drying to develop the bond; press them together and they just stick. They consist of large molecules – large enough to be viscous but small enough to flow into an intimate contact with the surface.

Other adhesives don't feel like this. Wallpaper paste and woodworking glue are not tacky at all, and even superglue in its original state is a runny liquid. These glues function in one of two ways. Some of them are solutions or suspensions of a solid, runny enough to allow the adhesive molecules to flow into good contact with the surface. Subsequent evaporation of the solvent leaves the solid behind to hold the join together. Wallpaper pastes and woodworking glue are like this. Alternatively, there may be a chemical reaction on the surface, so that the glue we apply as a liquid polymerises and turns into a solid. This may be because the user makes a mixture of two reagents before applying it to the joint (like epoxy adhesives) or because the surface initiates the reaction. The so-called 'superglue' is of this type. It is a cyanoacrylate, whose polymerisation is initiated by any nucleophile, the most common of which is water (see Figure 11.1).

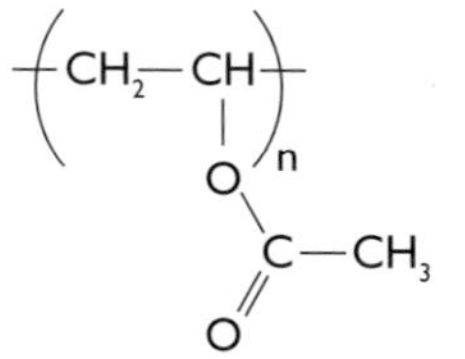

PVA woodworking glue

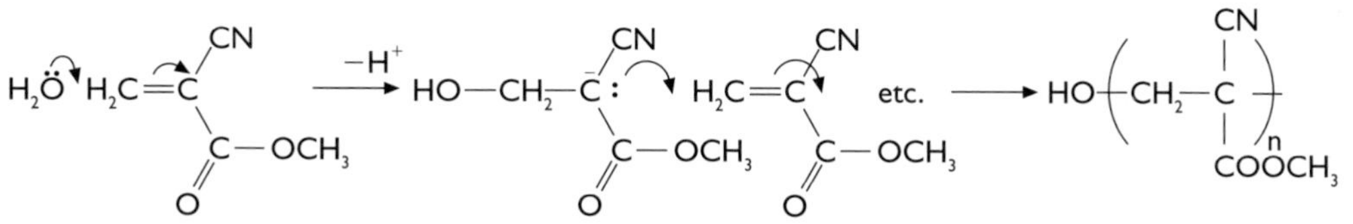

Setting of a cyanoacrylate superglue

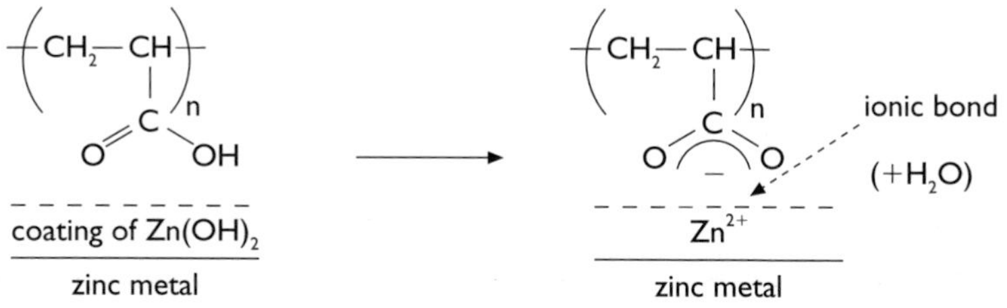

coating of Zn(OH)₂

zinc metal

ionic bond

$(+H_2O)$

Zn^{2+}

zinc metal

Binding of a polyacrylic acid to an oxidised zinc metal surface

Figure 11.1

Once the join has formed, what is it that keeps it together? There are three main theories of adhesion, and it is probable that different theories are applicable to different glues.

1. **Mechanical interlocking** assumes that the two objects to be joined have surface roughnesses, at a molecular level, and it is the hooking up of these roughnesses that is responsible for holding them together. A sort of molecular-scale Velcro, in fact. Evidence for this seems to come from the observation that if the surfaces to be joined are roughened prior to gluing, a stronger joint

is often made. So, for example, polythene can be used to fasten metals together: the polythene is melted, the metals coated with the melt and pressed together. Research showed that the joint was strongest if a thin rough coating of metal oxide was first produced on the metal surface. On the other hand, it appears that, except in a few cases, it is not that the rough areas catch on each other, but that roughness creates a larger area over which interactions can operate.

2. **Diffusion theory** is applicable mainly to the gluing together of polymers using a solvent-based adhesive, or even just the solvent itself. It is suggested that the presence of the solvent dissolves a thin layer of the surface of each piece to be joined. The polymer chains are now much more mobile because they have gone into solution, albeit only in a thin layer. These mobile chains can now migrate and tangle up together before the solvent evaporates. In a very real sense, the two separate lumps of polymer have been made into one, although the extent of mingling of polymer chains in the region of the join will not be as great as in the bulk solid. The forces holding the joint together are therefore the same as those holding the solid together: van der Waals' forces, dipole–dipole interactions, hydrogen bonds or even ionic interactions. The use of dichloromethane-based glues for perspex is an example of this sort of adhesion.

3. The so-called **adsorption theory** proposes that the contact between glue and surface is so intimate that the particles of both (atoms, ions, molecules, whatever) are close enough together for the normal inter-particle forces to operate. Calculations have been made of the magnitude of these forces. For example, if perfectly flat surfaces were pressed together until they were 10^{-7} m apart, van der Waals' forces would hold them together with a force of about 10^4 N cm^{-2} – far greater than the experimental strength of most adhesive joints. Physicists talk of optically flat surfaces, but this sort of calculation assumes that the surface is about 10^3 times smoother – hardly achievable in practice. Nevertheless, it shows that the forces involved are big enough if we can get the glue close enough to the surface. Of course the forces involved may not just be van der Waals' forces; stronger forces may occur. The traditional starch-based pastes and woodworkers' PVA glue presumably adhere by means of hydrogen bonds and other dipole–dipole interactions between the glue and the wood or paper (see Figure 11.1). There may even be covalent bonding; silicon-based paints applied to steel surfaces may be attached by covalent Fe−O−Si bonds.

Often the adherence of the glue is improved by surface treatment. Anodising of aluminium thickens up the surface oxide coating, and adsorption of water into this creates a scattering of −OH groups across the metal surface. The anodised aluminium can now be glued with cyanoacrylates: there is hydrogen bonding between these surface −OH groups and the oxygens in the glue. It is not possible to glue polyethene satisfactorily, but if it is oxidised by treatment with a flame, UV light or chromic(VI) acid, surface C=O groups are created that can hydrogen bond with many adhesives. Surface oxidation of zinc producing a surface layer of zinc hydroxide can enable it to be glued with polyacrylic acid by salt formation, leading to an ionic bond (Figure 11.1).

Further reading

Adhesion and Adhesives, A J Kinloch, Chapman and Hall, 1987 (3)

'This Yankee dodge'

Our memory for pain is short – it requires an injury to make us realise just how wonderful the invention of anaesthetics was. Imagine an amputation without it. Before the 1840s the mainstays of pain relief during surgery were opium, laudanum, mandrax and alcohol. Mesmerism, a sort of hypnosis, was also popular.

Then, on December 10th 1844, one Gardner Colton gave a demonstration of dinitrogen oxide (nitrous oxide, N_2O) in Hartford, Connecticut. He was a former medical student who had not taken his degree and who now made his living travelling up and down America giving lectures. A local dentist, Horace Wells, was in the audience, and he noticed that one of the volunteers from the audience had banged his shin while under the influence of the gas and made it bleed, but afterwards had no memory of the pain. A private demonstration the next day was followed by the first surgery. Colton administered the nitrous oxide and a colleague removed one of Wells' wisdom teeth. The following year, Wells tried to demonstrate it at the Harvard Medical School. Unfortunately, too little nitrous oxide was used, the patient shrieked with pain and Wells was hissed from the room.

Ether (ethoxyethane) had been used by Dr Crawford Long of Jefferson, Georgia in an operation to remove cysts from a young man's neck in March 1842, but it was William Morton – a former partner of Horace Wells – who successfully demonstrated its use for pain-free surgery when the senior surgeon at Massachusetts General Hospital removed a neck tumour in October 1846. Within two months it had crossed the Atlantic. Robert Liston, professor of surgery at the University of London, used it when he amputated a gangrenous leg at the thigh. The anaesthetist was a 21-year-old medical student, and, as usual, the operation was fast – it was timed at 27 seconds (the record was said to be nine). When he woke up, the patient is said to have cried 'Take me back to the ward. I can't go through with it! I'll have to live with the leg.' Liston turned to the assembled audience and said 'Gentlemen, this Yankee dodge beats mesmerism hollow.'

It is, perhaps, worth reminding ourselves about the conservatism of medical communities then – and perhaps still today, too – by recalling that operations were still being performed without anaesthesia *25 years later*.

The last of the famous trio of 19th Century anaesthetics, trichloromethane (chloroform), was discovered within a year by James Simpson, professor of midwifery at Edinburgh. He was much attacked – by men, presumably – for use of chloroform in childbirth (for as it says in Genesis chapter 3 verse 16: 'in sorrow thou shalt bring forth children') but when Dr John Snow gave it to Queen Victoria for the birth of her last two children, 'that blessed chloroform' became respectable.

Each of the three compounds had disadvantages. Chloroform was toxic, ether caused high levels of post-operative nausea and vomiting, and nitrous oxide was difficult to administer. So over the next hundred years, a large range of other substances was used, but by about 1940 it was clear that new anaesthetics were needed, and Imperial Chemical Industries in Britain embarked upon a search.

The trouble was that nobody knew how anaesthetics worked. The range of molecules that can act in this way is so huge that it is difficult to think of one chemical mechanism by which all these differing substances could operate. From quite early on, therefore, it was assumed that if there was a general mechanism, it must be physical, a consequence of some physical effect on the body. In about 1900 two German pharmacologists established that the effectiveness of an anaesthetic correlated well with its solubility in a lipid, such as olive oil.

Figure 11.2 summarises data for 22 different anaesthetics in three different animals. It is clear that the higher the solubility in lipid, the lower the pressure of gas needed for anaesthesia – in other words, the more effective the gas is. The Meyer–Overton theory assumed that anaesthesia was something to do with the effect of the molecules on the structure of the membrane. This meant that the anaesthetic molecule had to be substantially non-polar, so that there were no strong interactions (such as dipole–dipole or hydrogen bonds), and it could then dissolve in the lipid, where the interactions were presumably only weak van der Waals' forces.

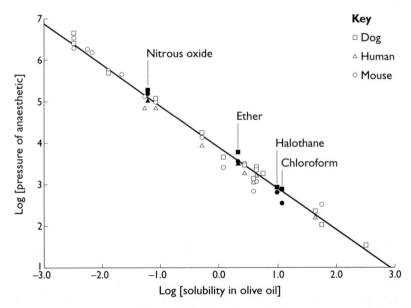

Figure 11.2 Plot of anaesthetic pressure versus olive oil solubility

On the other hand, establishment of the anaesthesia and recovery afterwards are rather slow with very non-polar molecules. It was suggested that this was because the compound also had to dissolve in the blood so that it could be transported to the brain, and this required some water solubility, and therefore some slight polarity.

With this rather limited theory, ICI were able to establish criteria for their research programme. The molecule had to be stable, unreactive, volatile, pretty soluble in lipid but with some water solubility, and non-flammable. By 1956 they had come up with halothane, $CF_3-CHClBr$ and 40 years on it is still one of the most widely used compounds. Use of the best of all – sevoflurane – is restricted because of cost implications, although most anaesthetists will use it for children.

Even today, 150 years on from the first pain-free operation, exactly how anaesthetics work is still not known. It seems clear that they must in some way interfere with the operation of impulses in the brain. Like most cells, the neurones of the brain have concentrations of Na^+ and K^+ ions which are different on the two sides of the membrane: high K^+ and low Na^+ inside the cell, low K^+ and high Na^+ outside (see Figure 11.3). This concentration imbalance means that there is a potential difference between the inside and the outside of the cell of about 30 mV.

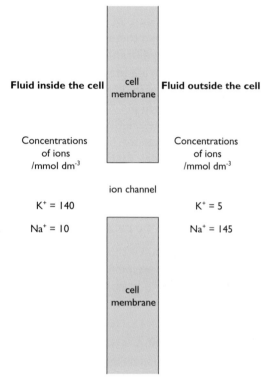

Fluid inside the cell | cell membrane | Fluid outside the cell

Concentrations of ions /mmol dm^{-3}

Concentrations of ions /mmol dm^{-3}

ion channel

$K^+ = 140$

$K^+ = 5$

$Na^+ = 10$

$Na^+ = 145$

cell membrane

Figure 11.3 Ionic concentrations inside and outside the cell

When the neurone is stimulated, ion channels open in the cell wall and sodium ions rush into the cell down the concentration gradient, altering the potential difference. Milliseconds later, potassium ions diffuse out. However it is controlled, this ion movement – sodium in then potassium out – results in a change of the potential difference between inside and out. This electrical impulse, which slides along the nerve cell, is one part of the mechanism of transmission of nerve impulses. It is assumed that anaesthetics act by disruption of this, perhaps by interference with the ion channels.

Direct evidence of this has come from the study of lipid bilayers. These are synthetic membranes made across a hole in a piece of plastic, rather like the soap bubble formed when you dip a wire loop into a soap solution. These synthetic membranes are made of lipids with a polar group at one end, and they arrange themselves in a double layer two molecules thick, with the polar groups facing

81

outwards on each side, into the aqueous solution on either side of the membrane, and with the long non-polar fatty acid chains tangled together in the centre.

It was some time before the means to incorporate ion channels into lipid bilayers was found, first using the antibiotic gramicidin, but then separating natural ion channels from biological tissues and inserting them into the artificial membranes. And now, in a series of elegant experiments, researchers showed that anaesthetics close the sodium channels. This means that on arrival of an electrical impulse, no sodium ions flow, nerve conduction is blocked and no impulse passes. No impulse, no pain.

How does this closure of the sodium channel occur? It is not fully understood, but there are two broad theories. It is possible that when the anaesthetic dissolves in the lipid of the membrane, it alters it in some way that affects the sodium channel. Certainly work on alkane anaesthetics showed that the thickness of the lipid bilayer increased – in other words, the layer swelled – when the alkane dissolved, and the researchers put forward a theory which exactly, and *quantitatively*, explained the anaesthetic effect of the alkane. On the other hand, the dissolving of the anaesthetic into the lipid may not be as important as direct binding to one or more of the proteins that are incorporated into all membranes. Direct binding of anaesthetics to proteins has not only been demonstrated, but this binding has also been shown to be related to the anaesthetic effect. The sodium channel is one such membrane protein, and it may be that the effect is achieved by the anaesthetic binding to one of the hydrophobic regions of the protein.

Further reading

A Short History of Anaesthesia, G B Rushman, N J H Davies, R S Atkinson, Butterworth-Heinemann, 1996 (fascinating history – 1 – but quite technical science)

Hydrophobia

Oil and water don't mix; soap cleans; the very nature of proteins and biological membranes – all these depend largely on so-called hydrophobic interactions.

The idea looks simple. *Of course* oil and water won't mix, we might think, because if oil molecules get in between the molecules in liquid water, they break the hydrogen bonding, and this will be so unfavourable energetically that the process just cannot occur.

Let's look at some data. Given in the following table are some ΔH, ΔS and ΔG values for a process in which a given hydrocarbon solute molecule is transferred from a hydrocarbon solvent to an aqueous solution.

Solute	Solvent	ΔH kJ mol^{-1}	ΔS J (mol K)$^{-1}$	ΔG kJ mol^{-1}
CH_4	C_6H_6	-11.7	-75.8	$+12.1$
C_2H_6	C_6H_6	-9.2	-83.6	$+15.7$
C_4H_{10}	C_4H_{10}	-3.3	-96.3	$+25.3$
C_6H_{14}	C_6H_{14}	0.0	-95.3	$+28.4$

A glance at the data confirms that ΔG is positive; the process is very unfavourable. If we had a solution of methane in benzene and shook it up with water, the methane would not go into the aqueous layer. Like dissolves like, and unlikes don't mix. So the solubility of methane in water at room temperature and pressure is *tiny* – only about 1.4×10^{-3} mol dm^{-3}. But this insolubility of methane in water is not due to the ΔH term. If we could persuade the methane to dissolve in water, the process would be *exothermic*. As far as the enthalpy term goes, dissolving methane in water is *favourable*. It is the entropy term which is not, and it is so unfavourable that it outweighs the ΔH and makes ΔG positive.

How can this be? How can dissolving methane in water have a negative entropy term? After all, water is a well-ordered liquid to start with, as a result of hydrogen bonding: how can dissolving methane make the system *even more ordered*?

If we introduce a methane molecule into water, it has to make room for itself, and in doing so, it has to elbow aside some water molecules and disrupt their hydrogen bonding. Creating this cavity for the methane is thus endothermic – so far. But it now seems that the water molecules arrange themselves around this hole in such a way that they make new hydrogen bonds with each other around the surface of the cavity, new hydrogen bonds which more than compensate for those lost in the first place. Thus the ΔH term for dissolving methane is negative (although as the size of the hydrocarbon increases and more hydrogen bonds have to be broken to make room for it, the ΔH value becomes more positive). The methane molecule thus induces an ordering of the water molecules around its cavity. It is this which causes the ΔS value to be so negative and prevents the methane from dissolving.

All this has massive implications. For example, what will be the nature of any water within biological membranes, the centre of which consists largely of non-polar lipids? And consider this – because $\Delta G = \Delta H - T\Delta S$, as we lower the temperature, the entropy contribution becomes less and less important compared to that of the ΔH term. In this system, it is the entropy term which prevents the hydrocarbon dissolving, so because the ΔH term is favourable, we may reach a temperature at which ΔG becomes zero, and below which dissolving actually becomes preferable. For methane being partitioned between hexane and water, this happens at about 150 K; below this temperature, ΔG becomes negative and methane would dissolve better in water than in hexane. I don't have data for the equilibrium:

$$CH_4(g) \rightleftharpoons CH_4(aq)$$

but the same idea applies here too – there will come a temperature when the equilibrium tips in favour of the aqueous solution. If the system is also under pressure, then by Le Chatelier's Principle the right-hand side becomes even more favoured. This is true: if we cool a mixture of water and methane under pressure, we find that a solid separates, of composition about $CH_4.(H_2O)_{5.8}$.

Chlorine hydrate, $Cl_2.(H_2O)_{6.9}$, was the first of these peculiar compounds to be found (by Humphrey Davy, in 1810), and their full elucidation has proved awkward. There is a whole range of them, of general formula $X.(H_2O)_n$:

X	n (approx)
Ar	6.1
Kr	6.9
Xe	7.6
CH_4	5.8
C_2H_6	6.9–8.2
C_3H_8	17.9

It turns out that there are two different types of solid. X-ray studies have shown that they are *clathrate* compounds – the water molecules form a solid lattice which is different from the usual ice lattice. The water molecules form hydrogen-bonded cages which *trap* the gas molecules inside them.

There are two different types of lattice, and each type has two different sorts of cage. Figure 11.4 shows the type I lattice and its two different cages, one made up of 12 pentagons (called 5^{12}) and the other made of 12 pentagons and 2 hexagons ($5^{12}6^2$). (The type II lattice is slightly different so the cages are of different sizes.)

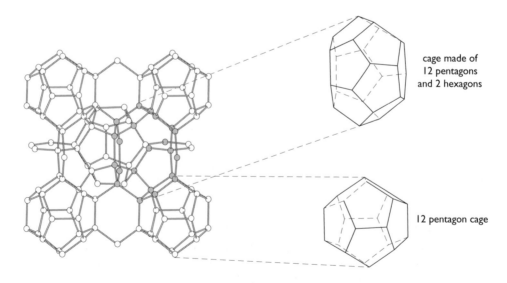

cage made of 12 pentagons and 2 hexagons

12 pentagon cage

Figure 11.4 The type I gas clathrate structure

Depending upon the size of the molecule, it can fit into one or other of the cages:

	Type I		Type II	
	5^{12}	$5^{12}6^2$	5^{12}	$5^{12}6^2$
Diameter of cage/nm	0.492	0.576	0.490	0.646
Ratio gas:water	1:5.75	1:7.67	1:5.75	1:17.0

It appears that each gas molecule goes into the cavity which best fits it, interacting with the water molecules forming the walls of the cage by van der Waals' forces. The 'formula' of the compound will depend on which sort of cage is occupied. (Not all the possible sites are occupied; typically only 70–90% are filled, which makes things look even more odd.)

These structures are similar, but not identical, to normal ice. Just as in ice, the O···O···O bond angles are close to the tetrahedral angle. But the O−H···O distance in the clathrates is about 0.29 nm, compared to the 0.276 nm in ice: they have a slightly more open structure. There are other more subtle differences.

For pure water, then, the ice lattice is more stable than the clathrates, but in the presence of non-polar gases at high pressure or low temperature, the balance is tipped so that the clathrate lattice becomes more stable.

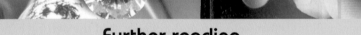

Further reading

The Real Reason Why Oil and Water Don't Mix: T P Silverstein, *J Chem Ed* **75**: 116, 1998

Water, F Franks (ed.), Plenum Press, 1973: Volume 2, Chapter 3 (2)

Clathrate Hydrates of Natural Gases, E Dendy Sloan Jr, Marcel Dekker, Inc., 1990 (2–3)

Cement

The effect of heat on blue hydrated copper (II) sulphate, $CuSO_4.5H_2O$, is a familiar demonstration. White, anhydrous copper (II) sulphate is produced:

$$CuSO_4.5H_2O \rightarrow CuSO_4 + 5H_2O$$

If this anhydrous copper sulphate is now allowed to cool and a small amount of water added to it, there is a violently exothermic reaction, and the solid $CuSO_4.5H_2O$ is reformed. Of course, you don't get nice crystals, but if just the right amount of water is used, you do get a solid. This is the sort of thing that happens when cement sets.

Cement is made by heating a very intimate mixture of aluminosilicate clays and limestone to about 1450°C. This is done in a long cylinder inclined at a slight angle to the horizontal, so that the solid reagents can be dropped in at the top and as the cylinder rotates they slowly migrate to the bottom, reacting as they go. Heating is by a huge natural gas jet blown in at the bottom, or by premixing coal with the reagents and burning it as the mixture descends. The $CaCO_3$ loses CO_2, and the whole mass partially melts, ultimately forming a solid called clinker. This is then cooled, gypsum is added (see below) and the mixture is ground very finely.

The end product is usually considered to be a mixture of four compounds:

- ~50% Ca_3SiO_5, which can be treated as if it were $3CaO.SiO_2$, and for simplicity is abbreviated to C_3S (but of course the C doesn't stand for carbon, nor the S for sulphur!)

- ~30% Ca_2SiO_4, treated as if it were $2CaO.SiO_2$, abbreviated to C_2S

- ~10% $Ca_3Al_2O_5$, treated as if it were $2CaO.Al_2O_3$, abbreviated to C_3A

- ~10% $Ca_4Al_2Fe_2O_{10}$ treated as if it were $4CaO.Al_2O_3.Fe_2O_3$, abbreviated to C_4AF

The proportions of the various compounds will vary a little, depending on the nature of the starting materials.

Setting of the cement is a hydration, essentially similar to that of anhydrous copper sulphate, and it too is exothermic. There are differences, however. For one thing, the products of the reaction of cement are insoluble in water, so whereas use of excess water will produce a copper sulphate solution, the cement still sets to a solid. Cement will therefore set even under water. And the setting is not only a hydration; the calcium silicates also undergo hydrolyses, producing more complex salts, such as $Ca_3Si_2O_5.3H_2O$ (or $3CaO.2SiO_2.3H_2O$, abbreviated to $C_3S_2H_3$), together with $Ca(OH)_2$.

$$Ca_3SiO_5 + 6H_2O \rightarrow Ca_3Si_2O_5.3H_2O + 3Ca(OH)_2 \ (+ \ heat)$$

It is the $Ca_3Si_2O_5.3H_2O$ ($C_3S_2H_3$) which is primarily responsible for the developing strength of the cement. The heat produced in the reaction can be a problem. In cold climates it is useful in that it tends to prevent the water freezing during the setting process (which would be disastrous). On the other hand, if a large mass of cement is being used in a hot country, cooling pipes may have to be embedded in the structure so that the heat can be pumped out; they can be left in place as reinforcement. The calcium hydroxide is doubly significant. It makes an important contribution to the structure and hence the strength of the final solid. But the wet mix should be washed quickly off the skin, and even the dry powder is dangerous to eyes or lungs, because the rapid hydration leads to high temperatures and to very alkaline products: cement burns are a well-known hazard.

Because cement is a mixture of anhydrous salts, hydration and hydrolysis occur in steps. Although the amount of C_3A ($Ca_3Al_2O_6$ or $3CaO.Al_2O_3$) is small, typically between 5% and 15%, it hydrates very violently, leading to a rapid stiffening of the cement paste known as flash set. This would make the cement unworkable within a very short time, so to prevent it happening, gypsum, $CaSO_4$, is added to the clinker before it is ground. This reacts with the C_3A, preventing the flash set and thus ensuring that the cement remains workable for several hours.

The progress of the set can be observed by following the rate of heat production of the mixture as it solidifies (see Figure 11.5).

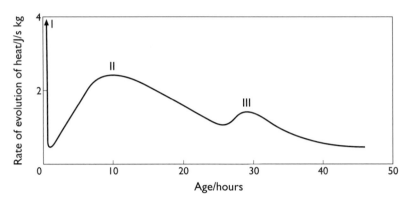

Figure 11.5 The evolution of heat as cement sets

The very high initial peak, occurring within less than an hour of mixing, corresponds to the surface reaction of the cement particles and, despite the addition of gypsum, is probably due mainly to hydration of C_3A. The grains of cement have now become covered with a layer of hydrated salts such as $C_3S_2H_3$, and because these are insoluble in water, they tend to stop further water diffusion into the interior of the cement grains. For a while, therefore, the rate of setting slows down and the cement remains workable for at least a couple of hours. Water penetration cannot be held up for ever, though. Eventually it percolates through the layer of $C_3S_2H_3$. This generates an osmotic pressure, which eventually ruptures the $C_3S_2H_3$ layer, and a small amount of the contents will shoot out through the hole. As soon as this meets the water outside, however, it reforms the insoluble $C_3S_2H_3$ layer, and so the process goes on. As the setting proceeds, then, spiny growths reach out from each grain of cement, and as these meet and interlock, the cement gathers strength (see Figure 11.6).

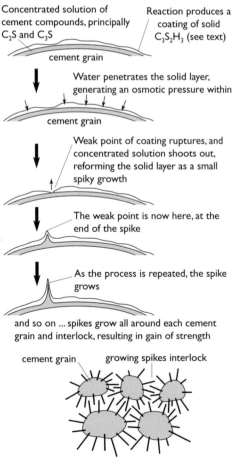

Figure 11.6 The setting of cement

Even after 30 hours or so, there are further reactions going on, and indeed cement goes on getting stronger for up to a year after mixing as the calcium silicates slowly achieve more complete hydration.

Hydration of copper (II) sulphate requires a water:salt mole ratio of 5:1, or a mass ratio of 90:159.5, or 0.564:1. Calculations of this sort cannot be performed for a cement, not least because it is a mixture. Empirical determination of the optimal water:cement ratio for complete hydration shows that about 0.38:1 by mass is required. (Of course, there are no weighing machines on building sites; bricklayers use their experience. On the other hand, suppliers of premixed concrete do weigh all the ingredients, water included.)

Hydrated copper (II) sulphate has two different types of water in the crystals, bonded by ion–dipole interactions and hydrogen bonds. Cement has many more types of water, but as with copper sulphate, they are structural, responsible in part for the strength of the material. Binding will be the whole range of forces: van der Waals' forces, ion–dipole interactions and hydrogen bonds, while much of the strength of the final cement will be due to the $Si-O-Si$ covalent bonds created as products like $Ca_3Si_2O_5.3H_2O$ are formed.

Cement is used mixed with some sort of aggregate, such as sand or gravel, because these are much cheaper than the cement itself, and, provided appropriate aggregates are used, the strength of the final mix will be unaffected. Both cement and concrete are very strong in compression, but typically 8–10 times weaker in tension. This low tensile strength has been related to the presence of small flaws: pores, tiny cracks, air bubbles and so on. This means that stresses may not be transmitted uniformly throughout the solid. As a result, concrete which will have to stand up to tensile stresses is usually reinforced with steel. Bonding of steel and concrete arises chiefly from friction (achieved by the shaping of the metal surface so that interlocking occurs) although there may be some influence of chemical bonding. Intriguingly, the presence of rust is advantageous – so long as the rust is firmly attached to the metal surface – because it allows for better 'keying' of concrete to metal. There may also be hydrogen bonding between the concrete and $-OH$ groups in the rust.

If the temperature is high, setting may be unduly rapid; under these conditions, retarders may be useful. These are substances that slow down the set, and include sugars, carbohydrates, soluble zinc salts and soluble borates. Their mechanism of action is unknown, although it is clearly no accident that all of them can form extensive hydrogen bonding. Indeed if sugar is added to the extent of 1% by mass, the cement will not set. During the construction of the Channel tunnel, molasses was used to clean the machinery, as washing with large quantities of water was not possible underground.

12

FREE RADICALS

Free radicals are species with unpaired electrons and they range from the furiously reactive atoms like Cl· or groups such as CH_3· to the really rather unreactive species such as O_2. They all share the characteristic that their reactions are pretty unspecific – they tend to react with whatever they hit – so that cascades of different products may ensue, especially if the radical is one of the more reactive ones.

Flames

Light a candle. Sit down quietly beside it and let the air become still. As the candle burns the wick will become longer and will develop a curl, so that the end of it eventually pokes out of the edge of the flame and glows red-hot.

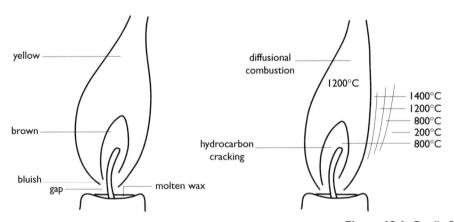

Figure 12.1 Candle flame

As you try to light the candle, the match melts a pool of wax and the molten wax flows up the wick, getting further heated as it goes. It takes a little time for it to get hot enough to evaporate and burn – for it is the wax vapour that burns – hence the small gap of unburnt wick between the top of the candle and flame. Most of the energy loss from the flame is by convection, and as the heated gases rise from the top of the flame, air is drawn in from the sides and below the flame, thus providing the necessary oxygen. If you blow the flame out, there is a brief swirl of what looks like smoke from the top of the wick. Of course, it isn't smoke – there is no longer any combustion going on. If you put a flame into this 'smoke' it reignities. The 'smoke' is in fact wax vapour. Once the flame has been extinguished, the hot vapour goes on evaporating from the wick but it now cools and recondenses back to liquid and solid wax.

The colours reveal that the flame is not simple. The base of the flame is a faint blue, almost colourless, becoming more yellow towards the top. In the middle there is a roughly cone-shaped region which is a paler yellow, even brownish in colour. You can show that this brown region contains unburnt wax vapour: a small piece of glass tubing put into this region allows unburnt wax vapour to flow along the tube out of the flame and be ignited at its end. In fact the situation is more complex: sampling and analysis of this region shows that it contains products of cracking of the wax. If you put a cold surface into the yellow part of the flame, above the brownish cone, a black deposit of solid carbon is produced on the cold object. This region of the flame is one of diffusional combustion – the cracked wax and oxygen are diffusing together and combustion reactions are occurring. Carbon is formed during this stage, but by the time the top of the flame is reached, it has all been fully oxidised.

The temperatures shown in Figure 12.1 may look rather startling, and it is certainly true that you cannot use a candle to heat an object – a test tube or a kettle, for example – as hot as this. These values are obtained with microscopic thermocouples – any larger object will lose heat so rapidly that the maximum temperature it will achieve will be hundreds of degrees lower.

The flame from a Bunsen burner shows similar features. If the air hole is closed, the only oxygen available to the flame is that which diffuses into it from outside, so the flame is similar in structure and colour to the candle flame. There is no gap between the top of the burner and the flame as there is with a candle, as the gas does not take as long to heat up to its combustion temperature. And because the gas is issuing from an aperture which is about 1 cm across, the blue region at the base of a candle flame is not so evident. The bulk of the flame is therefore a mixture of the brown and yellow regions of the candle, and we should expect similar sorts of reactions. Certainly there is an abundance of soot, as you can readily show by trying to heat something with a yellow flame.

Open the air hole, though, and things change. The mixture of gas emerging from the tube now has enough oxygen premixed with it to start burning. (The flame does not slide down the burner because the rate of supply of gas is faster than the rate of propagation of the flame through the gases.) There is still not enough air for complete combustion, however, so more has to be supplied by diffusion, as with a candle. The flame is now much bluer, with a central cone of bright blue and an outer one of a more violet blue, mixed with some yellow. This inner bright blue conical surface is the primary reaction zone, only a fraction of a millimetre thick. Inside it, there has been essentially no reaction – a piece of glass tubing can be used to extract unburnt gas, burning it at the end of the tube.

Because of the deficiency of air, the products of this primary reaction include carbon monoxide and *hydrogen*, and these, together with unburnt methane, undergo full reaction at the outer flame front where these gases meet the oxygen diffusing in from the surrounding air.

So what actually is a flame? It is that region in space in which reactions are occurring, producing heat and light. What we see as the flame is just the various different light emissions due to hot, excited particles in the reacting gas. Exactly what these particles are can vary widely.

In the non-luminous Bunsen flame, with the air hole fully open, the first reactions occur in the fractions of a millimetre that we see as the blue cone. Spectroscopic studies of this region show strong emissions from the following free radicals:

Species	Wavelength/nm	Colour
C_2	516.5	green
	437.7	blue
CH	431.5	violet
OH	306.4	UV
HCO	420 and below	violet and UV (weak)

However these free radicals are formed (see below) they must be in some sort of excited state, and they return to the ground state by emission of light. (It so happens that this light is in the visible region of the spectrum. In addition to these emissions, the major radiation from a Bunsen flame is in the infra red, which you can feel as radiated heat. This comes from all regions of the flame, and is mainly due to emissions from water and carbon dioxide.)

We can see, therefore, why the inner conical surface in a Bunsen flame is blue or blue-green in colour: it is because of the production of these free radicals and their emission of light in the blue-green region of the spectrum. The outer cone of the Bunsen is paler in colour. C_2 radicals are never found here, although CH and OH may be, especially if the gases are being chilled by a cold surface. The major contributor to the colour of the outer cone is the familiar blue flame of combustion of CO, which has been formed in the earlier reactions. There may also be some continuous emissions in the visible, from incandescent particles of carbon.

But spectroscopy tells only a small part of the story. It has long been known that flames contain charged particles. So a charged plate will be discharged if brushed with a flame and it is easy to demonstrate that a flame conducts electricity. Presumably these charged particles arise as the high temperature causes ionisation of radicals, producing cations and electrons.

But the relatively recent application of mass spectrometry to flame chemistry has shown that things are much more complicated than was thought – *much* more complicated!

It is now clear that a methane flame contains *larger* species than you started with, as well as a range of other intermediates. For example, ethane, C_2H_6, ethene, C_2H_4, and ethyne, C_2H_2, have all been detected, as well as methanal, HCHO, and a host of intervening radicals.

The first steps involve collision of methane and another hot molecule, M*:

$$CH_4 + M^* \rightarrow CH_3 + H + M \qquad [1]$$

or O atoms
$$CH_4 + O \rightarrow CH_3 + OH \qquad [2]$$

or OH radicals
$$CH_4 + OH \rightarrow CH_3 + H_2O \qquad [3]$$

and the resulting methyl radical can then react with oxygen:

$$CH_3 + O \rightarrow HCHO + H \qquad [4]$$

or with OH radicals
$$CH_3 + OH \rightarrow CH_4 + O \qquad [5]$$

or even with another CH_3 radical $CH_3 + CH_3 \rightarrow C_2H_6 \qquad [6]$

Reaction [6] involves the production of a stable molecule from two radicals – so is a typical chain termination step familiar from the methane–chlorine reaction – but at these high temperatures many of the radical–radical reactions produce more radicals instead (as in [4] and [5]).

The C_2 radical, responsible for much of the blue colour of the Bunsen flame, presumably arises from the various C_2 species, possibly from C_2H. Or it may be that bigger radicals are formed: C_6H_2 and even C_8H_2 are known from ethyne flames, and these may fragment to give rise both to C_2 and ultimately to the multi-atom carbon particles that we call soot and whose incandescence gives us the yellow of the luminous flame. It may seem odd that these final steps are still not well understood, but so it is. Until recently soot had been no more than a nuisance, but with the discovery of C_{60} and other fullerenes in soot from hydrocarbon flames, a whole new game has begun.

further reading

Fire, J W Lyons, *Scientific American*, 1985 (1)
Flame Structure and Processes, R M Fristrom, Oxford University Press, 1995 (3)

Internet: search on 'fullerenes' if you have a few hours to spare.

Oxygen in the body

Bathed in oxygen, we cannot survive for long without it. If the brain is starved of it for even a few minutes, irreversible damage ensues. But more is too much of a good thing – oxygen at higher pressures is increasingly toxic. Breathing 50% oxygen for as little as six hours causes chest pain and coughing, and longer

exposure causes irreparable lung damage. Indeed there is some evidence that even atmospheric levels cause ill effects. How could this be?

Oxygen is itself a radical (see page 36) and is rather reactive. It has been suggested that its toxicity is due mostly to the formation of superoxide ions (which are radicals as well as ions, remember – see page 37). These may be produced by a range of reactions and it has been estimated that as much as 6% of the oxygen taken up by the cell is transformed into O_2^-. There is much evidence that superoxide ions damage biological systems. When exposed to O_2^- ions, heart mitochondria, lung tissue, synovial fluid, skin and a huge range of systems all showed damage and loss of function. As it is charged, O_2^- is a powerful nucleophile as well as a radical. Furthermore it is both a reducing agent (being oxidised back to O_2) and an oxidising agent (when it is converted to H_2O_2) and disproportionations are possible:

$$2O_2^- + 2H^+ \rightarrow H_2O_2 + O_2$$

(this reaction is catalysed by SODs: see page 176). Hydrogen peroxide is still a nasty molecule to have in the body: because the $O-O$ bond is so weak (a consequence of non-bonded repulsions, of course), the molecule can split:

$$H_2O_2 \rightarrow 2OH\cdot$$

or it can react with more O_2^-:

$$H_2O_2 + O_2^- \rightarrow O_2 + OH^- + OH\cdot$$

so in one way or another a whole family of potentially harmful ions and radicals can be produced.

Free radicals in the body! Just think of the rapid reaction of chlorine with methane, leading to CH_3Cl, CH_2Cl_2 and so on, as well as small amounts of C_2H_6. Imagine the indiscriminate savagery of a radical in complex bags of organic chemicals like us! Just as well we have batteries of defences!

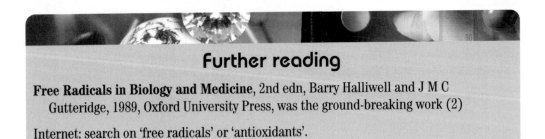

Further reading

Free Radicals in Biology and Medicine, 2nd edn, Barry Halliwell and J M C Gutteridge, 1989, Oxford University Press, was the ground-breaking work (2)

Internet: search on 'free radicals' or 'antioxidants'.

Getting ill, growing old

Why do our bodies wear out? One suggestion rather in favour at present is that free radicals damage body chemicals, and as this damage builds up, it ultimately overwhelms us, and we die.

Certainly oxygen gives rise to a range of free radicals (see page 93) which vary widely in reactivity. The table below gives the approximate half lives in the body of some oxygen-containing species.

Species	Symbol	Half life (s)
Molecular oxygen	O_2	$>10^2$
Hydroxyl radical	$\cdot OH$	10^{-9}
Superoxide radical-ion	$O_2 \cdot^-$	10^{-6}
Hydrogen peroxide	H_2O_2	10 (less in the presence of catalase)

Hydroxyl and superoxide radicals are so reactive that they damage whatever they hit, immediately. Molecular oxygen and hydrogen peroxide both have much longer lifetimes and can diffuse throughout the body, but at any stage they can give rise to the more reactive superoxide and hydroxyl radicals. We must think of radicals as uniquely damaging, able to wander at will throughout the system creating havoc as they go. So what sorts of damage do they do?

Probably the most widely studied reaction of oxygen radicals in the body is that with lipids. These are naturally occurring compounds that are defined solely by one physical property – that they are non-polar. They include a wide range of compounds: triglycerides (more correctly called triacylglycerols), steroids, phospholipids (also called phosphatides) and so on (see Figure 12.2).

Note that the side chains of triglycerides and phospholipids can have a wide range of structures, saturated or with one or more double bonds.

If we represent a lipid by LH, the sort of reaction that can occur might be represented by:

$$LH + R\cdot \rightarrow L\cdot + RH \qquad [1]$$

where R· represents a radical, such as ·OH (when the product RH would be water) or $O_2\cdot^-$ (when RH would be HO_2^- which could protonate to H_2O_2 and split in turn to form more ·OH). The lipid radical (L·) may now react with oxygen to form the lipid peroxy radical:

$$L\cdot + O_2 \rightarrow LOO\cdot \qquad [2]$$

which can react with more lipid molecules:

$$LOO\cdot + LH \rightarrow LOOH + L\cdot \qquad [3]$$

and so on, thus propagating the chain reaction. Peroxides have weak O–O bonds,

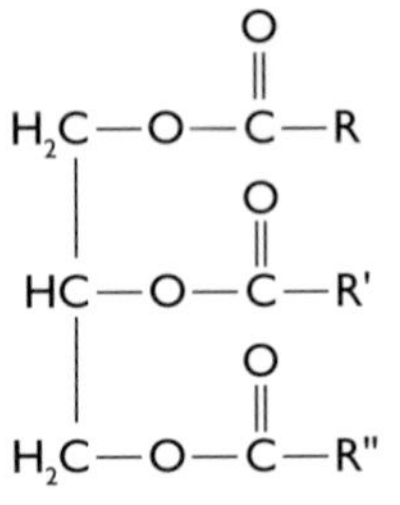

$$H_2C-O-\underset{\underset{O}{\|}}{C}-R$$

$$HC-O-\underset{\underset{O}{\|}}{C}-R'$$

$$H_2C-O-\overset{\overset{O}{\|}}{C}-R''$$

a triglyceride: R, R' and R" are typically $C_{11}-C_{19}$ chains

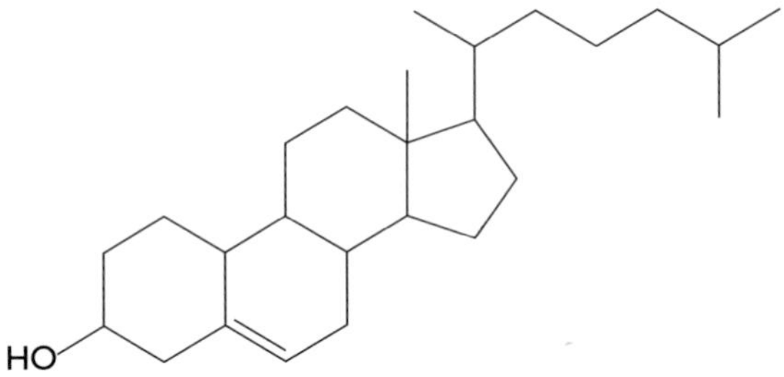

HO

cholesterol

$$H_2C-O-\overset{\overset{O}{\|}}{C}-R$$

$$HC-O-\overset{\overset{O}{\|}}{C}-R'$$

$$H_2C-O-\underset{\underset{O^-}{|}}{P}-O-CH_2-CH_2-\overset{+}{N}(CH_3)_3$$

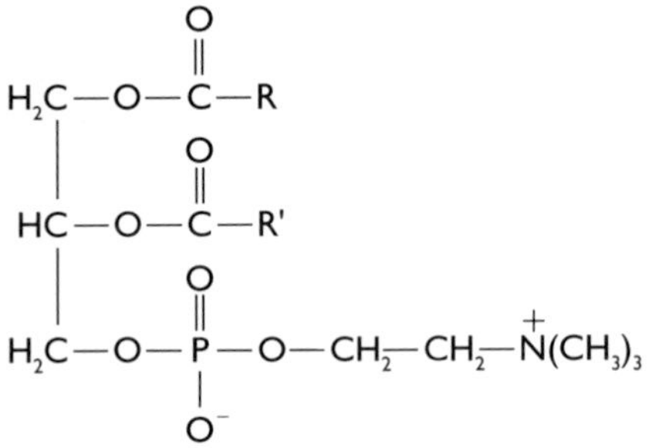

phosphatidyl choline

Figure 12.2 Structure of a triglyceride, cholesterol and phospholipid

so the LOOH can also break down to LO· and ·OH. In addition, Fe^{2+} and Fe^{3+} ions can act as catalysts:

$$LOOH + Fe^{2+} \rightarrow LO· + Fe^{3+} + OH^- \qquad [4]$$

$$LOOH + Fe^{3+} \rightarrow LOO· + Fe^{2+} + H^+ \qquad [5]$$

Lipids are major components of cell membranes so if these sorts of reaction occur to any great extent, the membranes will be damaged and the cells may leak.

And here's a particularly nasty little point. Saturated fats are a high risk factor for coronary heart disease, so there has been a substantial move towards the use of unsaturated or polyunsaturated fats in the diet. The table opposite gives the bond dissociation energies for various C–H bonds.

Bond	Bond dissociation enthalpy/ kJ mol^{-1}
CH_3-H	436
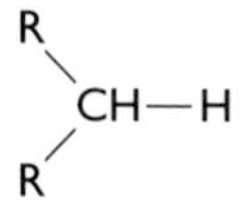 (R)(R)$CH-H$	403
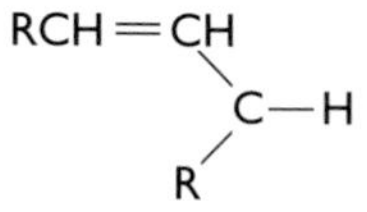 $RCH=CH$ ... $C-H$ (R)	355
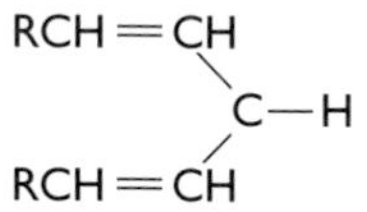 $RCH=CH$ ... $C-H$ ... $RCH=CH$	318

Figure 12.3 Bond energies of C—H bonds

Loss of the hydrogen from the middle carbon of a 1,4-diene is clearly very much easier than loss of H from a saturated or even an unsaturated fat. (This is because when the radical is formed delocalisation can occur that is not possible in the 1,4-diene: see Figure 12.4.)

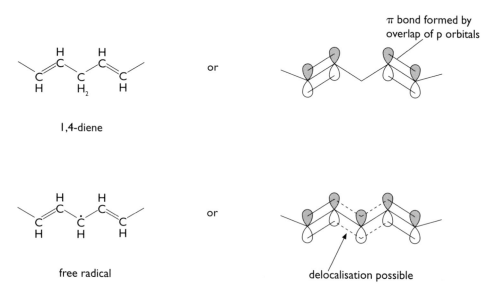

Figure 12.4 Delocalisation in the radical from a 1,4-diene

It may be desirable to have unsaturated fats in the body as far as protection from heart diseases is concerned, but an unsaturated fat is much more vulnerable to attack by radicals.

It has been estimated that there may be as many as 10 million $O_2 \cdot^-$ radicals being formed each day in every cell in the body, so the body has developed ranks of defences:

Type of defence	Location
Catalase, Mn SOD	Mitochondrial matrix
Tocopherol (vitamin E)	Inner mitochondrial membrane
CuZn SOD	Mitochondria
Glutathione peroxidase	Cytoplasm
Ascorbic acid (vitamin C)	Serum, cytoplasm, etc.
Glutathione, etc.	

SODs are superoxide dismutases (see page 176)

But what of the free radical theory of ageing? Is there any evidence to support it? If indeed this sort of free-radical oxidation is as serious as this theory proposes, we should expect to find that the longer-lived species have better defence systems. Figure 12.5 examines this. It shows the SOD concentration in various mammals (divided by their metabolic rate, so as to remove effects due to differences of metabolism) against the maximum lifespan of the mammal.

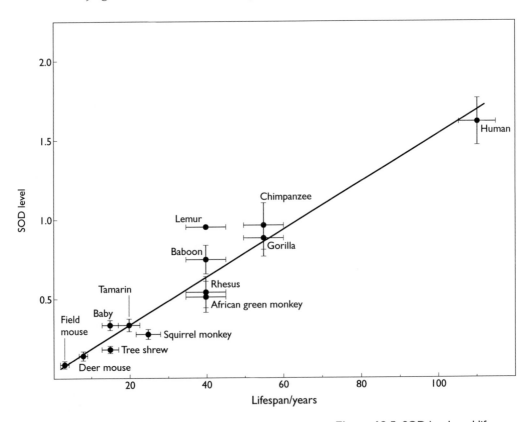

Figure 12.5 SOD levels and lifespan

The correlation is clear and remarkable: the longer-lived mammals have higher SOD levels. In other words, the higher the concentration of SODs (and therefore the better the defences against free-radical oxidations) the longer the animal lives.

And what of illnesses? Are there any that are linked to the presence of free radicals in the body? Both the major killers – cancer and heart disease – are now thought to involve free radicals. The most detailed study so far, that of over 6000 people working in Basel and extending over many years, has shown that the risk of death from cancer and cardiovascular disease was significantly raised in people with low levels of carotene and vitamin C.

What can we do? The first thing we must consider is reducing our intake of polyunsaturated fat – it is just so easy to oxidise. We need some, of course; linoleic acid (*cis, cis*-9,12-octadecadienoic acid) is an essential part of our diet for prostaglandin synthesis. (Nor should we replace polyunsaturated fats with saturated ones; as far as possible we should attempt to reduce our total fat intake.) We must pay attention to our use of cooking oils, too; they undergo oxidation during use and if we reuse them for too long, we will be eating oils which already contain peroxides.

Clearly we should boost our antioxidant levels. This is the reason behind the current popularity of ACE-selenium tablets, and they may do some good. (Selenium is essential for the functioning of glutathione peroxidase mentioned above.) On the other hand, the human body was designed by evolution to get all the nutrients it needs from the diet, and if we are deficient in any, it is probably because we are no longer eating the sort of diet our ancestors did during the millions of years that our bodies took to evolve. Studies on the few surviving hunter–gatherers left in the modern era have shown that their diet consists of a wide range of fruit and vegetables with little meat. (How often would you eat meat if you had to chase it down and kill it with a stone axe?) Hence the current recommendation that we eat at least five and preferably nine portions of fruit and vegetables a day.

further reading

Free Radicals in Biology and Medicine, 2nd edn, Barry Halliwell and J M C Gutteridge, Oxford University Press, 1989 (2)

Internet: search on 'free radicals' or 'antioxidants'

13

FUELS

It seems clear that within the lifetime of people now alive, oil will run out. And although coal reserves could last for several hundred years, in the UK, at least, most of these have now been abandoned and the pits sealed. New energy sources will be needed. This section mentions just two of the possibilities.

Vehicle fuels

Oil will run out. To be sure, new discoveries mean that it will not disappear as fast as once seemed likely, but run out it must, one day. Replacements must be found.

The introduction of a new fuel is a huge undertaking, and consideration will have to be given to the performance of the vehicles, ease of refuelling, environmental impact, costs and so on. Here are some data for five fuels.

Fuel	Gasoline	Natural gas	Liquid petroleum gas (LPG)	Methanol	Ethanol
Octane rating	91–98	>127	104	112	111
Air:fuel ratio	14.6	16.2	15.8	6.5	9.0
Enthalpy of vaporisation (MJ/kg)	0.30	–	–	1.08	0.84

First, we must think what effect changing fuel will have on the efficiency of the engine.

Engines are basically air pumps. Many of the difficulties of engine design revolve around getting enough air into the engine to burn the fuel (hence the use of superchargers and turbochargers). A liquid fuel (which will not vaporise until it gets into the cylinder) will occupy very little volume. (Think of the volume of 1 mole of liquid and gaseous water, for example: 18 cm^3 compared to about 24 000 cm^3 at room temperature and pressure.) But the two gases in the list above will occupy a significant volume – between 4% and 15% of the intake volume – so there is less room for the air, resulting in a power loss of about 4% for LPG and 9.5% for natural gas.

For a gasoline engine the efficiency of the engine also depends on the compression ratio – the higher the better – and this in turn depends on the octane rating of the fuel. All four of the alternative fuels have a higher octane rating than gasoline, so a higher compression ratio could be used with corresponding efficiency gains. Of course, if the engine is not designed specifically for the new fuel, but is a gasoline engine modified slightly to allow it to burn the new fuel, the efficiency gain will be less.

Emissions are likely to be an important consideration. Figure 13.1 shows the total net emission of greenhouse gases for a variety of fuels and sources.

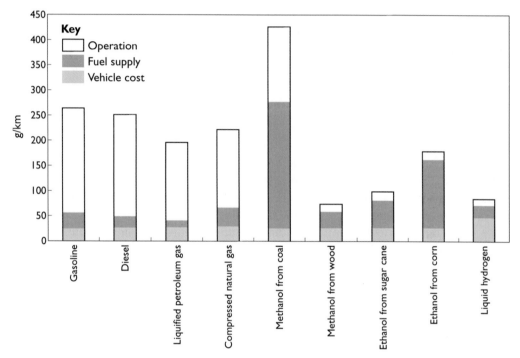

Figure 13.1 Net greenhouse gas emissions from various fuels (in g of carbon dioxide equivalent per km)

Note that this shows the total amount of gas given off: from manufacture of the vehicle, manufacture of the fuel and operation of the vehicle. The emissions produced by the alcohols made from wood, corn or sugar cane are so low because this is *net* emission – when the original plant grew, it absorbed carbon dioxide, and combustion of the fuel just puts this back into the atmosphere again. But combustion of methanol from coal puts back fossil carbon dioxide; the greenhouse impact of both fuel production and use is huge.

Emission of other pollutants will be less with all these fuels than for gasoline. The smog-forming hydrocarbons are primarily the larger and more branched ones, so even LPG (liquified petroleum gas, consisting mainly of propane) will emit smaller quantities than gasoline or diesel. The alcohols might emit aldehydes, perhaps, but these can effectively be removed using conventional exhaust catalysts.

Refuelling represents perhaps the major barrier to introduction of any new fuel. Popular uptake of the fuel is likely to be low unless there is a good network of filling stations, but there will be no incentive to construct this sort of network until there is a large user base. In addition, some of the fuels are more awkward to transport and to replenish. Natural gas has to be transported either as the liquid (in thermos-type vessels at temperatures below $-151°C$) or compressed, typically to around 200 atmospheres. The tank is therefore a more highly engineered item for natural gas than for gasoline: typically it will consist of a steel or aluminium liner with a Kevlar outer skin. Also, because a given volume of compressed or liquefied methane produces less energy than the same volume of gasoline, the car must carry a larger volume of methane. Instead of a gasoline tank of volume 20 gallons, or 90 dm^3, the compressed natural gas tank would have to be about 400 dm^3. The other fuels have a greater energy density, so their tanks could be smaller. For example at a pressure of about 15–20 atmospheres, an LPG tank would need to be only about 45% bigger than the gasoline tank. Refuelling pressurised tanks seems to present problems, too, and could probably only be done by trained operatives. This might limit use of these fuels to public service fleets.

All the fuels are reckoned to be safer than gasoline. This may seem bizarre given the high storage pressures for methane, but it is much less dense than air, so will dissipate rapidly if released, and its flammability range is much smaller than that of gasoline. LPG is much more similar to gasoline, but the stronger construction of the fuel tank (typically capable of sustaining a pressure of at least four times the operating pressure) makes rupture or leakage less likely. Methanol and ethanol are safer still in that their enthalpy of vaporisation makes generation of a vapour/air mixture pretty difficult. Indeed, this may make for poor starting at low temperatures, when electrical cylinder heaters (as with diesel engines) will be necessary.

The alcohols have another problem. They are more corrosive to engine components than gasoline, and they both absorb water, making them more damaging still. This necessitates careful redesign of all components that will come into contact with the fuel.

What are the current prospects for these fuels? There are some 800 000 vehicles operating at present world-wide using natural gas, but the biggest share of the market must surely be held by LPG vehicles, with probably 4 million vehicles at present in use.

Alcohols have long been considered as possible fuels. Methanol has been used in motor racing for decades, chiefly because of its higher octane rating and Germany has added 15% of methanol to its gasoline for years, but it is Brazil that has put alcohols at the forefront of national policy. This was provoked by a foreign-debt crisis in the 1970s caused by rising oil prices and interest rates, coupled with a crash in sugar prices. Between 1975 and 1979, the government-sponsored programme, Proalcool, increased the percentage of ethanol in fuel to 20%. Then in 1979 they began to promote ethanol-dedicated cars – as opposed to those using fuels enriched with alcohol – by offering incentives to purchasers of ethanol cars and guaranteeing that the pump price of ethanol would be cheaper than petrol. Ethanol cars reached 90% of all new car sales in 1985 and amounted to some 30% of the total car population by 1988. Recently, however, the world sugar market has improved and the cost of producing ethanol from sugar is now higher than that of petrol.

Methanol can be manufactured from methane, coal or biomass, and estimates suggest that methane-based methanol would become competitive when oil costs reached $27 a barrel. (Current cost of crude oil can be found from the business section of any newspaper – at the time of writing it is about $17.) Ethanol is chiefly made by fermentation of sugars, either from cane or maize, and estimates of costs depend on the use that can be made of the residual protein after extraction of the sugars. The break-even oil cost seems to be about $60 a barrel.

And what of hydrogen? Its virtually zero emissions make it very appealing, but the major problem is one of obtaining the gas in the first place. Current technologies use electrolysis of water, gasification of biomass or coal, or partial oxidation of hydrocarbons; none of these are cheaper than twice the cost of natural gas. Direct photolysis of water using sunlight is a hope for the future, but is not yet viable. Then there is the question of storage. Liquefaction is too costly in energy terms, and reversible formation of transition metal hydrides, although feasible, is still too slow and stores too little gas.

There is also the question of safety. The Hindenberg tragedy is etched on everyone's memory – surely hydrogen is too dangerous to use? To be sure, there are problems. Because it is so small, hydrogen diffuses much faster through a small orifice than methane so leaks are more of a problem. But this rapid diffusion can be an advantage – in the event of a spillage, it rapidly disperses, unlike liquid fuels which lie about waiting for a cigarette end. The range of composition of gas:air mixtures which are explosive is wider for hydrogen than for any other fuel, but its ignition temperature is high: 585°C compared to 258°C for gasoline. All in all, then, hydrogen is no more dangerous than any other fuel. We make and use, world-wide, tens of millions of *tonnes* of the stuff each year without catastrophe.

Further reading

Encyclopedia of Chemical Technology, 4th edn, Kirk–Othmer, Wiley Interscience, 1994 (2)

Alternative Fuels, T T Maxwell and J C Jones, Society of Automotive Engineers, 1995 (but it works in units like BThU and feet!; 3)

Burning snowballs, Bermuda triangle

There is a picture in one of the books listed at the end of this section showing a snowball burning. It's not snow at all, of course, or not quite – this snow-like stuff is actually methane hydrate, in which water molecules are hydrogen bonded together to make a cage in which the methane molecule is trapped (see page 82).

The stuff was first made in 1888, and it turned up again in the 1930s causing blockages in natural gas pipelines. This was a serious problem for the Soviet Union, much of whose gas came from Siberian deposits where the low temperatures inevitably favoured hydrate formation. As a result, much of the early work on methane hydrate was done in the Soviet Union.

The phase diagram for methane hydrate is shown in Figure 13.2.

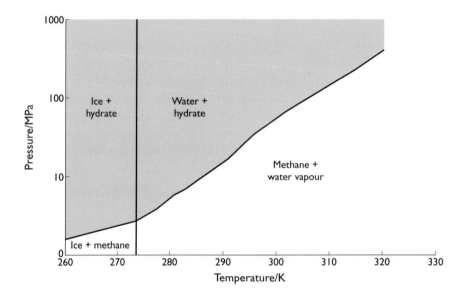

Figure 13.2

The hydrate can exist only in the shaded regions of the diagram, in equilibrium either with ice (to the left of the vertical line) or with liquid water. Note that the hydrate is stable only at very high pressures and/or low temperatures.

This sort of regime of pressure and temperature exists in many regions of the Earth. For example, in many places the permafrost exists down to 600 m. Below this depth, the heat flow from the Earth's core raises the temperature above 273 K, but the increased pressure with depth means that methane hydrate could in theory exist from about 200 m to below 1000 m. It was not until 1965, however, that the first discovery of the naturally occurring compound was made in the northern Soviet Union. It is now accepted that there will be other widespread permafrost deposits. The locations of currently known methane hydrate fields are shown on the map, Figure 13.3.

It's obviously rather difficult to estimate just how much hydrate there is world-wide; current estimates suggest that there are about 10 Tt (Tera = 10^{12}, so this is 1×10^{13} tonnes) of carbon locked up in methane hydrate. Compare this with the total quantity of carbon in fossil fuel deposits, detritus in soil, peat, dissolved as carbon dioxide in the sea, as atmospheric carbon dioxide and combined in living tissue in sea and on land; all that, the whole lot, adds up to only about 9 Tt.

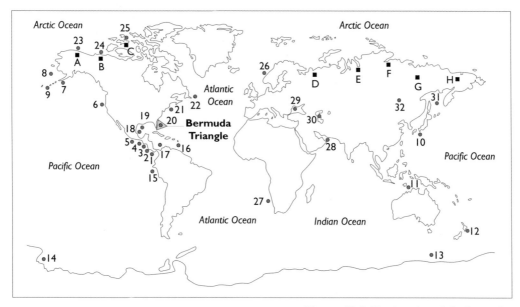

Figure 13.3 The location of the Bermuda triangle and methane hydrate deposits

A fuel source for the future, maybe. Perhaps the next century: there are several problems to be sorted out first. For one thing, the hydrates may not be simple. Analysis shows that a given hydrate may contain a wide range of hydrocarbons. Below are data from two sites in the Gulf of Mexico.

Site	Composition of gas/mol %				
	C_1	C_2	C_3	C_4	CO_2
Orca basin	99.1	0.34	0.28		0.24
Green Canyon-204	61.9	9.2	22.8	5.8	0.2

Gas produced from the Orca basin could be used directly as a replacement for methane supplies, but the other contains such large amounts of the C_2 to C_4 hydrocarbons that it would need refining first.

And just how could the hydrocarbons be obtained from their hydrates? The phase diagram (Figure 13.2) shows that if the temperature is raised, the equilibrium will always be shifted in the direction of free methane. Or to look at it another way, because the equilibrium:

$$CH_4(g) + aq \rightleftharpoons CH_4 \text{ (solid clathrate)}$$

is exothermic (see page 82), Le Chatelier's Principle shows that increase of temperature will shift it to the left. (This is why most gases get less soluble in water as you increase the temperature.) It has been suggested that this can be done by drilling separate injection wells alongside the production wells and forcing hot water or steam down into the hydrate deposit. The temperature is raised and methane is expelled up the production well.

Alternatively, both the phase diagram and Le Chatelier's Principle show that lowering the pressure will also have the effect of producing gaseous methane from the hydrate. The Messoyakha field in Siberia (about 85° east, 68° north; well inside the Arctic circle) started production in the late 1960s. At Messoyakha the hydrate is found associated with free methane, and it is this methane which in part maintains the pressure necessary for hydrate formation. As the gas is extracted, therefore, the pressure falls, and the hydrate decomposes. The well produced methane for 19 years.

Production of methane is therefore feasible and the quantities of hydrocarbons held in hydrates are about twice those in all other known fossil fuel reserves added together. Moreover, because methane has the highest hydrogen:carbon ratio, its use emits less greenhouse gas than gasoline, diesel, kerosene or fuel oil.

But if methane hydrates promise much for fuel production, they may also be an explanation of an old mystery. The so-called Bermuda triangle is a region of sea off the coast of Bermuda (see Figure 13.3). About 100 ships and aircraft have disappeared here since 1854, including five TBM Avenger torpedo bombers of the US Navy on a navigation exercise in December 1945, the MS Marine Sulphur Queen, lost in 1963, and the sailing vessel 'Marques' which foundered suddenly during the Tall Ships race in 1984. The sea floor appears to be unstable in this region – there are reports of frequent damage to telephone cables all along the North American continental shelf. The geochemist Richard McIver has suggested that if a landslip exposed a pocket of methane and its hydrate, large quantities of gas could be released almost instantaneously. Such a bubble of gas could cause a ship or even an aircraft to plunge to the bottom in seconds, maybe.

Further reading

Clathrate Hydrates of Natural Gases, E Dendy Sloan, Jr, Marcel Dekker, Inc, 1990 (2–3)

The Internet is a good source of information: search on 'Bermuda Triangle'.

14

GROUP I ELEMENTS

The elements of Group I have a chemistry that looks pretty straightforward.

- They have one electron in the outer shell and this is easily lost, so the elements have a valency of one.

- All the elements are very similar.

- The compounds of Group I metals are ionic and generally soluble in water.

- Significant complex formation occurs only with polydentate ligands, where the loss of water on formation of the complex from an aqueous ion leads to favourable entropy terms.

- The cations are classified as hard, so the complex formation is by electrostatic interactions with hard ligands, generally those possessing O or N atoms.

- The stability of the complexes is generally inversely related to the ionic size, so the order of stability is
$Li^+ > Na^+ > K^+ > Rb^+ > Cs^+$.

Lithium differs from the other members of Group I and resembles magnesium in many ways: the metal forms a nitride when heated in nitrogen, the carbonate is pretty easily decomposed by heat, it forms hydrated salts, and the fluoride and hydroxide are relatively insoluble.

Crowns and cryptands

In comparison with aluminium and the transition elements, group I and II elements do not form many complexes, and those that do form are of relatively low stability. So when Charles Pedersen announced in 1967 that he had synthesised cyclic polyethers which formed stable complexes with these elements, there was a great deal of interest. And when it was discovered that the stability of these complexes depended on the number and arrangement of the atoms, and that in some cases the most stable complex was formed with K^+, Na^+ or even Rb^+, as well as the more usual Li^+, the excitement became intense.

Pederson was trying to prepare something else, and a by-product turned out to be the cyclic ether dibenzo-18-crown-6 (see Figure 14.1).

Subsequently a whole family of cyclic ethers and similar compounds with N atoms in place of some or all of the oxygens has been prepared (some are shown in

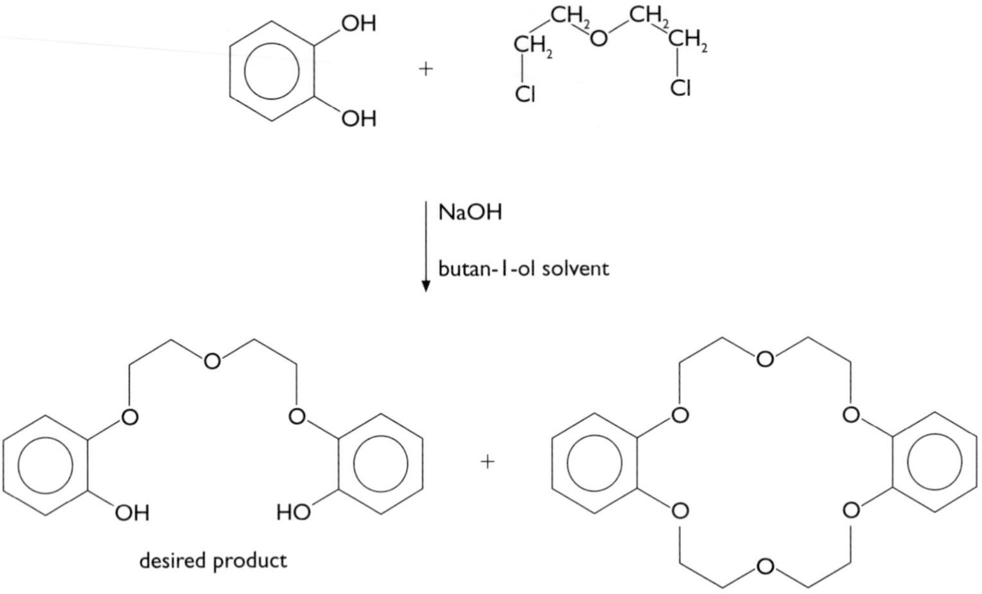

Figure 14.1 Initial synthesis of dibenzo-18-crown-6

Figure 14.2). (The first number gives the total number of atoms making up the ring, and the second gives the number of oxygens.) Later the two-dimensional crown ethers were joined by the three-dimensional cryptands, with a third chain bridging the molecule. (The names here give the number of oxygens per 'bridge'.) The structures of a variety of crowns and cryptands are shown in Figure 14.2.

These molecules form complexes with the group I (and other) ions in which the metal ion lies at the centre of the crown, and it is the interaction between the cation and the slightly negative oxygen which results in a negative ΔH of formation. It was suggested that the strength of the interaction might depend on the size of the hole in the centre of the molecule. If the hole was too small, the cation wouldn't be able to get into the most favourable position for interaction, while if it was too big, the ion would rattle about loosely in it. Only if the hole was just the right size would the cation and the δ- oxygens be able to interact to the maximum extent, and therefore produce the most stable complex. We can examine this by looking at the stability constants, the constant for the equilibrium:

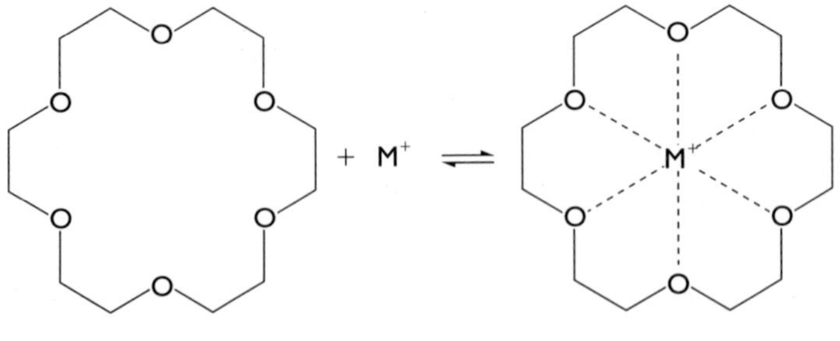

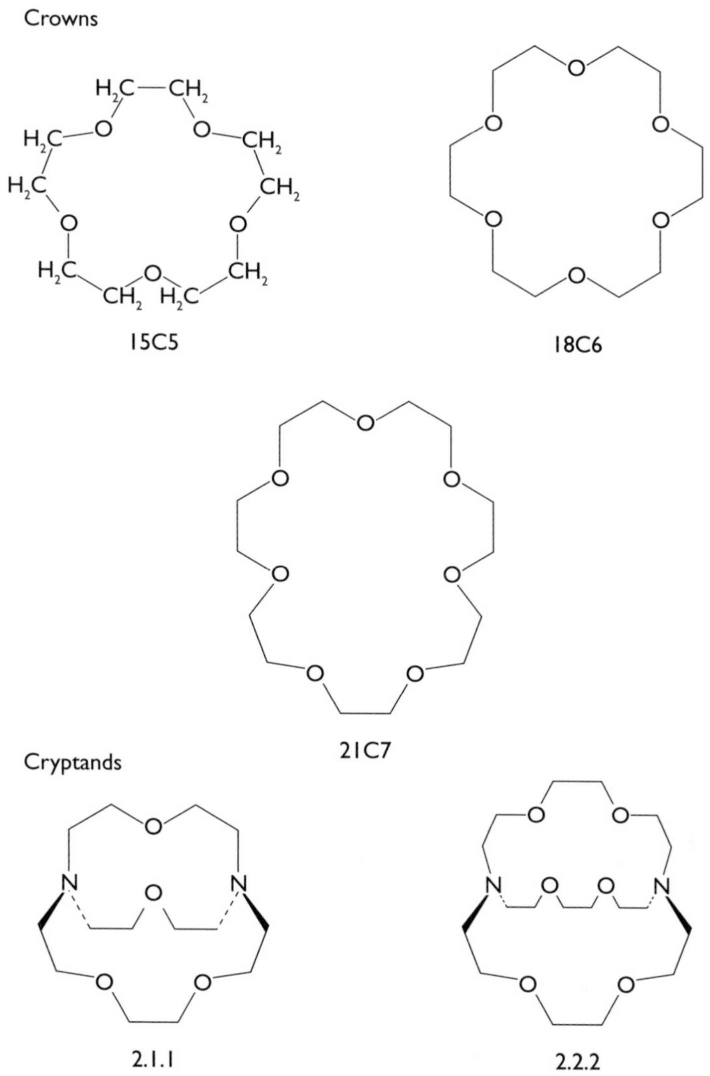

Crowns

15C5

18C6

21C7

Cryptands

2.1.1

2.2.2

Figure 14.2 Some crowns and cryptands

Figure 14.3 gives a plot of the log of the stability constant for the group I ion complexes with various cryptands. It seems that the suggestion is right. For example, cryptand 2.2.1 forms the most stable complex with the Na^+ ion, presumably because the cavity is just the right size for it, but if we look at a larger cryptand, say 2.2.2, we find that it is the larger K^+ ion that complexes most effectively.

It is perhaps this aspect of these compounds that is the most exciting: here we have simple systems that we can make and study easily in the test tube, but which can distinguish between Na^+ and K^+ ions solely on the basis of their size, and in so doing can perhaps help us to understand the role of these and other ions in the body.

In 1987 Pedersen, Donald Cram and Jean-Marie Lehn were awarded the Nobel Prize for chemistry for their work.

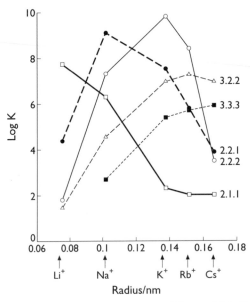

Figure 14.3 Cryptand complex stabilities

Further reading

Designing the Molecular World, Philip Ball, Princeton University Press, 1994, chapter 5 (1)

Any modern advanced inorganic chemistry text will have some coverage of this topic. **Chemistry of the Elements**, N N Greenwood and A Earnshaw, Pergamon, is good. (2)

For a more advanced treatment still:
Crown Ethers and Cryptands, George Gokel, Royal Society of Chemistry, 1991 (2)

Internet: search on 'crown ether' or 'cryptand'.

Pumps

It seems to be an almost universal rule of living systems that they keep the composition of the intracellular fluid different from that of liquids outside the cell. The classic example is, of course, that of mammalian cells, which typically will have the following concentrations (units are mmol dm^{-3}):

	Na$^+$	K$^+$
Inside	10	140
Outside	145	5

Maintenance of an ionic imbalance is crucial (for example, nerve conduction depends on it) and all cells will expend significant amounts of energy in doing so, perhaps 30–50% of their total energy consumption.

Figure 14.4 gives a schematic diagram of the animal sodium–potassium pump.

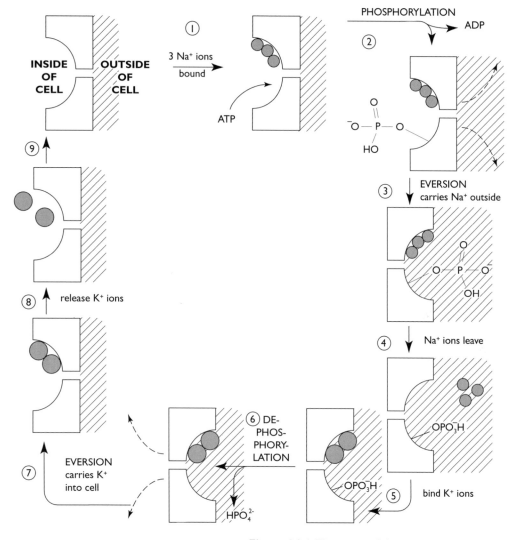

Figure 14.4 The action of the enzyme Na–K–ATPase

The two L-shaped pieces are meant to represent the business bits of one ATPase molecule. This is a protein of relative molar mass 110 000 found in the cell membrane, which hydrolyses ATP only in the presence of Na^+ and K^+ ions (in addition to the Mg^{2+} that all ATPases require). The operation of this pump is thought to be as follows:

Step 1 The ATPase takes up three sodium ions. Complex formation by group I ions is purely electrostatic in origin, an attraction between two ions or between an ion and a dipole; there is virtually no covalent bonding. So this is not a binding like, say, that of iron in haemoglobin; rather it is to be thought of as the sodium ion entering a channel in the surface of the protein. It seems that the channel is made of helical portions of the protein, lined with water molecules. The sodium enters this channel as the hydrated ion and remains hydrated. It is possible that it keeps its own hydration sphere which then interacts with the water molecules lining the channel, or it may become hydrated by the waters of the channel. Hydration, of course, alters the effective size of a cation, and for group I, the smaller the ion, the more strongly it is hydrated, and the larger its hydrated radius:

Ion	Radius/nm	
	Unhydrated	Hydrated
Na^+	0.102	0.33
K^+	0.138	0.28
Tl^+	0.150	

It seems that the hydrated potassium ion is too small to interact strongly enough with the hydrated Na^+ channel.

Step 2 The ATPase–sodium compound now reacts with ATP (Figure 14.5), converting it to ADP (Figure 14.5). This releases the energy needed for

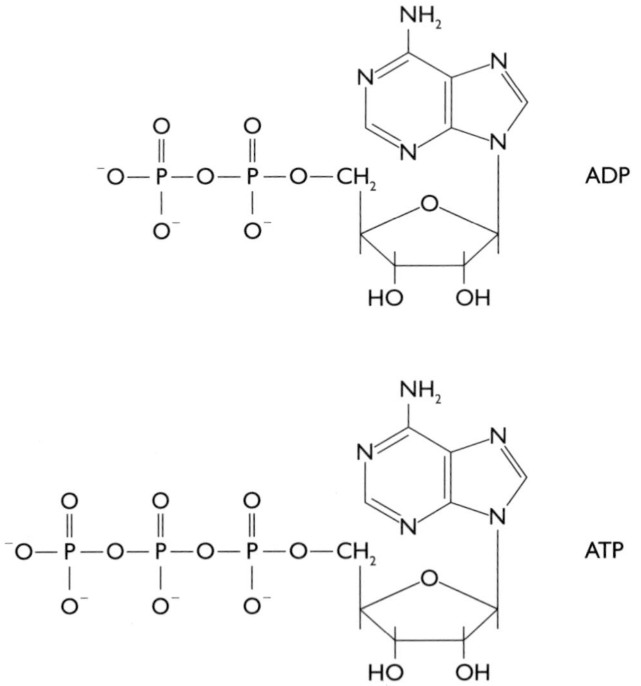

ADP

ATP

Figure 14.5 ADP and ATP

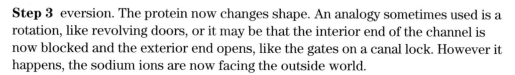

Step 3 eversion. The protein now changes shape. An analogy sometimes used is a rotation, like revolving doors, or it may be that the interior end of the channel is now blocked and the exterior end opens, like the gates on a canal lock. However it happens, the sodium ions are now facing the outside world.

Step 4 The sodium ions now leave and diffuse away from the protein surface, and

Step 5 potassium ions bind. The potassium channel seems to accommodate the unhydrated ion, and it has been suggested that it may be constructed from acidic or basic amino acid side chains, rather like a crown ether or a cryptand (see page 107). There is much evidence for its unhydrated nature. For example, H^+ ions readily migrate through the sodium channels, much as they do in water and by the same sort of mechanism, involving a co-operative rearrangement of bonds, rather than a physical migration of H^+. The sodium channels thus seem to contain water. The K^+ channels are not permeable to H^+ so they can have no water in them. Only Tl^+ ions come near the mobility of K^+ through these channels; all other ions are too big or too small. (This may explain the extreme toxicity of thallium compounds.)

Step 6 The phosphate group is now lost, and this releases the enzyme to carry out another

Step 7 eversion, carrying the potassium ions into the interior of the cell

Step 8 where they are released, and

Step 9 the enzyme is ready for the action once more.

This remarkable selectivity depends, therefore, solely upon size differences and differences in hydration. Note, too, that since three ions are pumped out for every two carried back in, there will be a potential difference set up between the inside of the cell and the outside, a difference of critical importance in the mechanism of nerve conduction.

Jens Skou shared the 1997 Nobel Prize for Chemistry for his work on this system.

Further reading

Any biochemistry textbook, for example, **Biochemistry**, L Stryer, W H Freeman and Co
   (2)
Inorganic Chemistry, 2nd edn, D F Shriver, P W Atkins and C H Langford, Oxford
   University Press, 1994 (2)

Lithium therapy

Manic depressive illness is terrible.

'My thoughts ran ... so fast that I couldn't remember the beginning of a sentence half way through ... I was spitting on a light bulb, thinking that if I watched the saliva burn, I could find the key to the cure for cancer.'

And then comes depression.

'... my friends require much more from me than I can ever possibly give, I seem a drain and a burden on them: the guilt and resentment are overwhelming. ... there is no point to anything. I am dead inside. What is the point of going on like this?'

Suicide is very common in manic depressives.

It is clear that these states are caused by changes in brain chemistry. Scans of the brain of a patient in the two phases of a manic depressive illness show big differences.

As is so often the case, a most effective treatment was found by chance and until recently its mode of operation was a complete mystery. In 1949, the Australian psychiatrist John Cade injected guinea pigs with a solution of lithium carbonate and found that they became quieter without becoming sleepy. Noticing this, he tried giving lithium to a severely manic patient. The results were little short of miraculous – the patient became perfectly well, and could go home and live a normal life. But the medical profession paid no attention, and it was not until the Danish psychiatrist Mogens Schou repeated the work and confirmed all Cade's results that lithium began to be used in Europe. It was not licensed in America until 1970.

Lithium salts are toxic, however, and whereas the optimum blood concentration is about 0.75–1.25 mmol Li^+ ions dm^{-3}, above about 1.6–2.0 mmol dm^{-3} toxic effects (vomiting, diarrhoea, thirst, hand tremor and even kidney damage or heart arrhythmias) become more marked. This ratio between the amount needed to have any effect and the toxic level is thus only about 2–3, which is very small, so regular monitoring is necessary. This is done by taking blood samples and measuring the lithium concentration. At first this has to be done quite frequently, but as the level stabilises the blood test is needed once every few months.

Lithium treatment is dramatically successful for mania (although its effectiveness in the depressive phase is slower to appear). Ten years after Cade's first suggestion, it had become clear that over 80% of people with manic depressive illness were improved by lithium. So it achieved widespread acceptance, although nobody knew how it worked. Indeed, a textbook written in 1972 said that lithium probably acted 'by virtue of its close chemical resemblance to sodium and potassium, interfering with the cellular metabolism and transport of these ions'. We now know that that is not so – the Na–K–ATPase does not pump lithium ions at all, presumably because the naked Li^+ ion is too small or the hydrated Li^+ too big.

Work published in 1995 shows that lithium acts by taking the place of magnesium in the body.

An understanding of the exact mode of operation of lithium is still hampered by the fact that we do not know exactly what causes manic depressive illness. But as long ago as 1922 it was shown that there is an increase in calcium ion concentrations in cerebrospinal fluid in depression and mania, and more recently that the calcium levels fall when the illness is controlled with lithium. But in the last 10 years or so it has been shown that calcium levels in cell fluid are controlled by levels of inositol-1,4,5-triphosphate (IP_3). If this is injected into cells, levels of calcium ions rise. It therefore seems probable that lithium ions act by lowering levels of IP_3 (and hence calcium) in the cell. We now know that they do this by interfering with an enzyme called inositolmonophosphatase (IMPase).

Inositol is stored in cell walls as a phosphate ester of a diacylglycerol. This is phosphorylated twice, and the glyceryl group removed to produce IP_3, which is released into the cell fluid (see Figure 14.6). This IP_3 triggers release of Ca^{2+} ions, which in turn affect mood. The IP_3 then undergoes successive loss of the three phosphate groups to produce free inositol, which is then recombined as the glyceryl phosphate ester in the cell wall, and is thus available for the whole cycle to continue. Removal of the last of the three phosphate groups in the conversion of IP_3 to inositol is catalysed by IMPase, and this is the point that is blocked by lithium ions. This means (see Figure 14.6) that the regeneration of free inositol is blocked, the whole cycle is stopped and the release of Ca^{2+} ions reduced.

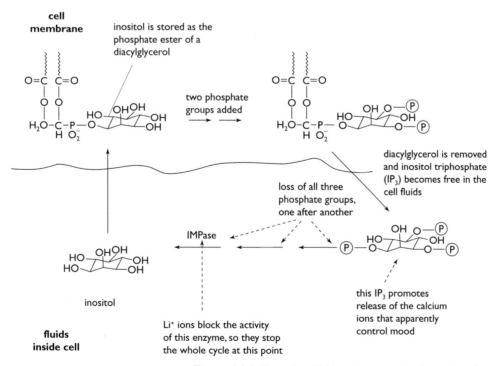

Figure 14.6 The role of lithium ions in manic depressive illness

IMPase, like all phosphatases, needs magnesium ions, probably to hold the phosphate group in the right orientation. Studies indicate that there are two Mg^{2+} ions per active site, one tightly held as a permanent occupant of the active site, the other more weakly bound, and alternately gained and lost as the hydrolysis proceeds. It is this second ion that is replaced by the lithium and, apparently, the lithium is more tightly bound, so once bound it isn't lost, thus blocking further reaction.

Why should lithium replace magnesium in this way? This is readily understandable: it is the basis for the diagonal relationship familiar to us in other areas of lithium chemistry. Like magnesium, lithium is a small cation (radius 0.076 nm, compared to 0.072 nm for Mg^{2+}), so it will fit wherever magnesium can.

But why it should be more tightly bound? That is more difficult. After all, it has half the charge of Mg^{2+}, and is slightly larger: any electrostatic interactions must surely be weaker. Even if we invoke covalency, it is hard to see why lithium should form covalent bonds which are stronger than those of magnesium.

The two different sorts of magnesium ion are presumably bound to the IMPase in different sorts of site. The first magnesium, the tightly bound one, might have a co-ordination number of 6 or more, whereas the second might be 4-coordinate, say. This would explain why the second is less firmly held, and also why the lithium is bound so much more firmly. When lithium is tetrahedrally co-ordinated, its observed ionic radius falls from 0.076 nm when octahedral, down to 0.059 nm. This smaller radius would certainly result in stronger electrostatic interactions with the lithium – in other words, stronger bonding.

The poet Robert Lowell quotes a friend of his, the author Robert Giroux: *'It's terrible . . . to think that all I've suffered, and all the suffering I've caused, might have arisen from the lack of a little salt in my brain.'*

Yes, lithium is indeed remarkable.

Further reading

Depression and How To Survive It, Antony Clare and Spike Milligan, Arrow (1)

An Unquiet Mind, K R Jamison, Vintage, 1995 (an account of her own illness by a world expert; 1). The quotations came from this and the next book.

Manic-depressive Illness, F K Goodwin and K R Jamison, Oxford University Press, 1990 is the standard tome (technical; 2–3)

Li–Mg: a Life-saving Relationship: T M Brown, A T Dronsfield and P M Ellis, *Education in Chemistry*, May 1997, p 72 (2)

15

ISOMERISM

Stereoisomers are compounds in which all the atoms are bonded to the same atoms, but arranged differently in space. The examples here are of two sorts. Geometrical isomerism is caused by restricted rotation about a double bond, so that the *cis* isomer – with two groups on the same side of the double bond – is distinct from the *trans* form. Optical isomerism arises because a molecule is different from its mirror image, usually because there is a chiral carbon in the molecule, with four different groups attached to it.

Old wives' tale 1

'Eat up your carrots; they'll help you see in the dark'

The orange and yellow colours of fruit and vegetables are mostly caused by two classes of compounds, the carotenes and the xanthophylls. Figure 15.1 shows one of these, called β-carotene. This absorbs light at the violet end of the visible spectrum (it has an absorption maximum at 455 nm), so it will appear a yellow-orange colour as this is what remains when the violet component of white light has been absorbed.

Figure 15.1 Structure of β-carotene

In the body β-carotene is converted to two molecules of retinol (see Figure 15.2), and it is retinol that is crucial to vision.

Indeed retinol, or one of its precursors, such as β-carotene, is a vital constituent of our diet and a deficiency has serious consequences. One of these, night blindness,

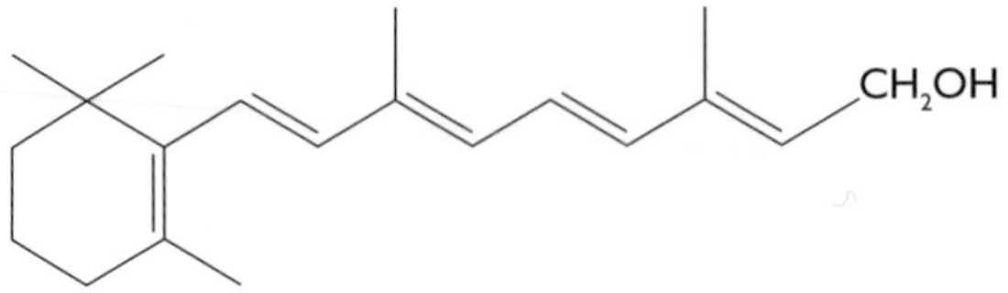

all-*trans*-retinol

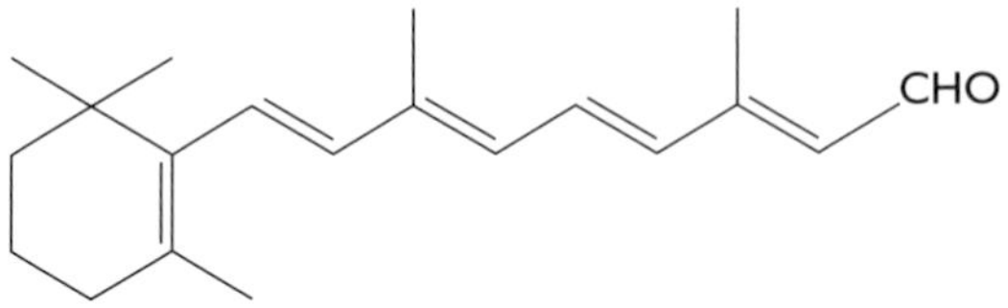

all-*trans*-retinal

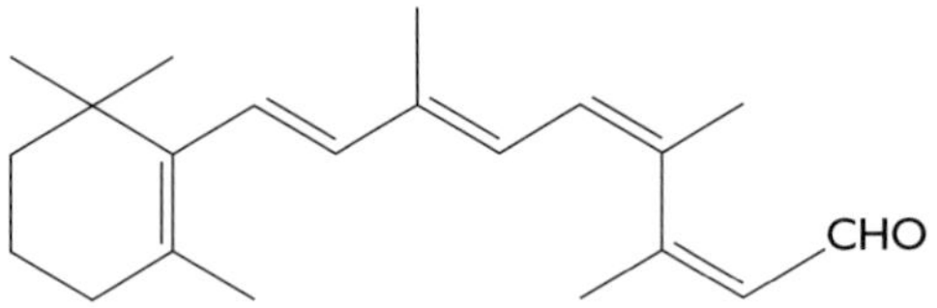

11-*cis*-retinal

Figure 15.2 All-*trans* and 11-*cis* retinol and retinal

was recognised during the first world war and the reasons for this are now becoming clear.

The retina at the back of a mammal's eye contains two different types of receptors. One type, called rods, is about 28 μm long and 1.5 μm in diameter in humans and is responsible for black and white vision. The rods contain retinol, which is converted to the aldehyde, retinal, by an alcohol dehydrogenase similar to the enzyme in the liver that oxidises ethanol. Like retinol, retinal can exist as a number of different isomers, depending upon whether each double bond is *cis* or *trans*. We should expect the all-*trans* form to be the more stable, as in this fully extended form the interactions between the various parts of the chain will be minimised. Calculations indicate that this is indeed so. But there is an enzyme system in the rods that converts all-*trans*-retinal to 11-*cis*-retinal, and as soon as the 11-*cis*-retinal forms, it immediately binds to the protein opsin to form the light-detecting system called rhodopsin.

Rhodopsin is formed by nucleophilic attack by an $-NH_2$ group of the protein on the $-CH{=}O$ group of the retinal (Figure 15.3). As a result, the 11-*cis*-retinal is covalently bonded to the protein and it also interacts with the remainder of the protein by van der Waals' interactions. This bonding together of retinal and opsin shifts the wavelength of maximum light absorption from just below 400 nm to 493 nm. It is this light absorption that triggers the nervous impulse and enables us to see.

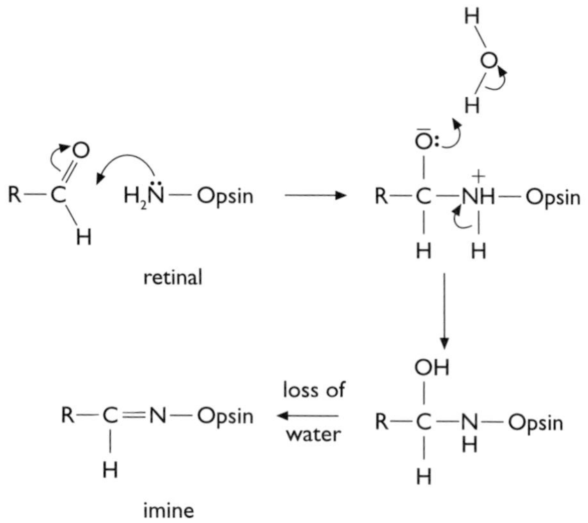

Figure 15.3 Formation of imine from opsin and retinal

The bonding in a carbon–carbon double bond is shown in Figure 15.4.

One sp^2 hybrid orbital on each carbon interacts to form a σ and a σ* orbital; since there are only two electrons, they occupy the σ orbital and the σ* orbital is empty. The two p orbitals, one from each carbon, interact to form a π and a π* orbital and as before, since there are only two electrons, they occupy the π orbital and the π* orbital is empty. Absorption of light energy, however, can excite the most weakly held electron – one of those in the π orbital – up to the next highest orbital, the π*. This π π* excitation can lead to a singlet excited state (with the spins of ground state and excited electrons still opposed), but this can be followed by transfer to the triplet state, when the spin of the electron in the π* orbital reverses. Return to the ground state is now much more difficult – the spin would have to switch back again – so the triplet excited state has quite a long lifetime. And the π bond has been considerably weakened. After all, there is now only one electron in the π orbital. So the 11-*cis*-retinal can convert to the all-*trans* form fairly readily, and it now does so because the all-*trans* form is so much more stable. It is that single event, the conversion of 11-*cis*- to all-*trans*-retinal, caused by the light, that enables us to see. But the all-*trans*-retinal is a very different shape from the 11-*cis* molecule (see Figure 15.5); indeed, in the laboratory, the all-*trans*-retinal will not combine with opsin at all.

So absorption of light changes 11-*cis*-retinal to the all-*trans* form and as a result the retinal and opsin come apart. This triggers the optic nerve. It does this by altering the permeability of the rod cell membrane to sodium ions. Normally, there are open pores in the membrane and sodium ions are flowing into the cell (and being pumped out again by the sodium pump: see page 110). When light hits the retina, these pores are closed and the influx of sodium ions is blocked: a single photon blocks the flow of up to a million sodium ions. Indeed, an elegant little experiment shows the change in electrical potential as light enters the eye. If you touch an electrode on the front of the eyeball and another on the scalp, let the eye become

Bonding in C = C

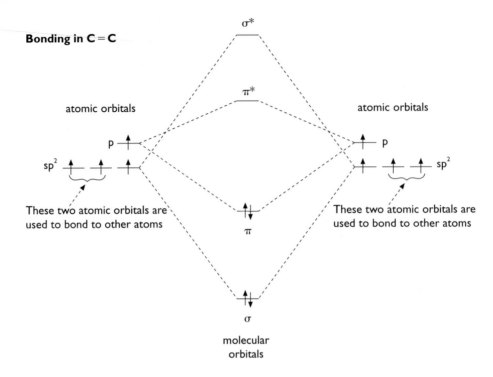

ππ* excitation of an alkene by light

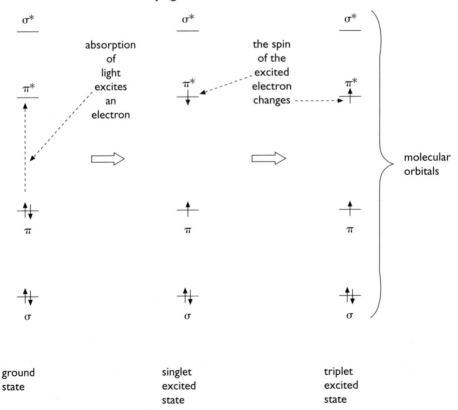

Figure 15.4

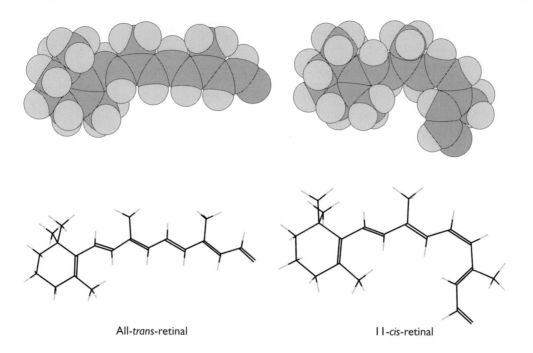

All-*trans*-retinal   11-*cis*-retinal

Figure 15.5 Shapes of the retinals

adjusted to darkness – in other words, become as sensitive as possible by building up maximum stores of rhodopsin – and then expose it to light, a potential difference of about 0.5 mV is detectable between eye and scalp.

The precise mechanism by which the arrival of the light causes this blockage of sodium ions is complex, and involves calcium ions and a transmitter molecule called cyclic guanosine monophosphate (cGMP). The anti-impotence drug Viagra also affects cGMP levels and, although the drug is very specific for enzymes in the penis, about 3% of patients experience blue tinges to the vision as it alters cGMP levels in the retina.

Some of the 11-*cis*-retinal has now been converted to the all-*trans* form, and so the final step is formation of new 11-*cis*-retinal, so that the whole process can occur all over again. As soon as it is released from the opsin, the all-*trans*-retinal is reduced to the corresponding all-*trans*-retinol, and transport mechanisms remove the retinol from the eye and replace it with fresh stocks from the liver. The dehydrogenase now catalyses oxidation of the all-*trans*-retinol to the all-*trans*-aldehyde and this is isomerised to the 11-*cis*-retinal. Since the 11-*cis* molecule is of significantly higher energy, some source of energy must be available to the enzyme – it presumably comes from hydrolysis of ATP.

Eat up your carrots? Oh yes, lack of β-carotene leads to a deficiency of retinol and ultimately to night blindness. Mind you, if you also eat dairy products and green vegetables, you are unlikely to be deficient in vitamin A even if you hate carrots. But with suggestions that the antioxidant properties of vitamin A tend to prevent cancer, there may be even more incentive to eat them!

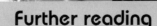

Further reading

Chemistry and Light, P Suppan, Royal Society of Chemistry, 1994 has a good summary, as has any book on photochemistry (2)

Biochemistry, L Stryer, W H Freeman and Co, 1988 (2)

Yellow babies

The lifetime of a red blood cell in the body is about 120 days, after which time it is broken down. The haemoglobin is converted to bilirubin which is normally filtered out by the liver. In newborn babies, however, the liver may take several days to achieve full function, and bilirubin can build up in the infant's blood. This is especially common in premature babies, causes the baby to look yellow, and if untreated, can lead to brain damage.

The bilirubin molecule has two C=C systems which can be *cis* or *trans*. In the form normally occurring in the body, both are *cis*, an arrangement which results in the formation of six hydrogen bonds within the molecule. Irradiation of the molecule with light in the visible and near ultra-violet excites a π electron in the double bonds to a π* orbital, allowing the *cis* double bond to convert to the *trans* arrangement, just as happens with rhodopsin (see page 117). This has the result that some or all of these intramolecular hydrogen bonds are broken and the *trans* form can now hydrogen bond to water. As a result, the molecules are much more water soluble than the original all-*cis* form, and can be separated out by the kidneys and excreted in the urine.

Treatment of jaundice in the new-born was discovered following the observations of an alert nurse that babies lying in cots in sunlight recovered much faster than those in shade, and is now a simple matter: the whole body is exposed to sunlight or to a lamp emitting near ultra-violet light.

Who were the first Americans?

Forget Columbus; there were people in North America long before then. Everyone agrees that they came from Siberia, either at the end of the last glaciation (around 14 000 to 12 000 years BP – before present) or long before that, perhaps as early as 35 000 years BP. Which? Perhaps most intriguing of all to an outsider is the fact that the argument has raged for a hundred years or more, and is still not settled. The 'late arrival' proponents point to the explosion of human activity starting around 11 500 years BP, characterised by the wide appearance of particular stone tools (called 'Clovis points'), and sudden disappearance of the American big mammals – mammoths, camelids, sloths, etc. – at about this time. Supporters of the early arrival argue that there is a handful of sites (the 'pre-Clovis' sites) throughout the North American continent that seem to be much older.

Evidence for this long chronology centred originally around ^{14}C dates for organic material found at these 'pre-Clovis' sites. In the early days, the original ^{14}C method required quite large quantities of wood, charcoal or bone. In the case of bone up to 100 g was needed, and there were further problems in that exchange of carbon atoms could occur between 'old' carbonates dissolved in ground water and the material of the bone. This could be overcome by extracting the collagen from the bone, but this meant that even more material was required. At that time, too, there was an upper limit to the age of material which could be examined, of about 35 000 to 40 000 years, because the residual amounts of ^{14}C were so low.

Then along came AAR, or amino-acid racemisation. Amino acids are chiral, of course – they contain a carbon atom with four different groups attached. Mammals synthesise only the L form. When the animal dies, however, formation of the L-amino acid stops, and the existing amino acids begin slowly to racemise. That is to say, the L forms start to convert to D forms (and vice versa); eventually there will be equal amounts of each. [Exactly how this happens is not certain; one proposal is that a proton is lost from the chiral carbon leading to a carbanion (Figure 15.6). Uptake of the proton again could occur from either side of this planar ion.] It is hardly surprising that the process is slow. But if we can assume that the conditions do not fluctuate wildly, the extent of racemisation can be used to date the remains of living material.

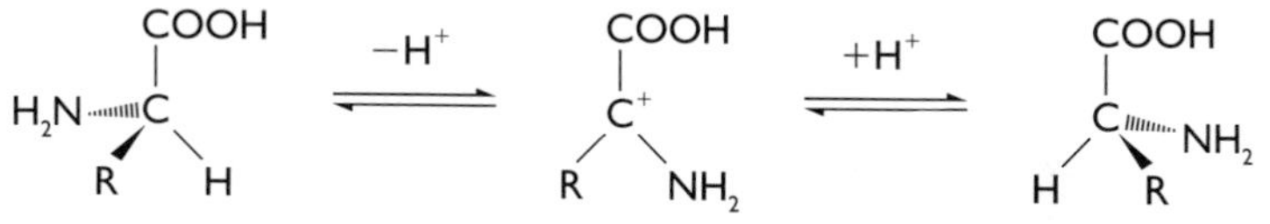

Figure 15.6 Racemisation of chiral amino acids

The debate over the date of the first Americans looks to an outsider so entrenched that it might be likened to a civil war. When AAR studies on aspartic acid from skeletons found near La Jolla, California, were published, showing D/L ratios from 0.16 to 0.53 and suggesting dates as old as 48 000 years BP, the furore was unimaginable. At first it looked as though the supporters of recent arrival were finished. But there were murmurs of dissent. Skulls of this age from elsewhere were obviously primitive, with big brow ridges; these looked like modern ones. How could they be so old, folk asked.

Fortunately, a major scientific advance now arrived, in the form of a vast improvement to ^{14}C dating. Accelerator mass spectrometry allowed the measurement of amounts of ^{14}C much lower than hitherto, making it possible to use much smaller amounts of material (a few *milligrams*, even) and also allowing much more rigorous chemical purification of the material to be tested. This new technique was immediately applied to the material from La Jolla and elsewhere, and the results published with the subtitle 'none older than 11 000 years BP'. (Can't you just hear the shouts of triumph from the supporters of the short chronology?)

The trouble seems to have been in the calibration of the AAR method. Because the rate of racemisation is dependent on many factors, including temperature, absolute estimation of age cannot be done. Instead you have to take a sample from the locality and date it by two methods, AAR and ^{14}C, perhaps. Once the AAR method has been calibrated for this particular location, you can go on to date other, perhaps older, objects. It seems that the original ^{14}C dating, of a skull found during road construction at Laguna beach, California, estimated at about 15 000 to 17 000 years BP was wrong. The revised date was ~5000 years BP, so all the AAR dates had to be shifted downwards, too.

Alas for the supporters of early colonisation. Alas, too for AAR as a technique, which seemed at first to have been seriously discredited, and is only slowly recovering. It is still used with caution for dates prior to the earliest dates accessible to ^{14}C (about 30 000–40 000 years BP).

But what of the early Americans? When did they arrive? Is there agreement? There is not. A recent publication lists four sites which are apparently earlier than the Clovis weapons, and which cannot be explained. So there is apparently solid evidence for settlement before 11 500 years BP, but still there is argument. As one writer has put it: 'one wonders exactly what evidence would be necessary to sway the contestants either way.' Who needs facts when a good prejudice will do instead?

Further reading

Archaeological Chemistry, A Mark Pollard and Carl Heron, Royal Society of Chemistry paperbacks (1–2).

Asymmetry in living systems

Any reaction giving rise to a chiral product will produce a racemic mixture of the two possible isomers. For example, reaction of HCN with ethanal could produce two possible isomers of 2-hydroxypropanenitrile, depending on which side of the planar molecule is attacked by the ^-CN nucleophile. And since attack from either side is equally likely, the two possible optical isomers are produced in equal amounts.

Yet all the naturally occurring amino acids exist as only one optical isomer, the L-form. On one level this is easy to understand: biological molecules, particularly enzymes, are themselves optically active and so can catalyse the reactions of one optical isomer but not the other. We explain this by saying that just as the right hand fits the right-hand glove (and not the left), so one optical isomer can fit into the active site of the enzyme and react, whereas the other isomer can't.

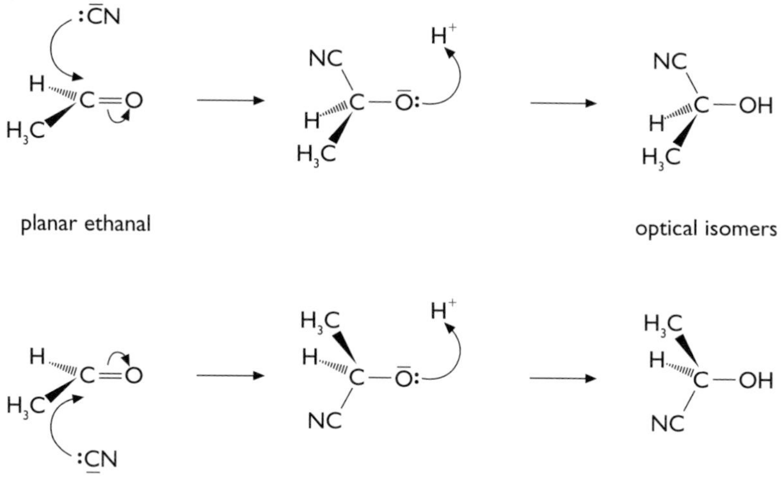

planar ethanal

optical isomers

Figure 15.7 Ethanal plus HCN

But how did it come about that living systems managed to select one optical isomer in the first place? And why should they do so? Let's deal with the second question first. There may be several reasons why life needs optical purity. Certainly, if the sugars of the backbone of DNA are a mixture of the D and L forms, a regular helical structure cannot be formed. Helices could be formed with all D or all L (though the helices would be oppositely handed), but a mixture of the two would not work. The existence of regular structures in nucleic acids or proteins requires the use of one optical isomer or the other, but not both. And if the active site of an enzyme is to bind the substrate very specifically – and this is usually the case – a precise arrangement of binding groups is required, and this will only work for one isomer and not the other. If living systems could not confine themselves to L-amino acids, for example, they would need twice as many enzymes, one set for the L-acids, and another set for the D-acids. Very wasteful! (You might like to ponder whether the two systems could exist side by side: one using L-amino acids exclusively, and the other using just the D-acids. Could there be a colony of D-tigers somewhere in India alongside the existing population of L-tigers?)

So there are good reasons why life uses just half the available chemicals. More difficult to understand, perhaps, is how this happened. After all, the initial syntheses of life molecules came about from little, non-chiral molecules: how could the developing system 'learn' to select one isomer instead of another?

The answer must be by chance, like all evolution. If this seems unlikely, remember that only 'correct' chance decisions would survive; organisms with 'wrong' choices would not. Realise, too, that life has had a long time to make wrong choices before the right ones happened. So we must suppose that the optically pure compounds, such as the L-amino acids, somehow arose by chance. There are several ways in which this spontaneous resolution of a racemic mixture might occur. One is by fractional crystallisation. If a supersaturated racemic solution of some amino acids is seeded with one isomer, that isomer crystallises out preferentially. Drop a crystal of L-glutamic acid into a racemic solution of the acid, and the crystals formed are

125

91% L-acid. Drop a D-crystal into the same solution and you get 88% pure D-acid. (The method is used industrially as part of the synthesis of monosodium glutamate.) If this still seems improbable (where would the seeding crystal come from?), we should realise that the smaller the crystal, the less improbable is its formation. Formation of a tiny L-glutamic acid crystal would be quite feasible, and if it were picked up by the wind and blown into a saturated racemic solution, we could suddenly get a huge amount of the L isomer. (Although since this is a chance process, we should expect to get the other isomer by the same means somewhere else.)

There is an alternative possibility. If we attempt to polymerise an amino acid, we find that polymerisation of the D or L form is faster than polymerisation of a DL mixture, often as much as 20 times faster. Moreover, the peptide from the pure L or D forms is longer than that made from the racemic mix. Again it seems that we need only a small excess of one isomer for a sort of amplification to occur.

Further reading

The Origins of Life on Earth, S L Miller and L E Orgel, Prentice Hall, 1974. Old, and incorrect in detail, but a classic (2)

16

KINETICS

The speed of reactions is not only critical to a chemical company making ammonia, it underlies everything we do. Often, a reaction will be first order and its rate will be directly proportional to the concentration of reagent:

Rate = k[reagent]

and the fall in concentration of the reagent will be exponential, with a constant half life.

Occasionally, however, the rate of a reaction will be quite unaffected by the amount of reagent present:

Rate = constant

We call this a zero order reaction. Higher orders are possible, and a third order reaction is considered here because of the immense importance of the molecule involved.

Drug dose

Drugs don't stay in the body – one way or another it gets rid of them. This may be by some reaction or other, converting the active drug into an unreactive product (see page 46). Very rarely, the drug will be converted into something that the normal chemistry of the body can cope with. Insulin is an example of this: it is a protein and when broken down it will produce amino acids that the body can use to synthesise new protein. Usually, however, the drug and its metabolites are foreigners and will have to be excreted. This may be via the lungs (as with inhaled anaesthetics, for example), through the skin (rarely and to a small extent) or in the urine or faeces.

Whatever the precise mode of elimination, as time passes the concentration of the drug in the body fluids will fall. Many drugs are lost in a simple first order reaction, in which the rate of loss of the drug is proportional to its concentration:

Rate = k[drug]

where square brackets denote concentration in moles dm^{-3}. This leads to an exponential decay of the drug concentration with time. Figure 16.1 shows this sort of thing: it plots the concentration of a drug in the blood at various times after a single intravenous injection. (A feature of first order reactions is their constant half life; the curve in Figure 16.1 has a half life of five hours.)

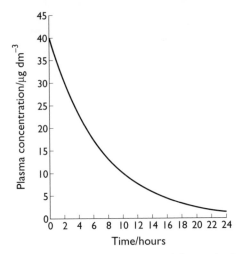

Figure 16.1 Exponential decay of a drug with a half life of 5 hours

But in order to have its effect, a drug will have to be present at some concentration above a minimum value, called the therapeutic level. Below this, it will be too dilute to work. On the other hand, all drugs have side effects. Get the concentration too high, and these side effects may become unpleasant or serious: antibiotics cause diarrhoea, antidepressants produce a dry mouth and so on. Ideally, there will be a large difference between these two concentrations. Pharmacologists talk of the therapeutic ratio:

$$\text{therapeutic ratio} = \frac{\text{concentration causing ill effects}}{\text{concentration needed for beneficial effect}}$$

The important thing in any drug therapy, then, is to get the concentration high enough to have the desired effect, yet not so high that the side effects become unbearable. (Of course, exactly what constitutes 'unbearable' will vary. Some people can put up with a dry mouth, others cannot stand it. And a side effect that is too serious in a cold cure might be quite acceptable in cancer therapy.)

Figure 16.2 illustrates the problem. This represents a drug which needs a plasma concentration of about 7 μmol dm^{-3} to work, but whose toxic effects become apparent at about 21. (In other words, the therapeutic ratio for this drug is about three.) Injection of a single dose once a day produces a toxic level for nearly five hours after every injection, but by 12 hours the concentration is so low that the drug has stopped working. Using half the amount morning and night would be better – the toxic levels are reached less frequently and for less time – but plasma concentrations are below the effective levels for over three hours out of the first twelve and for two or so thereafter. Injection of just a quarter of the original dose four times a day is better still: the levels of the drug are too low for about two hours on the first day, but for the rest of the time they are fine.

So now it is clear why some drugs are taken every few hours, while others are taken once a day or even less often: it depends on their half life in the body. The half life of amoxycillin, one of the most commonly prescribed penicillins, is

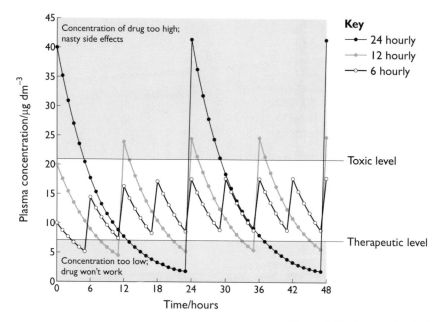

Figure 16.2 Graph of multiple dosing

60–90 minutes, so it has to be taken every four hours. Lithium ions, on the other hand, have a half life of 18–20 hours in young adults (but rising up to 36 hours in the elderly), so lithium carbonate is taken once a day. Chloroquine, a malaria preventative, is taken just once a week, because its half life in the body is about five days.

Matters aren't always quite so straightforward, though. For one thing, drugs aren't always injected. Swallowing pills is preferable to needles, so if it is possible, a doctor will use this route. The problem here is that it may take a little while to get the drug into the bloodstream: absorption through the walls of the stomach or the gut may take quite some time.

But there is an advantage to this slow absorption. It may take a while for the concentration of the drug to build up, but it doesn't get as high as with an injected dose, so it's easier to avoid toxic levels.

It gets still more complicated. All this assumes that the drug is absorbed into a simple solution in one solvent: the blood, perhaps. But almost all drugs will have some solubility in the body lipids as well, and will have to be removed from these lipid stores before they can be eliminated. This is the so-called two-compartment model of drug absorption, illustrated in Figure 16.3.

Elimination from the blood plasma will have one half life, and transfer from lipid stores back to blood plasma may have another. Even if we neglect the slow absorption and the time taken for transfer to the lipid stores, the decline of the plasma levels of the drug will be complex. A classic example of this is cannabis, which has high lipid solubility. This means that although the psychotropic effects last for perhaps 2–3 hours, tetrahydrocannabinol and its metabolites can be detected in the body for up to a week.

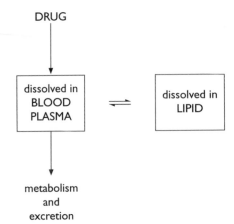

Figure 16.3 Diagram of the two-compartment model

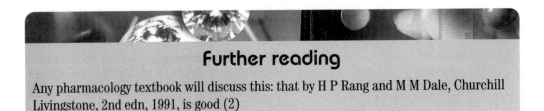

Further reading

Any pharmacology textbook will discuss this: that by H P Rang and M M Dale, Churchill Livingstone, 2nd edn, 1991, is good (2)

Drink driving

Ethanol undergoes extensive hydrogen bonding, so it is completely water soluble. On the other hand, since it is a small molecule and uncharged, it also has appreciable solubility in the non-polar molecules of the body that biochemists call lipids. As a result, it easily crosses the non-polar stomach wall and dissolves in the blood, so is rapidly transported around the body.

When you drink alcohol, the peak concentration in the blood is reached after 1–2 hours, and begins to decline thereafter. Figure 16.4 shows the level of ethanol in the blood at hourly intervals after rats were fed ethanol by stomach tube at the rate of 4.8 g/kg body weight. (For a 70 kg [11 stone] man this corresponds to 335 g of ethanol, or around 17 pints of beer). After an initial pause while the alcohol is being absorbed, the fall in blood alcohol is accurately linear with time. The rate of reaction does not depend on the concentration; breakdown of the alcohol is zero order.

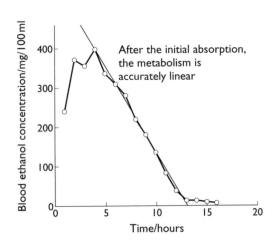

Figure 16.4 Breakdown of alcohol in rats

In other words, the ethanol is broken down at a steady rate. Similar data have been obtained for human subjects, where the rate of metabolism is again quite steady, at about 7.3 g per hour for a man. (Compare this with the usual rule of thumb: that a man will break down one unit of alcohol an hour. A unit is *about* 10 cm³, or 7.85 g of ethanol.) The rate of metabolism for women is much slower, at about 5.3 g per hour. But these figures hide huge variations: values for men have been found ranging from 4.1 to 11.1 g per hour.

Most of the countries of the world now limit the amount of ethanol that a driver is permitted to drink and continue to drive a car. In the UK and most states of the US this figure is 80 mg/100 ml of blood but some countries in Europe have the figure of 50 mg/100 ml (and at the time of writing, this lower limit is proposed in the UK). Some US states use 100 mg/100 ml.

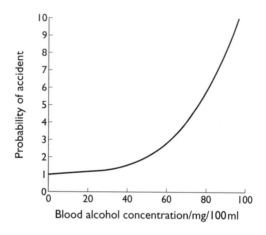

Figure 16.5 Accident rates and blood alcohol levels

Figure 16.5 shows the probability of having an accident for a man driving with varying levels of blood alcohol, relative to the probability if he has no alcohol on board.

It is clear both that any amount of alcohol increases his risk of accident, and that the decision as to where to put the legal limit is quite arbitrary. A 50 mg/100 ml level approximately doubles the risk of accident, whereas at 100 mg alcohol per 100 ml the risk is getting on for *ten times* greater. How do we decide what is acceptable?

There are several routes of metabolism in the body, but the major one occurs in the liver, catalysed by the enzyme alcohol dehydrogenase (ADH).

This oxidises the alcohol to ethanal, at the same time reducing the cofactor NAD to reduced NAD, given the symbol NADH (see Figure 16.6). The oxidation of the ethanol thus depends on the availability of NAD, which is reformed by oxidation of the NADH by other enzymes. Now the NADH cannot be reoxidised to NAD (and thus become available to allow more ethanol to be oxidised) until it has been dissociated from the alcohol dehydrogenase. The rate limiting step of the ethanol oxidation is dissociation of the ADH–NADH complex, and the rate of this is constant. As a result, therefore, the rate of breakdown of ethanol is constant, as we have seen: the metabolism is a zero order reaction.

It should be obvious, then, that the only thing that could speed up the metabolism of the alcohol is something that will remove the NADH from the enzyme more quickly. One of these is fructose – a sugar which requires NADH for its reduction – large doses of which cause a small increase in the rate of breakdown of ethanol.

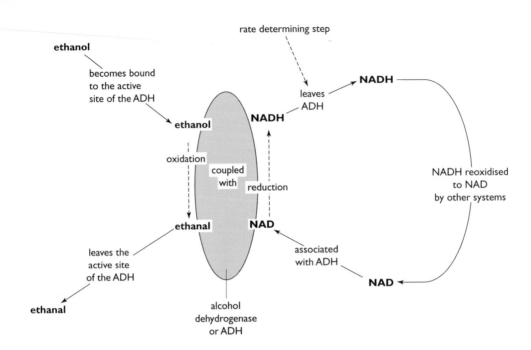

Figure 16.6 Ethanol metabolism

Not enough to help you sober up, however! Similarly, black coffee won't sober you up – the caffeine *may* make you more alert, but you are still drunk!

Further reading

Buzz, Stephen Braun, Oxford University Press, 1996 (1) is a delightful account of the effects of alcohol and caffeine.

Any pharmacology textbook will discuss this: that by H P Rang and M M Dale, Churchill Livingstone, 2nd edn, 1991, is good (2)

NO reactions

NO is almost unique in that many of its reactions – with oxygen, for example – are second order in NO, first order in O_2 and overall third order, and they get *slower* as the temperature rises: for example the rate of the NO/O_2 reaction drops by a factor of about two between 25°C and 200°C.

Clearly a single-step mechanism is out of the question. Collisions of three molecules, two NO molecules and one O_2, are so very unlikely that they could not give rise to the very rapid reactions, and we could not explain the effect of temperature. Instead one proposed mechanism supposes that the NO undergoes some limited reversible dimerisation:

$$2NO \rightleftharpoons N_2O_2 \quad \text{(plus heat; } \Delta H \text{ is negative)} \qquad [1]$$

Since a covalent bond – albeit a weak one – is being formed, this equilibrium will be exothermic. It is now followed by slow reaction of the N_2O_2 with the other reagent, the O_2.

$$N_2O_2 + O_2 \rightarrow 2NO_2 \qquad [2]$$

The equilibrium constant for reaction [1] is K_{eq}, given by:

$$K_{eq} = \frac{[N_2O_2]}{[NO]^2} \qquad [3]$$

Since the second step of the mechanism – in other words, [2] above – involves the collision of one N_2O_2 and one O_2, the rate of this step will be given by

$$\text{Rate} = k[N_2O_2][O_2] \qquad [4]$$

where k is the rate constant for step [2]. But the concentration of N_2O_2 can be obtained by rearranging equation [3]:

$$[N_2O_2] = K_{eq}[NO]^2 \qquad [5]$$

and substitution of [5] into [4] gives:

$$\text{Rate} = kK_{eq}[NO]^2[O_2] \qquad [6]$$

which is of the required third order kinetics.

Moreover, since the first equilibrium is exothermic, Le Chatelier's Principle predicts that it will be shifted to the left with increase in temperature. This will lower the concentration of $[N_2O_2]$, and thus – from equation [4] – reduce the rate. (Of course, increasing the temperature will also increase the rate constant k in the usual manner proposed by Arrhenius, and since this is exponential it will have the dominant effect over large ranges of temperature. Over relatively small temperature changes, however, the effect on the equilibrium [1] is more important.)

One important point follows from these kinetics. If the concentration of NO is low, because the rate of reaction is proportional to the *square* of the concentration, the reaction will be extremely slow. This is the reason why oxidation of NO to NO_2 in the atmosphere occurs via reaction with radicals like $CH_3-O-O\cdot$ rather than direct reaction with oxygen. The same logic is behind the use of inhaled NO to lower the blood pressure of new-born babies (see page 155).

Further reading

Any advanced physical chemistry textbook. The best is **Physical Chemistry** by P W Atkins, Oxford University Press, many editions (2).

17

LIGHT

Light supplies energy to a system. The consequences of this depend on the amount of energy supplied. Planck's formula gives $E = hf$; that is to say, the energy of the incident light is proportional to its frequency.

Infra red radiation is of such low energy that it can alter only the rotational and vibrational states of a molecule: this is made use of in infra red spectroscopy (see pages 197–199). Visible and ultra-violet radiation, however, can excite electrons. The excitation may result in useful absorption, as in sunscreens. If visible light is involved, colour is produced, as in precious stones or dyes.

The light absorption may be followed by a chemical reaction. Formation of free radicals in a mixture of chlorine and methane is a familiar example; another is the chemistry of photography or photochromic lenses in which the incident light induces a redox reaction, converting Ag^+ ions to metallic silver. Less well known, perhaps, is the light-induced conversion of a *cis* compound into the corresponding *trans* isomer, the very process by which you read these words (see page 117).

Photography

Photography is old; the alchemist Fabricius noticed that silver salts darkened in sunlight as far back as 1556.

Then in 1841, W H Fox Talbot used semi-transparent paper coated with silver iodide and 'developed' with gallic acid. Even now, so many years later, silver salts form the basis of the process and the full theory is still not understood.

The photographic film
Most black and white or colour films contain silver bromide as the main constituent. Depending on the speed of film required, small amounts of silver chloride and/or iodide will be incorporated as well. The compounds are formed by mixing aqueous solutions under carefully controlled conditions to precipitate the insoluble salts. A film for available-light photography might have crystals around 10^{-6} m in diameter, containing perhaps 10^{13} silver atoms.

When light hits the film, the energy causes the halide to lose an electron:

$$X^- \xrightarrow{\textit{light energy}} X + e^-$$

producing a halogen atom and an electron. The electron is picked up by the silver ion:

$$Ag^+ + e^- \rightarrow Ag$$

Normally it is pretty reversible, with the energy released when the electron is transferred back to the halogen being given out as thermal energy, which is lost to the surroundings. But it is not perfectly reversible (which is why silver bromide and iodide darken on standing) and it is this lack of reversibility that is made use of in the photographic process.

The electron is able to migrate through the AgX crystal, perhaps reversibly forming Ag atoms as it goes. All crystals will have flaws or defects in them – places where a lattice site is empty, or where an extra ion or an ion of a different type has been incorporated into the lattice. At this point, formation of the silver atom may be particularly favourable so this is no longer reversible, and the silver atom is trapped. As more light photons hit the film, more electrons are produced and they migrate until they find the same region where irreversible formation of silver atoms is favourable. Thus more silver builds up at the same spot, and the amount of silver depends on the amount of light that has hit that silver bromide crystal.

This is fine; we have the beginnings of a photographic process. But it suffers from two major disadvantages.

First, it is very slow. Even with the best of developers, exposure times would have to be measured in minutes, rather than fractions of a second. This was overcome very early by the fortuitous discovery of sensitisers. The early photographic plates were made of glass, and it was difficult to apply and to hold in place the necessary fine layer of silver salts. Photographers had to make their plates and expose them while they were still wet, but in 1871 R L Maddox began to develop plates coated with dry gelatine. Unknown to him, sulphur-containing molecules in his gelatine deposited sulphide ions on the surface of the crystals in place of two halide ions, and these sulphide ions act as very efficient traps for the latent image. Nowadays this sensitisation is achieved by addition of sulphur compounds during film production, and other sensitisers, most notably compounds of gold, may be used as well. Of course we no longer use glass – the gelatine is coated onto films of cellulose triacetate (more correctly called cellulose triethanoate). Films are now over a million times faster than Fox Talbot's original pieces of paper and another 10 to 100-fold increase seems feasible. This will enable photos to be taken with exposure times of 1/50th of a second, by *starlight* alone!

But there was a second snag. If we make a photographic film using just silver bromide, it will be sensitive only to light at the blue end of the spectrum, with wavelengths up to about 480 nm. Adding small amounts of AgI can extend the working range up to about 520 nm, but red light will still not be detected. If nothing was done, only photography of objects in the green and blue (and ultra-violet) regions of the spectrum would be possible. The answer, first discovered in 1873, is to add a very dilute solution of a dye (aqueous if the dye is water soluble, but more usually in some other solvent such as ethanol) to the silver halide crystals. The dye molecules are adsorbed onto the crystals, lying flat and in stacked arrays on the crystal surface. When they absorb light – and because of the extensive delocalisation in the molecules used, this is in the green or red region of the spectrum – excitation of their electrons to higher, presumably antibonding, molecular orbitals can be followed by transfer of these excited electrons to Ag^+ ions. In this way, reduction of the silver ions can be induced by absorption of longer wavelength light, and the film becomes sensitive to all wavelengths (the so-called panchromatic film). Figure 17.1 shows the effect of addition of increasing amounts of the dye 1,1'-diethyl-2,2'-cyanine iodide on light absorption by an AgBr crystal.

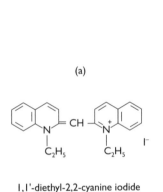

(a)

1,1'-diethyl-2,2-cyanine iodide

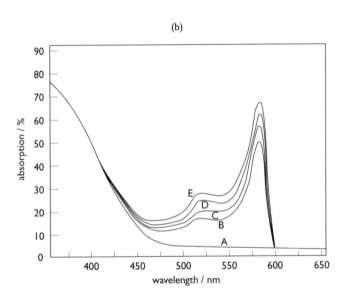

(b)

Figure 17.1 a) 1,1'-diethyl-2,2'-cyanine iodide; b) The effect of adding this sensitising dye on the absorption spectrum of silver bromide. (A–E have increasing amounts of dye, from 0 in A to 6.6×10^{-4} moles of dye per mole of AgBr in E)

But it is important for us to realise that in the fastest films, exposure may produce no more than 4–6 silver atoms at a given spot. Even if 10 times more atoms were deposited, that would constitute a speck of silver only 4×10^{-9} m across, far too small for us to see. So far the image is only latent; if we look at the film, we can see no change. The image has to be developed.

Development

This is done by reduction of more Ag^+ ions to silver atoms, using the mild reducing agent hydroquinone (1,4-dihydroxybenzene). Reduction of the Ag^+ ion occurs preferentially at the site of the newly formed silver atoms, spreading out from there ultimately to reduce all the Ag^+ ions. If we leave it in the developer for too long, then, the whole film will go black. It is vital that we avoid this. We want an image where the blackness will depend on the amount of light hitting each point of the film, and to do this the temperature and time of development must be closely controlled.

Exactly what happens in the development process is unknown. Why does reduction of Ag^+ ions occur faster where Ag atoms have already been formed by exposure to light? One theory supposes that the developer molecules are adsorbed onto these tiny clusters of silver atoms, and the electron transfer from developer to Ag^+ ions occurs here, possibly catalysed by the silver. However it happens, it is clear that formation of silver is much faster at those points where the silver atoms have already been formed by the action of the light, and that as reduction continues, silver filaments can be seen spreading out from these initial centres.

Once development has proceeded far enough to generate the image, it is stopped: the film is washed in the so-called 'stop bath'. All developing agents contain $-NH_2$ or $-OH$ groups and are oxidised in the developing process (see Figure 17.2).

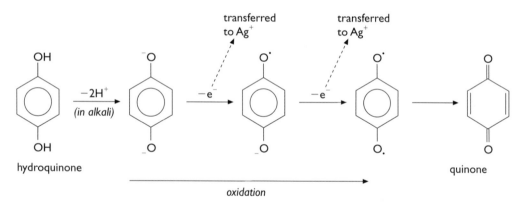

Figure 17.2 Structures of hydroquinone – in alkali and being oxidised

As the solution is made more alkaline, the $-OH$ groups of hydroquinone are ionised, and oxidation of the molecule becomes easier. (For the same reason, a precipitate of $Fe(OH)_2$ rapidly turns brown as it is oxidised to $Fe(OH)_3$; loss of electrons from a negatively charged species is easier than from a neutral one, which in turn is easier than from a cation.) Thus all developers are more effective in more alkaline solutions, and they will not work at all if the solution is too acidic. The developing solution is commonly made alkaline by addition of sodium carbonate. Stopping the developing process can thus easily be done by immersing the film in an acid, most usually ethanoic acid. But the process is not over yet.

Fixing the image

After development, the film still contains undeveloped silver halide crystals and if these are not removed, it will go completely black on further exposure to light. This is done by washing the film in a 'fixer' solution which dissolves the unreacted silver salts. The most common fixer is sodium thiosulphate which reacts with silver ions first to form the rather insoluble $[AgS_2O_3]^-$ ion, but then forms more soluble complexes in the presence of excess thiosulphate ions: $[Ag(S_2O_3)_2]^{3-}$ and even $[Ag(S_2O_3)_3]^{5-}$. When immersed in the fixer, after a short while the emulsion of the film becomes clear as the insoluble silver salts are converted to the soluble complexes and washed off into solution. To ensure very substantial removal of the silver salts, fixing is continued for longer (a useful rule of thumb is for twice the clearing time), although since these are equilibrium processes, complete removal of the unreacted silver salts is impossible.

Although the film will have been dipped into the acidic stop bath, some of the alkaline developer will have penetrated the film and may still be present. It is therefore necessary to add acid to the fixer solution. Unfortunately, however, thiosulphate reacts with acid to form the parent acid which breaks down to give sulphur:

$$S_2O_3^{2-} + 2H^+ \rightleftharpoons H_2S_2O_3$$

$$H_2S_2O_3 \rightleftharpoons H_2SO_3 + S$$

and the sulphuric (IV) (sulphurous) acid decomposes to give off sulphur dioxide:

$$H_2SO_3 \rightarrow H_2O + SO_2$$

Deposition of sulphur into the emulsion of the film would be a problem, in that not only would it fog the film, but it could also react with the silver causing the image to brown. The answer is to buffer the fixer, so that it is not too acidic. One recipe is as follows:

sodium thiosulphate	$Na_2S_2O_3.5H_2O$	250.0 g dm^{-3}	1.01 mol dm^{-3}
sodium sulphate (IV)	Na_2SO_3	10.0 g dm^{-3}	0.08 mol dm^{-3}
sodium hydrogensulphate (IV)	$NaHSO_3$	25.0 g dm^{-3}	0.24 mol dm^{-3}

The pK_a value for the HSO_3^- ion is 7.2, and simple buffer theory gives the pH of this mixture as 6.7 – slightly acidic so that small amounts of alkali will be neutralised, but not acidic enough that the thiosulphate ions will decompose.

But who wants black and white pictures?

Colour photographs

Objects look coloured because when white light strikes them, part of the visible spectrum is absorbed and the object appears to have the complementary colour. A tomato appears red because it absorbs green light; a lemon, yellow because it is absorbing blue and violet.

The same idea governs the production of colour negatives. Three layers of gelatine–silver halide emulsion are used. Each one is sensitised to a different region of the spectrum by incorporation of a different dye, so that each layer of the emulsion responds to only one region of the spectrum (see Figure 17.3). After development, each region of the spectrum produces a region of complementary colour: so blue light will produce a yellow area on the negative, red light a green one and so on. Printing of the positive colour print reverses the procedure to give the true colours.

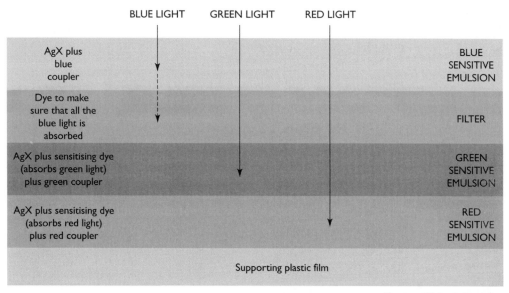

Figure 17.3 Colour film

But how are the colours generated? Although there are as many different processes as there are different types of colour film, the basic idea is common to all of them. It is the silver crystals in each layer of the emulsion that create the latent image, just as in the black and white process. Development occurs preferentially on the tiny cluster of silver atoms forming the latent image, just as before. But now we must focus our attention on the other half of the development process: the developer itself. As it reacts with the latent image to generate silver atoms, in numbers proportional to the amount of light that has hit the film, so oxidised developer molecules are produced in the same place on the film. These oxidised developer molecules are now made to react with special coupler molecules incorporated in each layer of the original emulsion to give rise to intensely coloured molecules. The developers are usually 1,4-diaminobenzene derivatives and a typical reaction might be as shown in Figure 17.4.

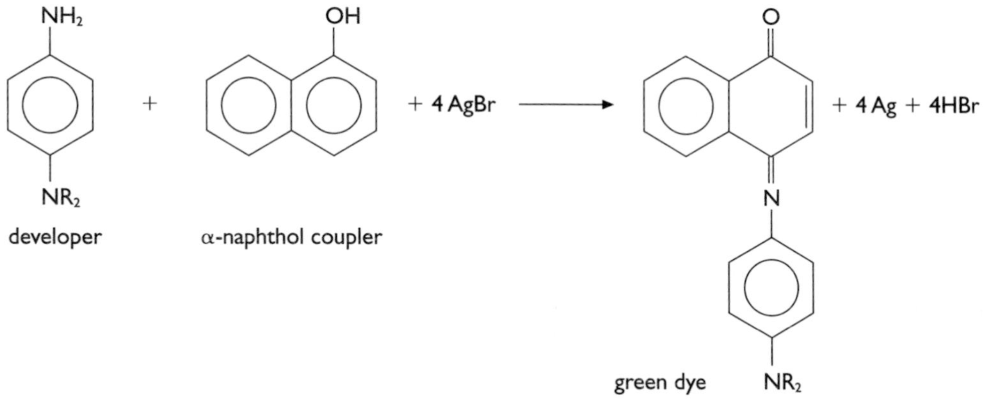

Figure 17.4 A coupling reaction

139

Note that this green-coloured dye is a response to exposure to red light, and when the print is made it will cause the printing paper to be exposed to green, resulting in a red colour on the final colour photograph.

Further reading

Encyclopedia of Chemical Technology, 4th edn, Kirk–Othmer, Wiley Interscience, 1994 has a good account of the theory (1–2)
Modern Photographic Processing, 2 volumes, Grant Haist, Wiley Interscience, 1979 (2)

Photochromic lenses

How nice not to have to put on sunglasses! As the day gets brighter, the glasses darken naturally, then as the clouds come over, the colour fades once more.

The key process is exactly the same as that used in photography – absorption of light energy to bring about the transfer of an electron from a halide ion to silver, producing small particles of metallic silver dispersed throughout the glass:

$$Ag^+ + I^- \rightarrow Ag + I$$

and it is the particles of silver which provide the darkening. It is critical that the silver halide crystals are of the correct size. If they are too small – around 10 nm across, say – the resultant silver particles are too small and the colour is not dark enough. If they are any bigger than about 20 nm across, scattering of the light leads to hazy vision. This critical size of silver halide crystal is achieved by careful heat treatment of the glass. After the correct mixture has been melted together to achieve a homogeneous glass, it is held at 500–$600°C$. There are only small amounts of silver halide present (typically of the order of 0.25% silver by mass) and holding the glass at this elevated temperature allows the silver and halide ions time to migrate together to form the small crystals. Of course, the length of time at this temperature is critical: too long and the crystals are too big.

Exposure to light brings about the electron transfer, and the glass darkens. Unlike in the gelatin of a photographic film, the electron cannot migrate through the glass, so the silver and iodine atoms are held where they were formed, ideally placed to reverse the process. Remove the glass from the light, and the electron is transferred back, with the emission of the absorbed energy as heat: the glass becomes colourless once more.

It turns out that copper (I) ions are a good source of electrons, so they are usually added to modern glass, so that the process:

$$Ag^+ + Cu^+ \rightarrow Ag + Cu^{2+}$$

takes place alongside the original one. The colour of the darkened glass can be altered from grey to brown by small changes in the size of the silver halide crystallites, or by adding trace amounts (3–4 ppm) of palladium or gold compounds.

Further reading

Encyclopedia of Chemical Technology, 4th edn, Kirk–Othmer, Wiley Interscience, 1994 (1–2)

Hair dyes

Hair consists of keratin fibres twined round each other, held in a matrix of sulphur-rich protein (see page 11). These threads are then surrounded by a sheath of small overlapping plates of protein which lie flat against the fibre. The plates are made of a protein which is extensively cross-linked by $-S-S-$ bridges; as a result, they constitute a very effective barrier to penetration of the hair by any applied chemicals.

If we want a permanent dye we have to get the colour molecules into the core of the hair or the colour will be washed off by the next shampoo. Because the hair proteins have twice as many acidic amino acids as basic ones, their isoelectronic points are below 7. As the hair is made alkaline, the $-COOH$ side chains ionise, the number of $-COO^-$ ions increasing with pH. The net effect of this is to make the hair fibres repel each other (making the hair difficult to manage) and it causes the protective plates to rise up off the surface of the fibre, making penetration by chemicals much easier. The first step in any permanent dying procedure is, therefore, application of a dilute solution of ammonia (commonly as part of the dye mixture) to make the hair surface permeable. But even with this treatment it isn't possible to get large dye molecules into the fibre, so we use small precursor molecules instead and synthesise the dye inside the hair.

The second component of most permanent hair dyes is hydrogen peroxide solution. This has two desirable functions. Natural hair is coloured by the pigment melanin, whose colour arises from electronic excitation in the extensively delocalised π systems of the melanin molecule. Hydrogen peroxide bleaches the melanin by oxidising one or more of its double bonds, probably to form an epoxide, thus reducing the extent of delocalisation and shifting the absorption to shorter wavelengths. (All bleaches will work in this way, by reacting with the $-CH=CH-$ system. Chlorine will form a 1,2-dichloro compound.) The presence of the hydrogen peroxide thus allows us to decrease the natural colour of the hair before we create the new colour in its place. Greater amounts of peroxide enable us to have a lighter final colour.

The other function of the hydrogen peroxide is the formation of the actual dye inside the hair fibre. Most hair dyes contain 1,4-diaminobenzene (*para*-phenylene diamine in old terminology) or 4-aminophenol (*para*-aminophenol), and the hydrogen peroxide oxidises these to form a reactive intermediate. This will react with one of a range of other compounds to form a variety of dyes (see Figure 17.5).

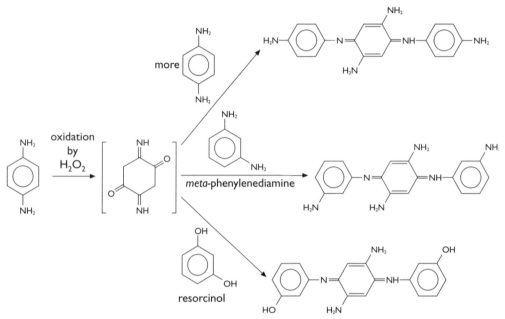

Figure 17.5 Dye formation from *para*-phenylene diamine

Use of larger amounts of 1,4-diaminobenzene tends to produce colours in the violet–red–brown range, whereas starting with relatively more 4-aminophenol gives lighter orangey browns.

After some 30 minutes or so the dye mixture is washed off the hair and an acid rinse applied. This lowers the pH of the hair, reprotonates the excess of $-COO^-$ groups on the surface (and thus removes the repulsions) and allows the protective scales to resettle around the fibre. The hair is now just as it was, but a different colour.

Well, not quite as it was. A side effect of the hydrogen peroxide is to oxidise the $-S-S-$ groups cross-linking the hair proteins, resulting in some loss of strength. Repeated bleaching or dyeing will continue this which is why hair that has been endlessly bleached starts to look frail and grassy.

Further reading

Encyclopedia of Chemical Technology, 4th edn, Kirk–Othmer, Wiley Interscience, 1994 (2)

Sunscreens

The lower the wavelength of light, the higher its energy. Biological systems are therefore most vulnerable to ultra-violet light, and elaborate systems have evolved to protect them. First in the line of defence is the thin layer of ozone in the stratosphere, at a height of around 50 km. Although the concentration of ozone is of the order of 10 parts per million – and if concentrated at a pressure of one atmosphere at sea level would be only about 3 mm thick – it removes much of the UV incident on the planet. But not all of it, and significant amounts do reach the Earth's surface.

Purely for convenience, it is divided into three regions:

Region	Wavelength range/nm	Energy/kJ mol^{-1}
UVA	320–400	3.3×10^2
UVB	280–320	4.0×10^2
UVC	200–280	5.0×10^2

Of course it is the UVC which is of the highest energy and is therefore the most damaging.

Some of the effects of UV on skin are familiar to us, from the acute – such as sunburn – to the long term, for example ageing and cancer. No doubt free radical formation is involved, leading to damage to DNA and to skin proteins. The skin attempts to protect itself against these effects – the sunlight stimulates it to produce melanin, a molecule with extensive delocalisation, which absorbs strongly in the UV and visible. Good though this protection is, it is not perfect and the build-up of melanin is quite slow, so if we are wise, when we jet off for our holidays, we will apply additional protection in the form of sunscreens. That these should screen out UVC and B has long been known but recent research has shown that unless they screen out UVA as well, they do not adequately protect us against skin cancer.

Sunscreens are of two types. First there are the sun blocks – creams containing mainly TiO_2 which completely prevent all radiation from reaching the skin. They are obvious as white masks obscuring lips and nose. For more general application the other type is used, containing large organic molecules which absorb strongly in the UV.

Because the energy of the incident light is quite high, it will result in electronic transitions. An electron in the highest occupied molecular orbital (called the HOMO) – usually a π or a non-bonding electron – is excited to the lowest unoccupied molecular orbital (the LUMO), commonly a π^* orbital, to form a singlet excited state (see Figure 17.6).

Excitation of any electron in this way can be followed by a number of processes. The spin of the excited electron may reverse, forming the more stable triplet state –

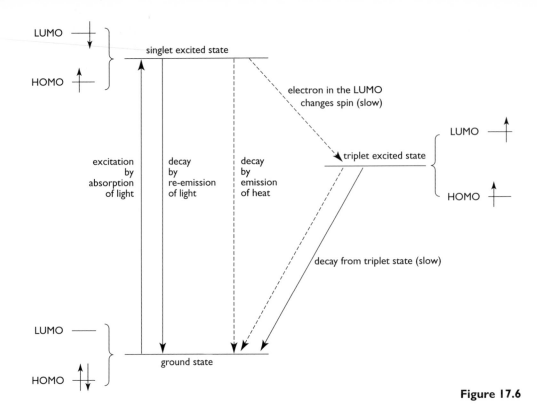

Figure 17.6

this is what happens in the eye (see page 117). But sunscreens must contain molecules which decay rapidly back to the ground state by emission of heat so we must choose molecules which do not readily form these triplet states. Figure 17.7 gives the structure of some of the common ones.

Commercial sunscreens quote a sun protection factor (SPF) which is experimentally determined by finding how long it takes a volunteer's skin to redden in sunlight with and without the sunscreen, applied at a standard rate of 2 mg of the compound per cm^2 of skin:

$$\text{SPF} = \frac{\text{time taken for skin to redden with sunscreen}}{\text{time taken for skin to redden without sunscreen}}$$

The higher the SPF, the greater the protection against sunburn and cancer. Unfortunately, the reddening is caused by UV light in the range 280–320 nm (UVB) so the SPF gives no measure of UVA protection, and manufacturers quote the UVA protection separately.

(The other components that you will find on any suncream container will include surfactants, to ensure that all the constituents stay well emulsified and do not separate out in the tube and thickening agents and preservatives – see page 11.)

Absorption spectra of three sunscreens are shown in Figure 17.8. Some of them protect primarily against UVA, some against UVB. Note that there is little or no protection against UVC. At present this does not matter, since the ozone layer does it for us, but if we continue to deplete it, sunscreens will have to be redesigned.

Structure	Common commercial name	Wavelength of maximum absorption/nm	Region of protection
	2-ethylhexyl-p-dimethylaminobenzoate (octyl-dimethyl PABA)	310	UVB
	octylmethoxycinnamate	310	UVB
	benzophenone-3	288 325	UVB UVA-B
	butylmethoxy dibenzoylmethane	370	UVA

Figure 17.7 Some sunscreen molecules

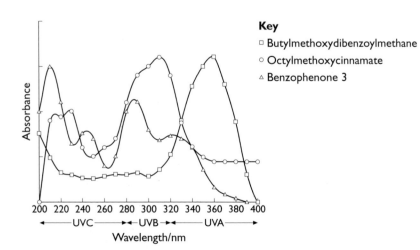

Key

□ Butylmethoxydibenzoylmethane

○ Octylmethoxycinnamate

△ Benzophenone 3

Figure 17.8 Spectra of sunscreens

further reading

Excitation of electrons is covered in any physical chemistry text; the best is by P W Atkins, Oxford University Press, many editions (2)
Chemistry in the Market Place, 4th edn, Ben Selinger, Harcourt Brace Jovanovich (1)

There is a little more on the chemistry of sunscreens in *J Chem Ed*, **74**: 51 and 99, Jan 1997 (2)

Jewels

Corundum is one form of Al_2O_3 in which all the aluminium ions are octahedrally co-ordinated by oxide ions. It's a pretty dull solid – white in colour, not valuable. If, however, about 1% of the aluminium ions are replaced by Cr^{3+} ions, we get the precious stone, ruby. The Cr^{3+} ion (radius 0.062 nm) is just a little larger than the Al^{3+} ion (0.053 nm), so it can replace it in the corundum lattice with little distortion. It is these octahedrally co-ordinated Cr^{3+} ions that give rise to the beautiful rich red colour.

The electron configuration of the Cr^{3+} ions is $[Ar]3d^3$. The oxide ions interact differently with the various d electrons of the Cr^{3+} ion because the orbitals are arranged differently in space. Ions in the horizontal x–y plane will repel the electrons in the $d_{x^2-y^2}$ orbital more strongly, because that orbital lies along the x and y axes. Similarly, the O^{2-} ions along the z axis repel electrons in the d_{z^2} orbital. The other d orbitals (the d_{yz}, d_{zx} and d_{xy}) lie between the axes, so they interact less with the oxide ions. The result is that whereas all the d orbitals of an isolated Cr^{3+} ion are of the same energy, those in a Cr^{3+} ion octahedrally co-ordinated in a corundum lattice are of different energy: the d_{yz}, d_{zx} and d_{xy} orbitals are of lower energy than the $d_{x^2-y^2}$ and the d_{z^2} orbitals. The three d electrons then occupy the d_{yz}, d_{zx} and d_{xy} orbitals (see Figure 17.9).

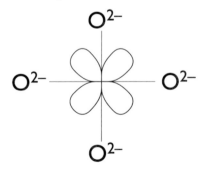

Oxide ions on the x and y axes do not interact very strongly with the d_{xy} orbital

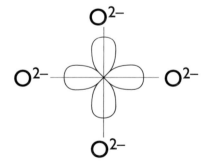

but the $d_{x^2-y^2}$ orbital is aligned along the axes, so it interacts more strongly with the oxide ions

Figure 17.9 Interaction of oxide ions with d orbitals

If the ruby crystal absorbs energy, one of these electrons can be excited to the higher d orbitals (see Figure 17.10). This energy can come from white light hitting the crystal, and it results in absorption of some wavelengths of the light. There are actually two absorptions (the reasons for this are complex), at about 570 nm (green light) and 414 nm (violet). The net result is that the red region of the spectrum is unaffected and the crystal thus appears red (see Figure 17.11). (There is also some red phosphorescence as well: see the inorganic textbook listed at the end of this section.)

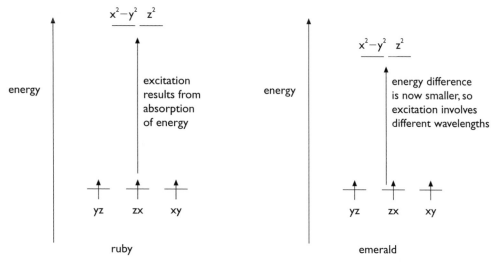

Figure 17.10 Absorption of light by ruby and emerald

Emeralds also owe their colour to electron transitions in Cr^{3+} ions, but in this case the host lattice is the mineral beryl, $Be_3Al_2Si_6O_{18}$ or $3BeO.Al_2O_3.6SiO_2$. In this lattice, the Cr^{3+} is again octahedrally co-ordinated, but slightly more weakly. That is to say, the splitting of the $d_{x^2-y^2}$ and d_{z^2} orbitals from the d_{yz}, d_{zx} and d_{xy} orbitals is slightly smaller (Figure 17.10). Thus the electron transitions are now of slightly lower energy, at longer wavelengths, about 600 nm (orange–red) and 490 nm (violet). There is very little absorption in the green, so this is the colour of an emerald (Figure 17.11).

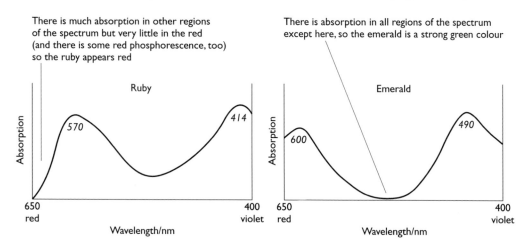

Figure 17.11 Absorption spectra of ruby and emerald

Like the ruby, the blue sapphire is based on the corundum, Al_2O_3, lattice, but the impurities which give rise to the colour are now iron and titanium. Titanium is usually present as Ti^{4+}; if the iron occurs as Fe^{2+}, electrical neutrality is maintained. The major contributor to the colour is now a charge transfer reaction: the incident light provides the energy for the transfer of an electron from an Fe^{2+} ion to a Ti^{4+} ion which is probably occupying an adjacent site, resulting in a redox reaction within the crystal:

$$Fe^{2+} + Ti^{4+} \rightarrow Fe^{3+} + Ti^{3+}$$

In addition there may be transfer of electrons between Fe^{2+} and Fe^{3+} ions. The net result is that there is absorption in all regions of the spectrum except the blue.

Further reading

Inorganic Chemistry, 2nd edn, D F Shriver, P W Atkins and C H Langford, Oxford University Press, 1994 (2)
The Physics and Chemistry of Color, Kurt Nassau, Wiley Interscience, 1983 (2)

18

METALS

This is such a huge topic that I have restricted myself a great deal. There is just a little discussion of the way in which we alter the properties of metals to make them do what we want, and how we join metals together.

Beer cans

Once upon a time, cans for beer, like those for baked beans, were made of steel coated in tin to stop them rusting. But since about 1970, the aluminium can has taken 99% of the drinks market (see Figure 18.1).

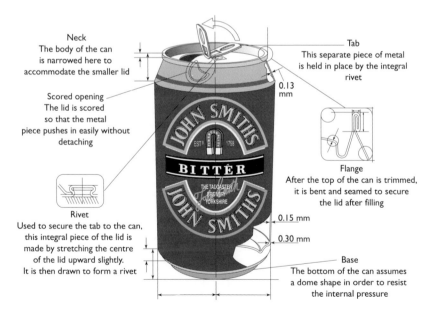

Neck
The body of the can is narrowed here to accommodate the smaller lid

Scored opening
The lid is scored so that the metal piece pushes in easily without detaching

Rivet
Used to secure the tab to the can, this integral piece of the lid is made by stretching the centre of the lid upward slightly. It is then drawn to form a rivet

Tab
This separate piece of metal is held in place by the integral rivet

0.13 mm

Flange
After the top of the can is trimmed, it is bent and seamed to secure the lid after filling

0.15 mm

0.30 mm

Base
The bottom of the can assumes a dome shape in order to resist the internal pressure

Figure 18.1 The aluminium can

Each can is made in two pieces. To form the body, a 14 cm disc is cut from a sheet of the alloy which is then pressed to make a cup 8.9 cm in diameter. A second machine lengthens the body and creates a dome in the base of the can (to withstand the internal pressure, which may reach 620 000 Pa, or over 6 times atmospheric). At the same time, the thickness of the walls is adjusted, from a maximum of 0.30 mm at the base to 0.08 mm at the top. All this in under 0.2 seconds! The lid has to be thicker (so that the ring-pull will work properly) and because this uses more aluminium, the can is narrowed at the top (from 6.6 cm to 5.3 cm) to reduce the diameter of the lid and hence the amount of aluminium alloy needed for it.

Since 1970, aluminium alloys have been designated by a four-digit number. The first digit indicates the other main element present in the alloy. Thus, for example, the 3xxx series has manganese as the main alloying element, whereas a 5xxx alloy has magnesium. The body of the can is made from the 3004 alloy, which contains 1.0–1.5% manganese and 0.8–1.3% magnesium, together with smaller amounts of silicon, iron, copper and zinc. Because the lid has to be more rigid than the body, it is made from 5182 alloy, containing about 4.5% magnesium.

Alloys are harder than the parent metal. When 'foreign' atoms dissolve into a solid metal, they may do so in two ways. If they are small enough, they may occupy the so-called interstitial sites – the spaces between atoms of the parent metal aluminium. Alternatively, they may actually replace the aluminium atoms at actual lattice sites. Because the sizes of the aluminium and the foreign atoms will be different, either method will introduce distortions to the lattice. Figure 18.2 shows why this results in a harder metal: the presence of larger magnesium atoms, for example, prevents the layers of aluminium atoms from slipping over one another. (Most metals are actually polycrystalline, and the impurity atoms perform the same function at the crystal boundaries, increasing the roughness of the surface of each

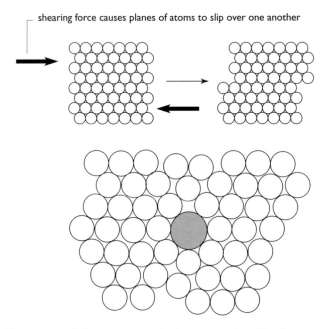

shearing force causes planes of atoms to slip over one another

The presence of a foreign atom wrecks the regular packing. The planes are no longer flat, so they can't slide over one another so easily. The foreign atom thus locks the planes together and makes the metal stronger.
(I have used an unusually large atom to exaggerate the effect)

Figure 18.2

crystal and so helping to lock them together.) Manganese and aluminium atoms are approximately the same size (0.137 nm and 0.143 nm, respectively), so the effect of manganese atoms on the strength of aluminium is fairly small: the 3004 alloy has about twice the tensile strength of pure aluminium. Magnesium atoms, however, are considerably bigger (0.160 nm) and their effect on the strength of aluminium is more marked. As a result of this greater size difference, magnesium is not very soluble in solid aluminium: at room temperature the maximum solubility is 1.8%. The 5182 alloy of which beer can tops are made has 4.5% magnesium dissolved in it, with a corresponding gain in strength. How is this done?

Figure 18.3 shows part of the phase diagram for the magnesium–aluminium system. The maximum solubility of Mg in Al is 1.8% at 0°C. The solubility of a solid in a solvent usually increases as you raise the temperature, and the curved line in Figure 18.3 shows that this is true for a solution of magnesium in aluminium: the solubility rises to a maximum of about 15% at around 420°C. The extra hardening needed in the aluminium for beer can tops is achieved by heating a mixture of 4.5% Mg and 95.5% Al to 450°C. The magnesium dissolves to give a solution in which the magnesium has replaced aluminium atoms at lattice sites. If we were to cool this solution slowly, at about 220°C the solid solution would start to separate into two different crystalline solids: the Mg atoms would diffuse through the solid aluminium to form crystals of the β-phase, Mg_5Al_8. If we cool it fast enough, however, the magnesium atoms don't have time to diffuse through the solid lattice and form the Mg_5Al_8, so they remain randomly distributed throughout the solid in a supersaturated solution. This extra magnesium (an extra 2.7% of it) confers yet more strength on the alloy: 5182 is over three times stronger than pure aluminium. This allows the lid to be thinner, with consequent savings in costs.

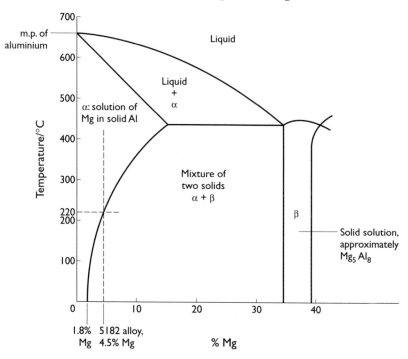

Figure 18.3 The phase diagram for the Mg/Al system

It takes about 2.3 MJ to produce one aluminium beer can: that would keep a 100-watt light bulb burning for over six hours. That's a large amount of energy invested in one aluminium can, so recycling – which saves 95% of this energy – makes much sense. But the construction of the can makes this difficult, because two different alloys are involved. What do we do? Do we try to separate lid from can? Too time (and energy) consuming. Do we ignore the differences in composition? Not possible: every use of aluminium requires a specific alloy. Instead, two methods are used. One involves shredding the metal. Because the 3004 alloy of the body is more ductile, it remains in larger pieces than the 5182 alloy of the lid, and they can be separated by passing through a screen. The second method involves melting the can and bubbling chlorine through the liquid. The chlorine reacts preferentially with the magnesium present, removing it as a slag of $MgCl_2$. The remaining metal, with manganese as the major impurity, can then have its composition adjusted and can be reused as 3004.

But beer cans hardly represent the most important use of aluminium metal. Think of aluminium and we probably think of aircraft, and here other strengthening techniques are employed. The duralumin alloys, the 2000 series, contain up to 4.5% copper. They undergo the same solution hardening process used with the 5182 Mg–Al alloy used in beer can lids. But now a further process, called age hardening, is brought into play. The alloy is heated to about 150°C and held there for a long time, perhaps 100 hours. This higher temperature increases the rate of migration of the copper atoms, and some of them start to form very small crystals of $CuAl_2$. These form randomly throughout the original solid solution and, because they are so big compared to an aluminium or copper atom, they exert an even stronger locking effect on the slip planes. (This is the same sort of effect as the Fe_3C in carbon steels.) The effects of these hardening processes are summarised in the table below:

Alloy	Composition	Hardening process	Tensile strength/N m^{-2}
1100	>99% Al	none	9.0×10^7
5182	4.5% Mg	solution	2.9×10^8
2024	4.5% Cu	solution + age	4.7×10^8
2090	2.7% Cu, 2.4% Li	solution + age	5.5×10^8

The 2090 alloy is used for aircraft skins; the airframes are likely to be made from 7075 (5.6% Zn and 2.5% Mg) which has a slightly greater tensile strength.

Further reading

Scientific American, Sep 1994, p 34 (1)
Engineering Materials 2, M F Ashby and D R H Jones, Pergamon, 1986 (2)
The Science and Engineering of Materials, D R Askeland, PWS Publishing, 1994 (2).
Light Alloys, I J Polmear, Arnold, 1995 (2)

Welding

Although metals can be glued together, if a very strong joint is required or if it has to conduct electricity, molten metal is used. For electrical circuits, solder was traditionally used – a tin–lead alloy containing 60% tin with a melting point of around 180°C. To join structural metals, however, a weld is needed in which the molten metal is a strong alloy compatible with the material of the structure and of similar strength. The melting points of these structural alloys are much higher, however, so the devices used to melt the metal are more complex than a simple soldering iron.

Although there is a huge range of welding methods, the two major techniques involve use of an acetylene (ethyne)–oxygen flame or of an electric arc to melt the metal. There are three different arc methods of increasing complexity. The simplest, that everyone has surely seen in use, is manual arc welding involving use of a hand-held electrode. A potential difference of between 15 and 45 volts is maintained between the electrode and the work piece. To start, the operator touches the electrode onto the work piece, then withdraws it to about 3–4 mm. As the electrode is withdrawn, the spark produced ionises the air and these resulting ions allow the arc to be maintained, generating a temperature of 6000–7000°C. The electrode thus melts, forming a bead of molten metal on the work piece which completes the join as it cools. The material of the join is thus dictated by the material of the electrode which will be used up as welding proceeds.

There are problems attached to this simple method. The presence of air at these high temperatures will result in the formation of metal oxides and nitrides which will seriously weaken the joint. For this reason the electrodes are coated with some material which will vaporise and bathe the work site in a protective vapour. The simplest of these are made of cellulose material which degrades providing CO_2 and probably water. The presence of hydrogen-containing compounds is sometimes undesirable, as free hydrogen is formed in the arc. The elements commonly being joined – those in the middle of the transition series – can dissolve it to some extent, and the presence of this hydrogen tends to expand the lattice and make the joint brittle and liable to cracking. For this reason, hydrogen-free coatings are used, mainly containing $CaCO_3$ and CaF_2. The $CaCO_3$ decomposes at the weld temperature, bathing the join in CO_2.

A more sophisticated variant of this welding technique uses a continuous wire in place of the electrode, and this is supplied to the work area at a slow, preset rate by means of a motor, so that it is renewed as fast as it melts away. To prevent reaction of the weld with oxygen or nitrogen or absorption of hydrogen the whole area is bathed in an inert gas (the so-called MIG, metal inert gas). Whereas the manual technique transfers the molten metal as droplets, the MIG technique permits use of higher currents producing a spray of molten metal. Carbon dioxide is the cheapest shielding gas, but dissociation to CO and oxygen can lead to oxidation of the weld metal. To get round this, the steel wire has more reactive elements added, such as manganese, silicon, aluminium, titanium and zirconium. Alternatively, argon can be used as the shield gas, sometimes with 1–2% oxygen added to give a higher temperature and a smoother weld.

Finally there is the so-called TIG welding method: tungsten electrode, inert gas shielded. Because tungsten has such a high melting point (3380°C) a separate wire of weld material has to be supplied to be melted to form the joint.

Aluminium is somewhat difficult to weld because it forms a very stable oxide and nitride. It is first degreased using a solvent such as chloromethane, then wire brushed to remove excess oxide coating. It can then be welded using MIG or TIG, with an aluminium alloy filler wire, shielding the work area with argon. Because aluminium becomes soft and fluid near the work temperature, the actual work area may need a ceramic support underneath to prevent sagging. Although MIG can be used, TIG is particularly suitable for aluminium because if the electrode is made positive with respect to the work piece, the positive ions in the arc (mainly Ar^+, presumably) will be repelled by the electrode, thus bombarding the surface and disrupting the coating of Al_2O_3.

Titanium is more tricky. Ultra-pure argon must be used, and it is important to ensure that reaction of the reverse face of the work piece cannot occur; titanium forms TiO_2, Ti_2N and TiN rather readily. This is usually done, if the weld is linear, by fitting a grooved plate to the back and feeding argon into the groove. If the weld is of an awkward shape, the whole thing will be fixed into a chamber with rubber seals and gloves for the operator; this will then be evacuated and purged repeatedly with argon, and the welding done in a flowing argon atmosphere inside this box. You can tell if oxygen is getting in as the weld discolours.

further reading

The Science and Practice of Welding in 2 Volumes, 9th edn, A C Davies, Cambridge University Press (2)

19

NITROGEN

Several factors make nitrogen interesting and uniquely valuable:

- it has an odd number of electrons in many of its compounds; they can thus act as radicals, albeit not very reactive ones. A wide range of reactions is therefore available to a molecule of this type, like NO.

- its triple bond is very strong and the single N—N bond is rather weak, a consequence of the repulsion between the non-bonding pairs of electrons, much as in difluorine or in peroxides. Reactions that have N_2 as one of the products are therefore unusually exothermic.

- it exhibits a wide range of oxidation states, from -3 in ammonia and ammonium salts to $+5$ in nitrates. There is therefore an extensive redox chemistry and interconversion of the various oxidation states may be easy.

- it has quite a high electronegativity, so its compounds with non-metals will be of low polarity.

From angina to impotence

Angina is the name given to the sharp pain in the chest which occurs when a sufferer exercises. It arises because the heart muscle is short of oxygen, often because the arteries of the heart are too narrow. As long ago as 1867 it was shown that if the coronary arteries could be widened, the increased blood supply that resulted would remove the symptoms. Amyl nitrite, $(CH_3)_2CH-CH_2-CH_2-ONO$, proved to be very effective – inhalation of the vapour removed the pain within seconds. A solution of the explosive nitroglycerine was equally good, requiring some 2–3 minutes for its action, but maintaining it for longer than amyl nitrite. Other drugs with a similar effect were developed but how they worked remained a total mystery until 1987, when it was shown that their effect was due to the production of nitrogen monoxide in the body.

Nitrogen monoxide? NO? The colourless gas that reacts instantly with air to produce the brown, very toxic nitrogen dioxide? In the body? Surely not! In fact NO has now been implicated in a vast range of body processes.

It is synthesised in the body from the amino acid arginine producing citrulline, which is recycled back to arginine (see Figure 19.1).

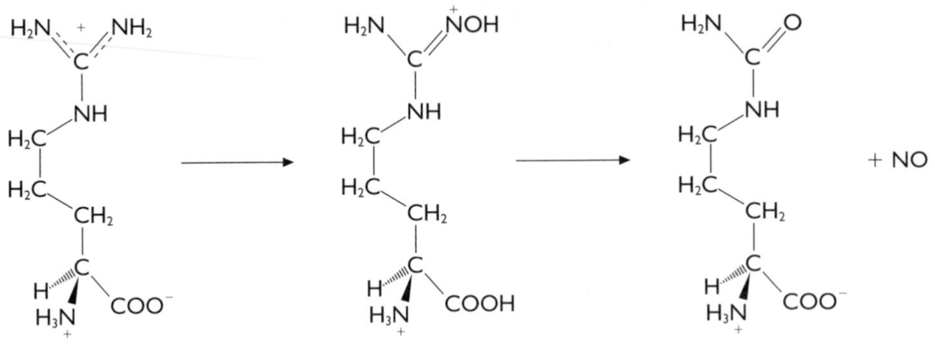

Figure 19.1 The biosynthesis of nitric oxide

Since this guanidino group of arginine is essentially an ammonia derivative in which the nitrogen has an oxidation state of -3, the reaction involves a five electron oxidation. It is catalysed by enzymes known as NO synthases (NOS); several have been isolated from human tissues. Some of these are found in the cells lining blood vessels, in blood platelets and in nerve cells, and they seem to generate small steady amounts of NO which carry out a range of physiological functions. NO, therefore, seems to act as a transmitter molecule, with an essential function in regulating the processes of the body.

What sorts of processes are controlled by this little messenger molecule? The first to be identified was the relaxation of the smooth muscle of artery walls, apparently by activation of an enzyme called guanylate cyclase. The NO binds to the iron in this enzyme, presumably via the lone pair on the nitrogen. It is probably this binding which activates the enzyme, leading in turn to relaxation of the muscles and widening of the arteries. This one function of NO has produced a number of therapeutic uses. Amyl nitrite and nitroglycerine reverse the symptoms of angina by giving rise to NO in the body. There are now occasions when direct inhalation of NO is being used to relieve high blood pressure – in new-born babies, for example, or after bypass surgery. In these cases a nitric oxide–air mixture containing 50–80 ppm NO is effective. At these low NO concentrations, the rate of reaction of NO with oxygen (which is second order with respect to NO, remember – see page 132) is far less than with haemoglobin or oxyhaemoglobin, so there is no danger of the toxic NO_2 being produced.

Nitroglycerine has also been of use in male impotence. This is a condition in which a man is unable to achieve or sustain an erection, and it has been estimated that half the male population will suffer from this at some time in their lives. Some time ago it was discovered that application of a solution of nitroglycerine to the penis caused good erections. It is now known that the mechanism of erection involves release of NO which activates the enzyme guanylate cyclase, which produces high levels of cyclic guanosine monophosphate (cGMP). The cGMP relaxes the walls of the blood vessels of the penis, allowing inflow of blood leading to erection. The new drug Viagra acts by inhibiting the enzyme which breaks down cGMP. So when sexual stimulation causes release of NO, cGMP levels reach higher levels than before. Prescription and black market sales of Viagra have broken all records.

But since NO synthases are ubiquitous, it is clear that the function of NO must be widespread and varied. Already we know that it inhibits blood clotting, and is involved in peristalsis in the gut and release of insulin from pancreatic cells. The high levels of nitrite ions in synovial fluid of arthritis sufferers may indicate a role for NO here, too.

It has long been known that nitroglycerine can relax uterine contractions. More recently it has been used to prevent premature births, a major cause of infant deaths. A recent study on women admitted to hospital starting to go into early labour showed that application to the abdomen of nitroglycerine patches could halt the contractions and prolong the pregnancy for up to a month with no ill effects to mother or baby. A baby born at 27 weeks has a much better chance of survival than one born four weeks earlier.

There are also other NO synthases which are spurred into action by infection. These enzymes were first identified in macrophages, but have since been found in other cells of the immune system. It seems, then, that NO has two broad roles in the body. In addition to its regulatory function, at much higher concentrations it acts to destroy invading microbes. Activation of the immune system results in the production of large amounts of NO. Then either the NO itself or, more probably, stronger oxidants, such as NO_2 (the NO is in much higher concentration here, remember, so the reaction with oxygen will be much faster) or peroxynitrites ($ONOO^-$, from reaction of NO with superoxide, O_2^-, see page 94) causes massive damage to the attacking organism. In some cases, the build-up of oxidants may reach such levels that the host organism starts to suffer damage, too: the classic is the condition known as septic shock, where severe infection is followed by a catastrophic fall in blood pressure. Excessive NO production might also be implicated in cerebral damage following stroke and Parkinson's disease.

Further reading

Biological Roles of Nitric Oxide: S H Snyder and D S Bredt, *Scientific American*, May 1992, p 28 (1)

This is such a new area that there are no books yet available. The Internet is a good source of current work; try searching on 'nitric oxide'.

Βlue babies and cancers

Just over 50 years ago, a couple of babies were admitted to hospital in rural Iowa with brownish-blue skin, first of the lips, spreading to fingers and toes and eventually the whole body. An alert paediatrician realised, however, that this cyanosis was actually due to a condition in which the Fe(II) ion of normal haemoglobin is oxidised to Fe(III). This form of haemoglobin, known as methaemoglobin, is unable to transport oxygen. When its concentration in the blood reaches 10%, the 'blue baby' symptoms are seen; higher levels produce lassitude, weariness and eventually coma. 60% is commonly regarded as the fatal level.

The transformation can easily be carried out in the lab using nitrite [nitrate (III)] ions:

$$Fe^{2+} + NO_2^- + 2H^+ \rightarrow Fe^{3+} + NO + H_2O$$

It has been proposed that something similar can occur in the body. Certainly nitrites are toxic: in 1946, 71 people in Leipzig ate soup flavoured using a 'curing salt' rich in nitrites; 37 required hospital treatment and seven died. It is reckoned that about 2–4 g sodium nitrite is fatal. Had the Iowa babies been poisoned with nitrite ions? It turned out that they had been reared on formula feeds made up using the local well water which contained a high level of nitrate ions, NO_3^-.

But nitrate ions are not toxic. Ammonium nitrate has been used as a medicine. One study quotes 268 patients who had consumed 2–9 g/day for *up to two years*; only two cases of methaemoglobinia were reported. Levels of nitrates in food are often high – one study estimated that a person might consume over 190 mg NO_3^- a day, with more coming from the drinking water. It now seems likely that any risk from consuming nitrate ions comes only from their conversion to nitrite in the body, and that this can be reduced to two main hazards: blue babies and stomach cancer.

Early research showed that blue baby symptoms occurred only in babies whose stomach pH was above 4. In the womb the baby is germ free, and it is contaminated only externally during birth. As the stomach and gut are initially free of bacteria, and as there is little acid secretion in the stomach, there are no barriers to colonisation of the infant's inside and the bacteria, therefore, flood in. But the composition of breast milk and commercial infant feed are very different, and as a result of this, the bacterial inhabitants of a baby's gut are determined by how it is fed. The effects of these gastric bacteria differ: it is found that the pH of the stomach of a 30-day-old breast-fed baby is about 4, while that of a bottle-fed baby is about 7. The less acidic stomach in bottle-fed babies allows nitrate-reducing bacteria to become established, with the greater risk of reduction of nitrates to nitrite.

Of course, this only poses a problem if too much nitrate is ingested, and the most usual route for this is by drinking water high in nitrates. For this reason the European Union has fixed a maximum admissible level of 50 mg nitrate per dm^3 (50 ppm), with a guide level of 25 ppm.

Blue baby syndrome is still with us. In Hungary where (unlike the UK) parents have to notify the authorities if the disease occurs, 1353 cases and 21 deaths were reported in the years 1976–1982. Intriguingly, there is a strong correlation between vitamin C ingestion and methaemoglobinia. In one study 42% of people who did not take a vitamin C supplement had a high methaemoglobin level, whereas levels were high in only 6% of those who did.

Nitrites have also been linked to cancer of the stomach, especially since it was shown that N-nitroso compounds are carcinogens (see Figure 19.2). These are formed when nitrous acid [HNO_2, nitric (III) acid] reacts with a range of nitrogen-containing compounds, such as secondary amines.

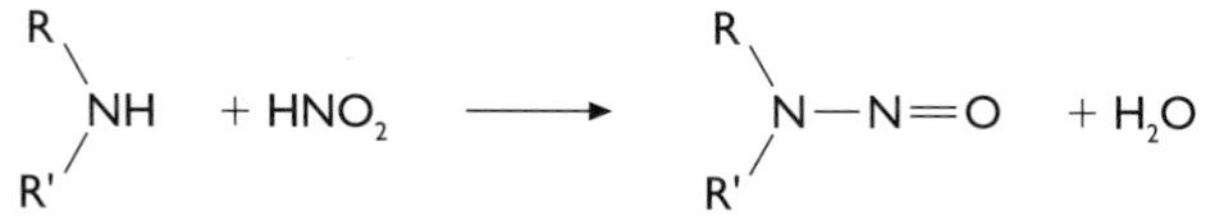

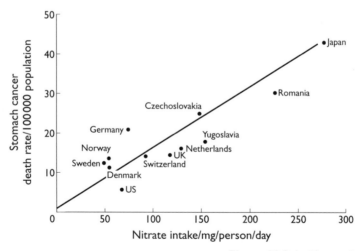

Figure 19.2 N-nitrosoamine formation from a secondary amine

Because this reaction requires the presence of free HNO_2, it will only occur to any significant extent in the presence of nitrites if the pH is low, and that means that the only site of their synthesis is likely to be the stomach, whose pH would usually be below 2.

But there is another route of nitrosoamine production. It has been found that there is a bacterial enzyme which catalyses their formation from nitrite *and nitrate*, but which functions best closer to neutral pH.

Figure 19.3 plots the incidence of stomach cancer against daily nitrate intake for a range of countries.

Figure 19.3 Incidence of stomach cancer as a function of nitrate intake

There does seem to be a correlation: the higher the nitrate intake, the higher the rate of stomach cancer. But the highest nitrate levels are found in lettuce, spinach, celery and so on, and nitrites are most abundant in green vegetables and potatoes, precisely those foods which form the staple diet of vegetarians, who are known to live longer than meat eaters. Epidemiological studies have shown that a high consumption of salad vegetables is actually *protective* against stomach cancer.

It seems likely that although vegetables may be high in one risk factor (nitrate and nitrite), they also contain compounds which reduce the risk. What might these be? The balance of probability is that they are antioxidants. Let's remind ourselves of the protective effect of vitamin C in methaemoglobin formation, mentioned above. Vitamin C destroys N-nitrosoamines rapidly and completely; combinations of vitamins C and E are even more effective. Perhaps these antioxidants reduce the nitrogen to a lower oxidation state. What do we do? Eat lots of fruit and vegetables.

Further reading

Nitrates and Nitrites in Food and Water, M J Hill, Ellis Horwood, 1991 (2)

Internet: search on 'nitrite'.

Air bags

Although the enthalpy and free energy of formation of sodium azide, NaN_3, are both positive, the activation energy for decomposition is high, so it is a reasonably stable solid and can be melted without much decomposition. On brief heating to a higher temperature, however – about 300°C is enough – the activation energy is supplied and decomposition back to the elements is initiated:

$$2NaN_3 \rightarrow 2Na + 3N_2 \qquad \Delta H = -44 \text{ kJ mol}^{-1}$$

This process forms the basis of the air bag. When the car collides with something, the rapid deceleration triggers a sensor which completes an electrical circuit, resulting in a heating current being applied to a coil embedded in the solid azide. Production of the nitrogen gas is very rapid, inflating the bag in fractions of a second and stopping the driver from hitting the steering wheel. About 150 g of azide is used, producing a maximum of 112 dm^3 of gas if decomposition goes to completion. The bag has vents in it, so that it is soft and yielding on impact.

The whole process is fraught with hazard and surely would not be considered were it not such a potential lifesaver. NaN_3 itself is relatively stable, but is extremely toxic. US standards for workplace exposure set a limit of 0.2 mg m^{-3} (compare that with the figure of 5 mg m^{-3} for NaCN). Interestingly the N_3^- acts rather like CN^- in the body, binding to Fe^{3+} ions in cytochrome oxidase. Fortunately, once it is initiated, the decomposition of the azide is relatively complete.

The products are also potentially dangerous, however. The sodium metal produced will be liquid at the temperature produced, so the azide is actually mixed with potassium nitrate, which reacts with the sodium as follows:

$$10Na + 2KNO_3 \rightarrow K_2O + 5Na_2O + N_2$$

usefully producing more gas. The two oxides are extremely corrosive, however, so silica (SiO_2) is also a constituent of the mixture. At the high temperatures generated it tends to react with the oxides to form a relatively inert glass, which also has the useful function of tending to seal all the products and any unreacted azide into a solid mass.

Other uses of metal azides are similar. Those of the heavy metals are much less stable, especially to shock, and are used in detonators for explosives. The most common is lead azide, made by a standard precipitation reaction:

$$Pb(NO_3)_2(aq) + NaN_3(aq) \rightarrow Pb(N_3)_2(s) + 2NaNO_3(aq)$$

Further reading

The Chemistry of the Elements, N N Greenwood and A Earnshaw, Pergamon, 1984 (2) has some more information on the azides.
Air Bags, A Madlung, *J Chem Ed*, **73**: 347–8, 1996

Explosives

They're not just about killing people – far from it, as we shall see. And almost all of them involve nitrogen, somewhere.

Explosion is not burning! Below are some data for a typical fuel, an explosive and, lying between these two, a rocket propellant.

	Fuel	Propellant	Explosive
Linear reaction rate/m s^{-1}	10^{-6}	10^{-2}	5×10^3
Energy output/J g^{-1}	10^4	10^3	10^3
Power/W cm^{-2}	10	10^3	10^9
Pressure developed/MPa	0.07–0.7	300–700	10^4–10^5

The linear reaction rate refers to the speed of reaction if the material is packed into a fuse. The shock wave in an explosive is transmitted at *five kilometres a second*! It is not the amount of energy released that makes explosives what they are: it is the rate of its release.

Although gunpowder was reputedly known to the Chinese over 2000 years ago and its main use was military, applications in mining began to appear as early as the 17th Century. By 1685 the practice of drilling shot holes and stopping them with clay so as to prevent escape of the gases had been developed. Setting the explosive off was a pretty risky business – it mainly seems to have involved lighting the touch paper and running – but by the start of the 19th Century, electrical firing had been developed. Today an explosive will have two components: the less sensitive primary charge which sets off the more stable secondary charge. The mercury fulminate detonator, $Hg(CNO)_2$, was discovered in 1865. Military explosives now tend to use lead azide, $Pb(N_3)_2$, but since this produces lead-containing fumes after detonation, it is being replaced in commercial explosives.

Ascanio Sobrero of Turin had invented nitroglycerine (Figure 19.4) in 1846, but because it is so shock-sensitive it remained just a curiosity until Alfred Nobel decided to develop it for commercial use. After a particularly serious explosion with this 'blasting oil' when his youngest brother was killed, Nobel set out to find a way to stabilise it. This he managed to do by absorbing it into keiselguhr, a type of clay. The result was dynamite – stable and easy to handle, but detonating with nearly all the power of nitroglycerine itself. But a quarter of its mass was inert clay, so Nobel replaced this with nitrocellulose – cellulose with all its −OH groups replaced by $-NO_2$ and itself an explosive. Blasting Gelatine, rubbery and waterproof, is still the most powerful commercial explosive.

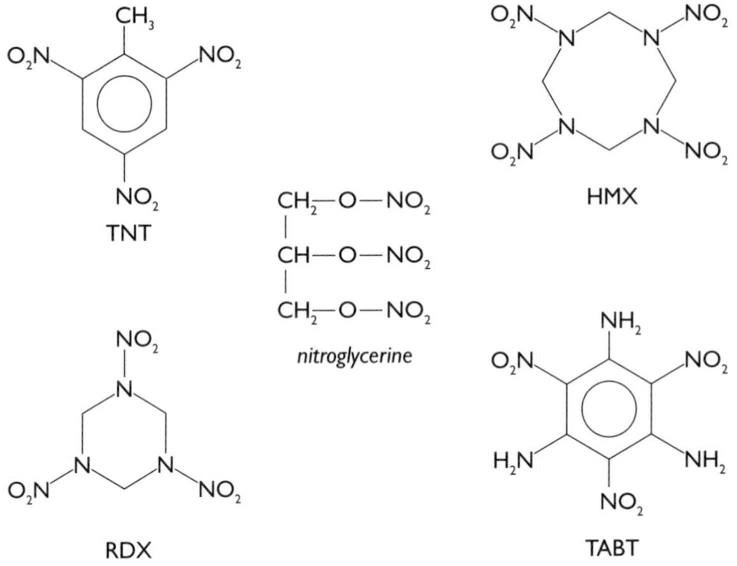

Figure 19.4 Some explosives

Almost all the succeeding explosives have also contained $-NO_2$ groups, because on detonation the nitrogen will result in the very stable N_2 molecule, and the oxygens can function as oxidisers for carbons or hydrogens in the rest of the molecule. So in 1900 TNT (2,4,6-trinitromethylbenzene) came into use, followed by RDX in the 1930s and HMX some 20 years later (see Figure 19.4). An interesting development is that of especially insensitive – and therefore safer – explosives, such as TATB (triaminotrinitrobenzene), whose extreme insensitivity is thought to be due to intramolecular hydrogen bonding between the $-NO_2$ and $-NH_2$ groups. Current developments pack more nitrogens into the molecule (as in HNIW, Figure 19.5) and research revolves around molecules with strained bonds so that the release of this strain increases the power output. Two possible substances are octanitrocubane and octa-azacubane (Figure 19.5). If it can be made, this last molecule will be the first explosive not to involve a redox reaction; its energy will come solely from the stability of the N≡N bond and the strain of the cube.

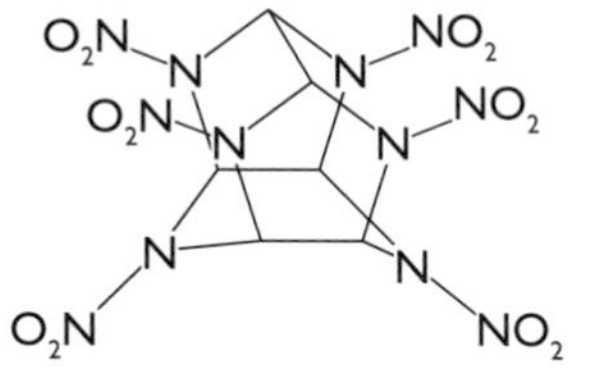

HNIW

(hexanitrohexa-azaisowurtzitane)

A recent introduction

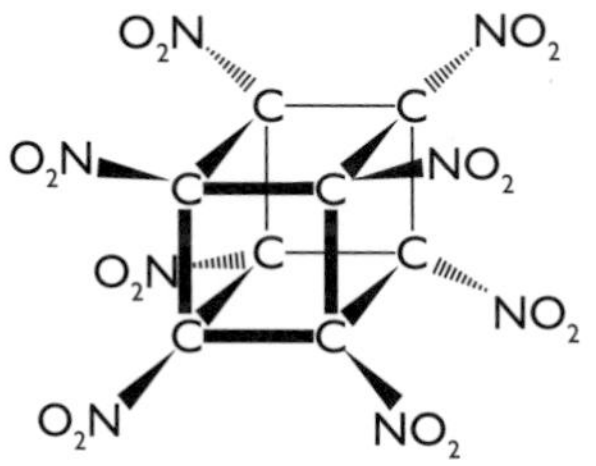

octanitrocubane

octa-azacubane

Possible future explosives

Figure 19.5 Some recent and potential future explosives

Present-day commercial explosives commonly consist of a mixture of TNT and RDX. The detonation of TNT is very different from the combustion:

combustion: $\quad 2C_7H_5N_3O_6 + \frac{21}{2}O_2 \rightarrow 14CO_2 + 5H_2O + 3N_2$

detonation: $\quad C_7H_5N_3O_6 \rightarrow 3.65C + 1.98CO + 1.60H_2O + 1.32N_2 + 0.46H_2$
$+ 0.16NH_3 + 0.10CH_4$

and since the oxidation on detonation is less complete, the energy released is reduced.

The activation energy is high so these explosives are safe and are routinely transported by road.

But what are they used for? Those of us not involved can have no idea of the breadth of use of these extraordinary materials. Demolition, of course; mining, naturally. Let's not forget construction, too: of canals, tunnels, roads and so on, and excavation for foundations for bridges and buildings. Then there are the explosive devices used to stimulate oil production from declining wells by firing bullets to perforate the surrounding rock.

And think of this: explosives are increasingly used to weld metals together. The two metals to be joined are placed together with the explosive on top (see Figure 19.6).

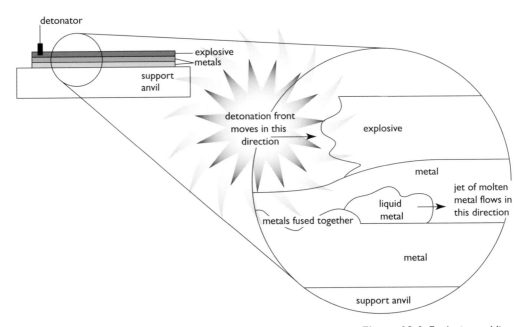

Figure 19.6 Explosive welding

Detonation is initiated at one end, and the shock wave flows along the work piece, melting the metal as it goes and fusing the two pieces together. The ripples in the interface result in an extremely strong bond, so that the resultant piece can be worked – cut, bent, machined – *as one piece*. This is particularly useful for ship construction in that unlike conventional joints, the interface is not accessible to the seawater and corrosion can only occur on the outer surface. We can use the technique to apply a thin layer of a corrosion-resistant metal – titanium, perhaps – to the surface of a structural metal such as steel.

War? Fireworks? There's more to explosives than that!

Further reading

Encyclopedia of Chemical Technology, 4th edn, Kirk–Othmer, Wiley Interscience, 1994 (2)

Explosives in the Service of Man, J E Dolan and S S Langer (eds), Royal Society of Chemistry, 1997 (2)

20

PERIODIC TABLE

Everything in this book is underpinned by the periodic table, of course. This section is just one aspect of it: the question of why living systems have chosen to use some elements but not others, and what they use them for.

Life elements

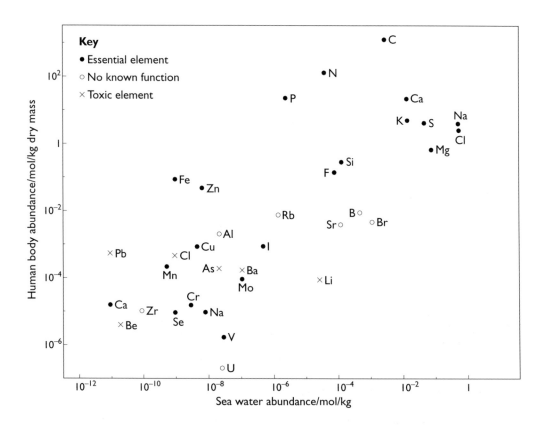

Figure 20.1 The abundance of elements in living matter and in the oceans

Life originated in the oceans. It had to: only in the sea could the delicate evolving molecules of living systems find protection from the blasts of ultra-violet radiation from the sun. But this meant that the original systems had to take what elements they could find in the Earth's oceans at the time, and until they could learn to select, these early organisms had to absorb whichever elements they were supplied with, in the quantities that were available. The composition of organism and surroundings cannot have been very different. Later on, of course, living systems had to develop ways of controlling their internal structure and composition, and the composition departed from this primordial recipe. But it seems reasonable to assume that changes will have been made only for improvements in function, so that much of the initial mix will remain unaltered, untouched from the beginning. This is seen in Figure 20.1 where the composition of the human body (dry mass, after removal of water) is plotted against the abundance of the elements in sea water (again omitting the water).

Although there is a wide scatter, there is clearly a significant correlation.

Development of an organism implies the development of a membrane, and moreover one that is permeable to at least some molecules, or the organism will rapidly run out of nutrients and accumulate waste products. But if the organism is to have any control over its metabolism, it must develop some means of choosing which elements and compounds it will employ.

So which ones do we use, and why? Figure 20.2 gives part of the answer: it shows part of the periodic table, with an indication of the role of each element.

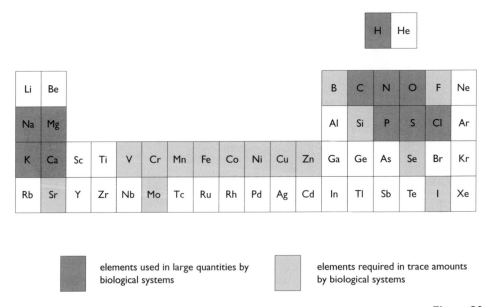

elements used in large quantities by biological systems

elements required in trace amounts by biological systems

Figure 20.2

That carbon would have to be the basis for the molecules of life is obvious. Its high bond strength and ability to form multiple bonds make for a huge range of stable molecules. The fact that it can form four bonds and that these are arranged at tetrahedral angles means that three-dimensional molecules are possible. Because its electronegativity is intermediate, its covalent bonds are not of extreme polarity, and thus the carbon may be $\delta+$ or $\delta-$, depending on its partner (which opens up possibilities of control of reaction mechanisms). As carbon has no low-lying empty orbitals, formation of more than four bonds is energetically very unfavourable. If we draw a hypothetical transition state for the S_N2-type reaction of a water molecule with CCl_4 and its silicon analogue (Figure 20.3), we can see that both require the central atom to be temporarily associated with 10 electrons. Silicon has empty 3d orbitals to allow this; carbon has only the 3s orbitals and they are miles away in energy terms. So $SiCl_4$ reacts explosively with cold water, whereas CCl_4 reacts only on prolonged heating. Carbon compounds are thus very reluctant to react – they are kinetically stable.

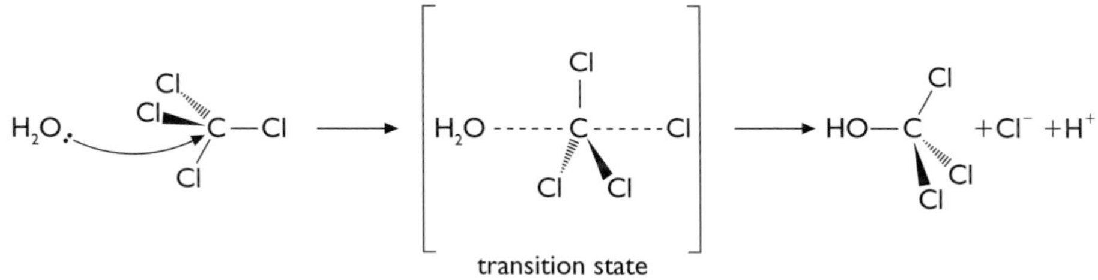

transition state

Figure 20.3 S_N2 reaction

And what of other elements? What do they do? The metals of the first two groups provide four of the most important elements: Na, K, Mg and Ca. These are associated with an ionic aqueous chemistry. Sodium and potassium form few complexes, and those that do form are of very limited stability, unless the ligands are chelating ligands, and even then their complexes are much less stable than those of other elements. Compare the stability constants for formation of $EDTA^{4-}$ complexes; i.e. K for

$$M^{n+} + EDTA^{4-} \rightleftharpoons [MEDTA]^{(4-n)-}$$

Ion	Na^+	K^+	Mg^{2+}	Ca^{2+}	Fe^{2+}	Zn^{2+}
Log K_{stab}	~1	~0	8.9	10.7	14.3	16.5

Sodium and potassium will therefore occur as free ions in biological systems, except where specific ligands have been evolved. These will be 'super chelators', rather like biological crown ethers or cryptands (see page 107).

Magnesium and calcium complex more strongly, but still up to a million times more weakly than the transition elements, and their inorganic chemistry is dominated by simple ionic substances. They occur both bound and free, therefore, in biological systems. The best-known complex of magnesium is chlorophyll, but it also complexes strongly with phosphate groups, in ATP, for example.

Calcium is everywhere – in extracellular fluids and in every cell of our bodies – and has a multitude of roles. There are several reasons for this, none of them easy.

167

First, like magnesium, it forms complexes of intermediate stability (inevitably with multidentate ligands), and whereas magnesium tends to bind more strongly to nitrogen ligands (perhaps because the N atoms are a little more polarisable than O), calcium binds preferentially to oxygen ligands. And because calcium is larger than magnesium it can interact with a large number of charged groups at once. Calmodulin is a calcium-binding protein of relative molar mass 16 500 found in every cell of every oxygen-using organism. It has four Ca^{2+} binding sites, all involving oxygen donor ligands. Every cell contains quantities of calcium held in this sort of reservoir; when needed, uptake or release can control the concentration of free calcium ions, and thus keep it within very fine limits. Calcium can thus act as a messenger ion, and these finely modulated changes in its concentration control muscle movement, blood clotting and bone growth.

With the transition elements matters become more complicated still. As you go to the right of the transition series, there is an increasing tendency for the elements to bind to nitrogen and sulphur ligands, resulting in a wider range of complexes of greater stability. And now oxidations and reductions are possible, often in easy single electron steps. But here we come to another constraint within which biological systems had to develop: the stability of water to reduction or oxidation.

Reduction of water produces hydrogen:

$$H^+ + e \rightleftharpoons \tfrac{1}{2}H_2$$

and when the H^+ concentration is 1.0 mol dm^{-3} (or pH = 1), the electrode potential for this process is defined as 0.000 volts. This doesn't correspond to biological reality, whose pH is around 7.0. Under these conditions, the $E°$ value for this process is about -0.4 V. The same sort of ideas apply to the oxidation of water. The corresponding equation is:

$$H_2O \rightleftharpoons 2H^+ + \tfrac{1}{2}O_2 + 2e$$

and at pH 7.0, the $E°$ value is about $+0.8$ V.

In other words, if a redox system with an electrode potential more negative than about -0.4 V occurs in an aqueous solution it will be a strong enough reducing agent to convert the water to hydrogen. Similarly, if the redox system has $E°$ more positive than about 0.8 V, it will tend to oxidise the water to oxygen. This limits the simple transition metal redox systems which can be used: the $E°$ value must lie between -0.4 V and $+0.8$ V. On the other hand, the redox potential of a transition metal is very sensitive to the ligand, so living systems can produce tailor-made redox couples by varying the metal complex formed.

Further reading

The Biological Chemistry of the Elements, J J R Fraústo and R J P Williams, Oxford University Press, 1991 (2)

21

POLYMERS

Amidst the bewildering range of available polymers, I have selected those used for just one purpose. It is, however, a pretty demanding purpose and it illustrates most of the strategies used in designing molecules for a particular purpose: for example, alteration of side chains to achieve different properties or increasing cross-linking for increased hardness.

Contact lenses

'Men seldom make passes
At girls who wear glasses'
Dorothy Parker

Not true, of course! There may be good medical reasons for use of contact lenses – such as extreme myopia – but if 99% of wearers do so for aesthetic reasons, what of it? It's hard enough for some of us to think well enough of ourselves; glasses may seem the final ugliness. To exchange specs for contact lenses may set the wearer free.

Any material we want to use for the lenses must meet some pretty stringent requirements. In particular, it must be strong enough to resist deformation when the wearer blinks, it must still allow the eye to be bathed in tears, it must enable the cornea to respire normally. And it must be transparent!

Early lenses were made of glass, but synthetic polymers were introduced at about the time of the second world war. The first polymer to find widespread use was perspex or PMMA (polymethylmethacrylate, more correctly called poly-methyl 2-methylpropenoate; see Figure 21.1a). This is a rigid solid, and if fitted carefully to the cornea so that a film of tears can circulate under the lens, it can be very comfortable.

Wearers of glass lenses had long been familiar with the so-called Sattler's veil which first announced itself as a slowly increasing haze in the vision, followed by the appearance of halos and eventually by irritation and soreness. Glass lenses had a practical time limit of about 3–4 hours as a result of this, and although PMMA wearers experienced it too, with careful design and fitting, PMMA lenses could be tolerated for up to 10 hours. Research showed that Sattler's veil was due to oxygen

(a) PMMA

(b) polydimethylsiloxane

Figure 21.1

deprivation. Because the cornea has no blood supply, it must acquire the oxygen needed by diffusion through the corneal surface. The lens should also be permeable to oxygen, therefore, or the cornea begins to respire anaerobically, producing lactic acid (2-hydroxypropanoic acid), which causes it to swell.

The next development, silicone lenses (see Figure 21.1b), were much more permeable to oxygen and less rigid than PMMA. Presumably the large silicon atom makes for an open enough structure to allow oxygen molecules to diffuse through. But the lenses suffered from the major disadvantage that water would not wet them and this, coupled with the lack of rigidity, meant that it was difficult to get a film of tears on the surface of the eye. One solution is to apply a hydrophilic coating to the surface, but there have been problems with this wearing away or being removed by enthusiastic cleaning.

Both these types of material are still in use world-wide, but they formed the basis for two new types of plastic that are in much greater demand. A small change to the PMMA monomer molecule (replacing the $-CH_3$ in the side chain with $-CH_2-CH_2OH$) produced the so-called hydroxyethylmethacrylate polymer (PHEMA, see Figure 21.2a). Whereas PMMA absorbed no more than 0.5% water, hydrogen bonding to the $-OH$ group allows PHEMA to take in up to 39%, swelling a little as it does so. The more open structure makes for a 70-fold increase in oxygen permeability, too, and a much reduced rigidity.

Now one might think that the more flexible the lens, the more comfortable it will be to wear, but although this is broadly true, the relationship is not quite so simple (Figure 21.3). There is the further problem that as the lens becomes more flexible, it may not adequately resist the deforming pressures of the eyelids, so the optical performance declines (region A in Figure 21.3). As the material becomes more flexible still, deformation occurs, but elastically (region B), and the lens rapidly reassumes the correct shape after blinking. As the plastic becomes even less rigid, the lens may lose its shape over time; this corresponds to C in Figure 21.3. The whole question of the rigidity of the material is therefore a tricky one.

Fortunately we can exercise a close control over the degree of wetting and of the rigidity of these hydrogels by using different side chains in the alkene monomer (see Figure 21.2b–c) and by using mixtures of monomers. The amount of water absorbed by the lens may be as high as 75%, and the lens can be as thin as 0.03 mm,

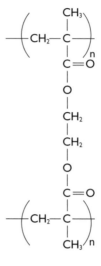

(a) PHEMA

(b) poly-(N-vinylpyrrolidine)   (c) poly-(acrylamide)   (d) Cross-linking of chains

Figure 21.2

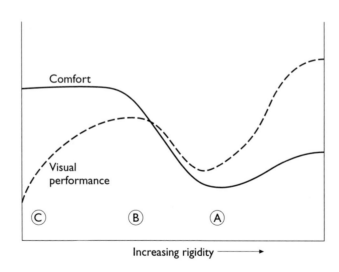

Figure 21.3

thus making for excellent oxygen transfer. Rigidity can be controlled by cross-linking the chains, for example by incorporating the bridging diene in Figure 21.2d.

These so-called hydrogel lenses are now in wide use, and will often be worn for extended periods, being removed only for cleaning and to allow the cornea time to recover. But because of the high water content and the consequent open structure of the polymer, it is relatively easy for contaminants to penetrate the polymer matrix, so scrupulous cleaning is required.

The desirable properties of silicone polymers – especially the high oxygen permeability – have been utilised in the rigid gas permeable (RGP) lenses. This has been done by attaching silicon-containing groups to the alkene monomer, as in Figure 21.4a. A similar effect is obtained by using long fluorocarbon chains, as in Figure 21.4b. Oxygen transport is now as good as or better than in the hydrogels. There is one big advantage over the hydrogels, though: because there is little water absorption, the polymer structure is more compact and surface contamination less of a problem. Extended wear is, therefore, likely to be more satisfactory than for the hydrogels.

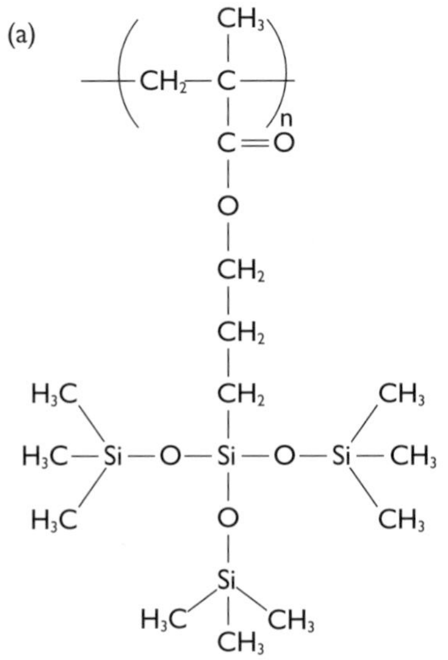

Figure 21.4

Further reading

Contact Lenses, 3rd edn, A J Phillips and J Stone, Butterworths, 1989 is a mammoth tome for the eye care professional. (3)

22

REDOX POTENTIALS

Three key points about electrode potentials are illustrated by the passages here.

1. One redox system will oxidise another if its potential is more positive than that of the other (and vice versa: it will reduce another if its potential is more negative).

2. The magnitude of the potential of an electrode is usually altered if the pH of the solution is altered.

3. Similarly, the electrode potential is changed by formation of complexes with different ligands.

THORP

Many of the fission products formed in nuclear reactors are themselves strong neutron absorbers, so if they are not removed, they will tend to stop the nuclear reactions before all the ^{235}U has undergone fission. To avoid this, the irradiated fuel elements are periodically removed from the reactor and the fission products separated from the unused fuel. The contents of the fuel elements vary from reactor to reactor, but in addition to the uranium and plutonium (both of which can be used for further fission), there will be a variety of transuranium elements (with atomic numbers above 92), and various isotopes of 30 or more other elements, mostly with atomic numbers between 38 and 48, and between 54 and 72. In the old British Magnox reactors, this complex mixture is contained inside a tube made of magnesium–aluminium alloy, but other reactors use different alloys for the canister: stainless steel for gas-cooled reactors and zirconium alloys for water-cooled ones.

British Nuclear Fuels' THORP plant started work in 1994, processing used nuclear fuel from Magnox reactors, although its future is still uncertain. Whatever you think about the desirability of nuclear electricity (and what might have happened if there had been a similar investment in renewables?), you have to admire the ingenuity of the whole process. There is the one problem mentioned above: that the irradiated fuel is an amazingly complex mixture, and its separation is very difficult. To that must be added the hazard of its intense radioactivity: the whole process must be done by remote control. As if that wasn't enough, care must be taken to make sure that there is never a critical amount of plutonium present in any system, either as solid or solution, or an uncontrolled nuclear fission will occur. The critical mass of a lump of solid plutonium is about 10 kg, corresponding to a sphere of radius *just under 5 cm*; but in solution the critical mass is probably around 500 g. Any error you make here will probably be your last. (There is no criticality problem with the uranium because the ^{235}U isotope is diluted with large amounts of non-fissile ^{238}U.)

Before anything can be done, the fuel rods are immersed in cooling ponds of water for three months or so. During this time, the shorter nuclides – such as ^{131}I, half life eight days – lose much of their activity. Then the chemistry can begin.

The whole process relies upon redox processes and solvent extraction. The relevant redox potentials are given in Figure 22.1, and the whole process is summarised in Figure 22.2.

Data: standard electrode potentials:

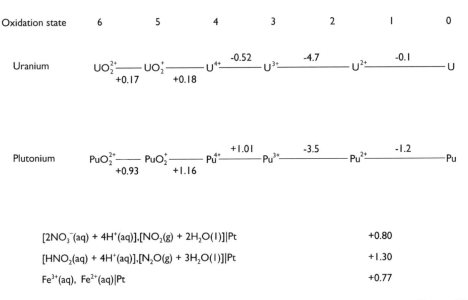

Oxidation state	6	5	4	3	2	I	0

Uranium: UO_2^{2+} —$+0.17$— UO_2^+ —$+0.18$— U^{4+} —-0.52— U^{3+} —-4.7— U^{2+} —-0.1— U

Plutonium: PuO_2^{2+} —$+0.93$— PuO_2^+ —$+1.16$— Pu^{4+} —$+1.01$— Pu^{3+} —-3.5— Pu^{2+} —-1.2— Pu

$[2NO_3^-(aq) + 4H^+(aq)],[NO_2(g) + 2H_2O(l)]\|Pt$	$+0.80$
$[HNO_2(aq) + 4H^+(aq)],[N_2O(g) + 3H_2O(l)]\|Pt$	$+1.30$
$Fe^{3+}(aq), Fe^{2+}(aq)\|Pt$	$+0.77$

Figure 22.1

The old fuel rods are chopped up and dropped into 7M nitric acid at 90°C. This is reduced to NO_2 and oxidises all the fuel rods and the casing. The redox potentials show that the HNO_3 can oxidise uranium all the way up to UO_2^{2+}, but that it should take plutonium no higher than Pu^{3+} (the Pu^{4+}, Pu^{3+} couple is more positive than that of nitric acid, so the nitric acid is not strong enough to oxidise the Pu^{3+}). In fact the plutonium *is* oxidised to Pu^{4+}: this is a consequence of the fact that the nitric acid is 7.0M, not 1.0M (as is required for the definition of E°, of course) and the reaction is done at 90°C, not 25°C.

The first of the solvent extractions is now carried out, using a 20% solution of tributyl phosphate (TBP) in kerosene. All the fission products remain in the aqueous solution whereas the UO_2^{2+} and Pu^{4+} ions pass into solution in the TBP/kerosene solvent. This solution is then treated with an aqueous solution of an iron (II) salt. The Pu^{4+} ions are reduced to Pu^{3+}, which dissolve into the aqueous

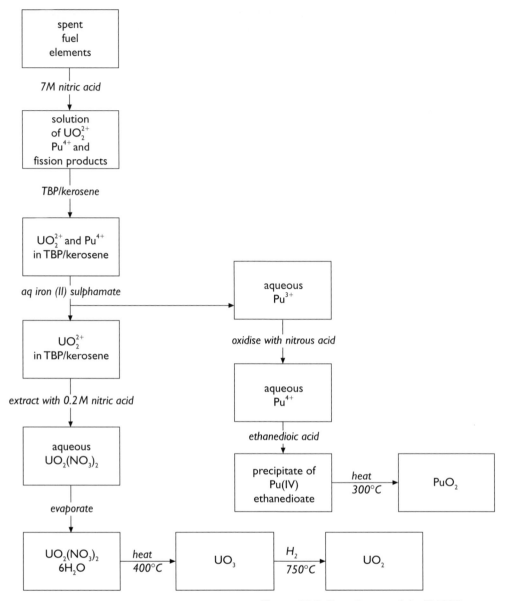

Figure 22.2 Flow diagram of the THORP process

solution, leaving the UO_2^{2+} unaffected in the TBP/kerosene solution. (An alternative to the iron (II) salt is to use a solution of U^{4+}. The Pu^{4+}, Pu^{3+} couple is more positive than any of the uranium couples, so Pu^{4+} should be able to oxidise any uranium ion all the way up to UO_2^{2+}, and the plutonium ends up as Pu^{3+}.)

The separation is now essentially complete (although in practice it is nothing like as perfect as this implies and much repetition may be needed). All that is required is work-up of the solutions into oxide fuel elements. There are two more redox processes: oxidation of Pu^{3+} to Pu^{4+} with nitric (III) (nitrous) acid and reduction of UO_3 to UO_2 using hydrogen.

Further reading

Chemistry of the Elements, N N Greenwood and A Earnshaw, Pergamon, 1989 (2)

SODs

Data: some standard electrode potentials:

Reaction	Standard electrode potential (V) at pH:		
	0	7	14
$O_2 + H^+ + e^- \rightleftharpoons HO_2$	-0.13		
$O_2 + e^- \rightleftharpoons O_2^-$		-0.33	
$HO_2 + H^+ + e^- \rightleftharpoons H_2O_2$	$+1.51$		
$O_2^- + 2H^+ + e^- \rightleftharpoons H_2O_2$		$+0.89$	
$Fe^{3+} + e^- \rightleftharpoons Fe^{2+}$	$+0.77$	$+0.2*$	$-0.86*$
$Cu^{2+} + e^- \rightleftharpoons Cu^+$	$+0.16$	$+0.9*$	$+0.14*$
$Mn^{3+} + e^- \rightleftharpoons Mn^{2+}$	$+1.5$	$+0.9*$	$-0.23*$

*These reactions are not as simple as written: see below.

As we have seen elsewhere (page 93), breathing oxygen is not a wholly satisfactory business (though admittedly it's better than the alternative). The superoxide ion, O_2^-, is very easily formed by a variety of reactions, and it is so damaging in the body that there are a number of enzymes devoted to its destruction, called superoxide dismutases, or SODs for short. These SODs catalyse the disproportionation reaction

$$2O_2^- + 2H^+ \rightarrow H_2O_2 + O_2$$

and the hydrogen peroxide is then destroyed by another enzyme, catalase. The SODs and catalase thus work together to protect us from the toxic effects of oxygen. One SOD consists of a protein containing an iron atom, and as the enzyme operates, the iron shuttles back and forth between its two common oxidation states.

The feasibility of this can be examined by looking at standard electrode potentials. Now E° values are normally quoted under acidic conditions, with the concentrations (or, strictly, the activity) of the H^+ ion set at 1.0 mol dm^{-3} (that is, at pH = 0). If we consider the equilibrium for the formation of superoxide, at pH zero this will be:

$$O_2 + H^+ + e^- \rightleftharpoons HO_2$$

and its value is -0.13 V. But of course biological systems function at a pH of around 7. As the pH is raised – i.e. as the hydrogen ion concentration is lowered – Le Chatelier's Principle would predict that this equilibrium lies more to the left, the couple becomes a better electron donor and thus more reducing and so the electrode potential should become more negative. At pH 7 the equilibrium becomes:

$$O_2 + e^- \rightleftharpoons O_2^-$$

and the electrode potential is now -0.33 V.

Similarly we have to find the value of the electrode potential for the Fe^{3+}, Fe^{2+} system at pH 7. Since the H^+ ion does not appear in the equilibrium:

$$Fe^{3+}(aq) + e^- \rightleftharpoons Fe^{2+}(aq)$$

it is less obvious why the electrode potential will alter as the pH increases. But if this equilibrium was set up at pH = 14, in the presence of OH^- ions at a concentration of 1.0 mol dm^{-3}, we should instead have:

$$Fe(OH)_3(s) + e^- \rightleftharpoons Fe(OH)_2(s) + OH^-(aq)$$

and the $E°$ value has become much more negative. This means that Fe^{2+} is more easily oxidised to Fe^{3+} under alkaline conditions, hardly surprising since the oxidation involves removal of an electron from neutral $Fe(OH)_2$ rather than the positive Fe^{2+} ion.

Whether iron (III) exists at pH 7 as aqueous ions or as the solid hydroxide depends on the hydroxide's solubility. The same is also true of the iron (II) ions, and of course the solubilities of the two solids are not the same. The details are not important; all this is merely to explain why the $E°$ value varies with pH and also why this variation is not simple. The electrode potential for the Fe^{3+}, Fe^{2+} couple is $+0.77$ V at pH 0 and $+0.2$ V at pH 7.

We need to examine the reactions:

$Fe^{III} \rightarrow Fe^{II}$ $\qquad\qquad$ $EFe^{3+} + O_2^- \rightarrow EFe^{2+} + O_2$ $\qquad\qquad$ [1]

followed by

$Fe^{II} \rightarrow Fe^{III}$ $\qquad\qquad$ $EFe^{2+} + O_2^- + 2H^+ \rightarrow EFe^{3+} + H_2O_2$ $\qquad\qquad$ [2]

(where EFe denotes the enzyme–iron complex.)

If reaction [1] is to occur, the electrode potential of the enzyme in its iron (III) form must be more positive than that of the O_2, O_2^- couple. In other words, it must be greater than -0.33 V. Since at pH 7 the value for $Fe^{3+}(sq)$, $Fe^{2+}(aq)$ is about $+0.2$ V, this is likely to be true (although – see below – the presence of the enzyme as a ligand might alter things a little).

For reaction [2] to occur, the Fe^{3+}, Fe^{2+} couple ($+0.2$ V) must be less positive than the O_2^-, H_2O_2 couple ($+0.89$ V) and, again, this is likely to be true.

This analysis enables us to understand how there can be a variety of superoxide dismutases, containing different metal ions. The requirement is that the metal must have two oxidation states, differing by one, and the electrode potential (at pH 7) for the couple $M^{(n+1)+}$, M^{n+} must lie between -0.33 and $+0.89$. In addition to the FeSOD described here, there is a copper–zinc–SOD and a manganese–SOD. Now the electrode potential for both the Cu^{2+}, Cu^+ and the Mn^{3+}, Mn^{2+} couples at pH 7 is about $+0.9$ V. This is more positive than -0.33 V, so a reaction like equation [1] above can clearly occur. On the other hand, $E°$ for both the Cu^{2+}, Cu^+ and the Mn^{3+}, Mn^{2+} couples seems to be greater than $+0.89$ V, so reaction [2] would not be feasible. How can this be explained?

This must be due to the alteration of the electrode potential by complex formation. For example, whereas the $E°$ value for the Fe^{3+}, Fe^{2+} couple is $+0.77$ V, that for the $Fe(CN)_6^{3-}$, $Fe(CN)_6^{4-}$ couple is $+0.28$ V. In this case, interaction of the CN^- ligands is stronger with the Fe^{3+} than the Fe^{2+} ions, so the electrode potential falls. A similar state of affairs must arise in the enzyme: interaction with the protein of both the Cu^{2+}, Cu^+ and the Mn^{3+}, Mn^{2+} systems must reduce their electrode potentials so that they fall into the crucial range: -0.33 to $+0.89$ V.

Further reading

There is likely to be something on this in any textbook of biochemistry or bioinorganic chemistry: I consulted **Principles of Bioinorganic Chemistry**, S J Lippard and J M Berg, University Science Books, 1994 (2)

SHAPES

The theory that the shapes of molecules are determined by the repulsions of pairs of electrons is covered well in a hundred textbooks, so I make no mention of it here. But its conclusions about bond angles – that three pairs of electrons about a central atom will mutually repel to an angle of 120°, or four to an angle of 109°28', for example – are an essential prerequisite to this section.

As well as the exact shape around an atom, however, we must also consider the shape of a molecule as a whole. Here computers can help us not only to visualise the molecule, but even to examine the operation of the electron-pair repulsion theory itself. The overall three-dimensional shape, along with other factors like its polarity, are crucial factors in determining the properties of a molecule – its ability to act as a painkiller, an antibiotic or a sweetener.

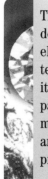

Computer models

Before long most chemists will start building models of the molecules they are working with. It's so much easier to work out what is happening if you can pick up a bigger version of the actual molecule, preferably to scale, and turn it over in your hands. As well as the familiar plastic balls and connectors, computer models are now being devised and used. Although they are not quite as easy to understand as a physical model, they have a number of special features.

First, it's useful to be able to see different representations of the molecule. Figure 23.1 shows several different ways of modelling ethanol: as a wire skeleton, a ball and stick model and a space-filling model, in which the atom is shown with dimensions equal to the van der Waals' radius of the atom. This last one is revealing: too often we forget that molecules are blobby objects.

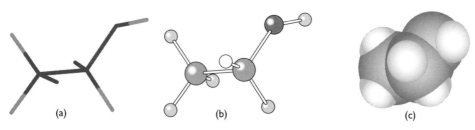

Figure 23.1 Different representations of a molecule of ethanol

The computer can be made to perform a range of calculations on the models. Figure 23.2 shows the results of using the modelling software Nemesis to determine the charges on each atom in a molecule of ethanol. The calculated value for the dipole moment is 4.67×10^{-30} C m (1.40 debyes); compare this with the data book value of 5.64×10^{-30} C m (1.69 debyes).

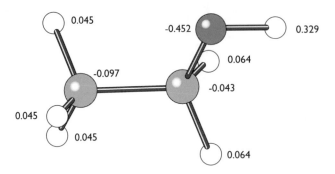

Figure 23.2 Charges on ethanol

The overall energy of a molecule can be thought of as being made up of several components, and these can be calculated and added together to find the total energy. Different programs do this in different ways. How Nemesis works can be seen by calculating the energies of the cyclic saturated hydrocarbons as the ring size increases. This is plotted in Figure 23.3.

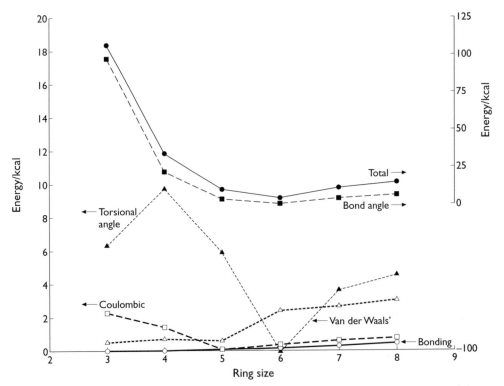

Figure 23.3 Energy vs ring size for cycloalkanes (from Nemesis)

(The energies are quoted in kcal; whatever IUPAC may say, many academic chemists still use the old unit!) In these calculations, Nemesis sums the following:

- bond energy – which varies if the bond has to change from its preferred length

- bond angle energy – this will rise if it is distorted away from the preferred angle. The high value for cyclopropane reflects the enormous strain energy as the bond angle is distorted from the preferred 109°28' down to 60°

- torsional angle energy – this represents interactions between atoms 1,4 to each other, like, say, the hydrogens in ethane

- van der Waals' interaction – if possible, the program calculates the magnitude of the van der Waals' interactions between all the atoms in the molecule.

- coulombic energy – this gives a value to the electrostatic interaction between atoms carrying full or partial charges.

A number of things emerge from these calculations. First, that the six-membered ring is the most stable, closely followed by five and seven. This pattern of stability is largely determined by the bond angle energy, resulting from the strain associated with squashing the bond angle down to 60° (for a C_3 ring) or 90° (for a C_4 ring). In a cyclopropane ring the hydrogens are eclipsed, so the torsional energy is quite high. It is higher still in the cyclobutane ring, because the eclipsed hydrogens on adjacent carbons are closer still, but falls to zero in the C_6 ring, because the hydrogens are now staggered.

Computer modelling programs allow investigation of the energy of the molecule as the shape varies. For example, ethane-1,2-diol can undergo rotation about the two C–O and one C–C bonds. The effects of rotation about the C–C bond are shown in Figure 23.4.

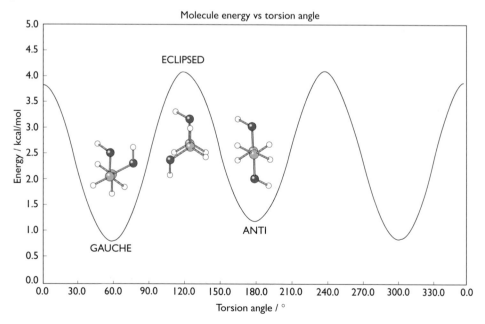

Figure 23.4 Energy of ethane-1,2-diol as the C–C bond is rotated

Not surprisingly, the various staggered arrangements are more stable than the eclipsed ones, but interestingly, it turns out that the gauche arrangement (where the angle between the two −OH groups is 60°) is more stable than the anti arrangement, where the two −OH groups are on opposite sides of the molecule. Presumably this reflects the charge interactions that can occur between the two −OH groups when they are closer. But this gauche arrangement, with angle 60°, is precisely the one required for ethane-1,2-diol to interact with a flavour receptor and taste sweet (see page 183).

There is much else that these computer models can do, with steadily increasing degrees of complexity. Of interest in drugs research is the matching of one molecule to another. The software can be made to superimpose one molecule upon another, and calculate the extent of match of the shape (see page 187).

Further reading

Reading is not much use here: it requires knowledge of quantum mechanics that few people have. The software may be quite hard to understand, too.

Nemesis, both the full version and a more limited sampler disc are available from Oxford Molecular Ltd, The Magdalen Centre, Oxford Science Park, Oxford OX4 4GA.
Molecular Modeller is less powerful than **Nemesis** because it was designed explicitly for school use. It is available from the IMPACT group, Department of Chemistry, University of Surrey, Guildford, Surrey GU2 5XH.

Sweets

Questions of how we smell and taste are proving difficult to unravel. So when Shallenberger and Acree proposed their theory of sweetness in 1967 it seemed like a breakthrough. They proposed that the molecule of every sweet substance must contain an AH, B grouping with the following conditions:

1. A and B are electronegative atoms

2. the distance between the nuclei of the hydrogen atom and the B atom should be 0.30 nm.

They proposed that the sweet molecule must interact with a receptor by two hydrogen bonds, as in Figure 23.5.

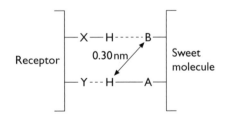

Figure 23.5 The sweet unit reacting with the receptor

X and Y must therefore also be electronegative atoms on the receptor molecule. Later proposals have attempted to modify this by suggesting that

3. if there is also another region which is non-polar or lipophilic, arranged about 0.31 nm from the A atom and 0.53 nm from the B atom, the molecule will taste even sweeter.

In practice, while it is certainly true that the presence of a lipophilic group does enhance sweetness, many sweet molecules seem not to possess one. As one worker in the field has put it: 'there seems little reason to over-complicate [the] original simple and elegant theory . . . in this way'.

And the theory *is* a good one. There is a wide range of substances that taste sweet, including peptides, nitrophenylamines and carbamide derivatives as well as various sugars. Unequivocal identification of the actual AH and B groups of a given molecule may sometimes be difficult, and rotation about single bonds may allow the distance between them to vary widely. For example, a molecule like ethane-1,2-diol may adopt a range of conformations. But if we build models, we can show that the two −OH groups must be in a gauche arrangement (see Figure 23.6). If they are anti to each other, they are too far apart, and the eclipsed arrangement will not only be of higher energy and put the two −OH groups rather too close together, but it also allows formation of hydrogen bonds in a five-membered ring within the molecule, rather than externally to the sweetness receptor.

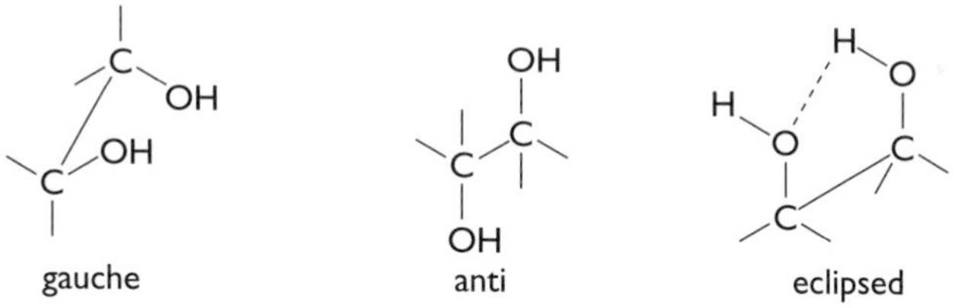

Figure 23.6 Gauche, anti and eclipsed ethane-1,2-diols

This is borne out by the simple sugars. Glucose exists predominantly as a six-membered ring in a chair conformation (see Figure 23.7). There are now several pairs of −OH groups in the appropriate gauche arrangement. But when the 3-deoxyglucopyranose is tasted (that is, glucose with the −OH on carbon 3 replaced by an H atom), the sweetness has gone; the 3-OH group must therefore function as the AH or B (Figure 23.7).

Similar studies implicate the 4-hydroxy group as B or AH. Quite why the 3- and 4-hydroxy groups must be acting in this way, and not, say, the 1- and 2-hydroxy groups, is not clear; it is presumably a function of the shape of the whole molecule.

Comparison of other sweeteners serves to confirm this general approach. Figure 23.8 shows the structures of some synthetic sweeteners, with their AH and B groups identified.

But there are problems. How do differences in sweetness arise? Lactose is only a sixth as sweet as sucrose, whereas saccharin is 350 times sweeter. Why does the

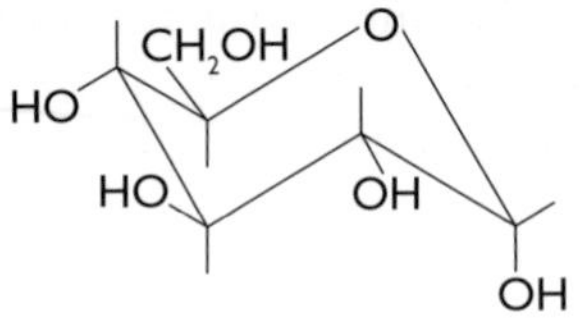

α-D-glucopyranose
(sweet)

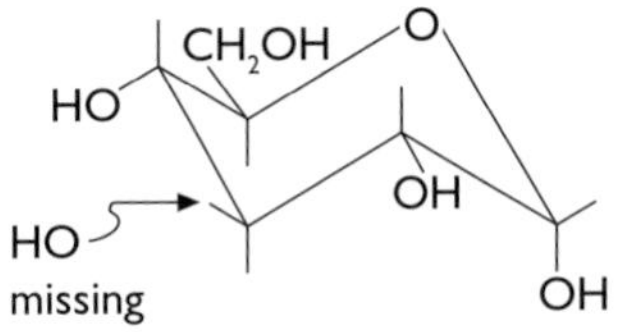

3-deoxy-α-D-glucopyranose
(not sweet)

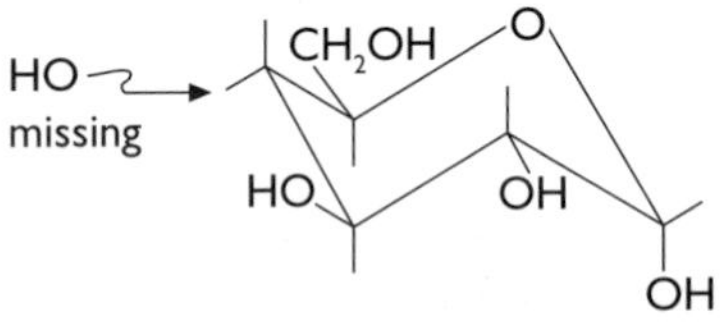

4-deoxy-α-D-glucopyranose
(not sweet)

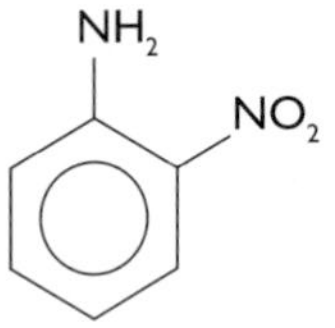

2-nitrophenylamine
[sweet (and very toxic)]

Figure 23.7

aspartame

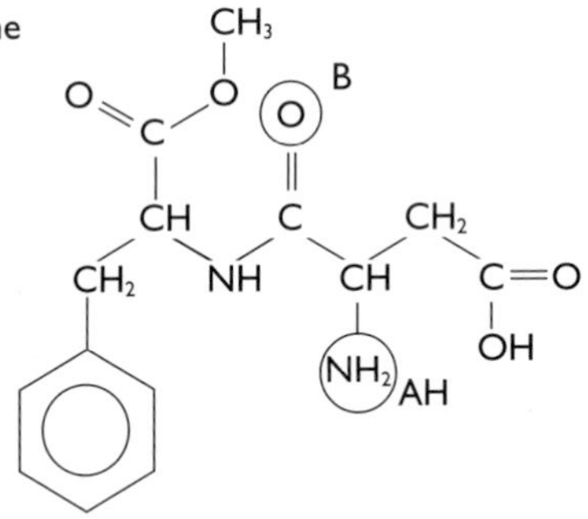

saccharin

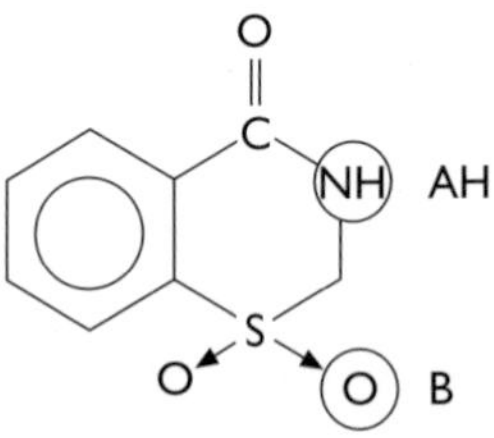

sodium cyclamate

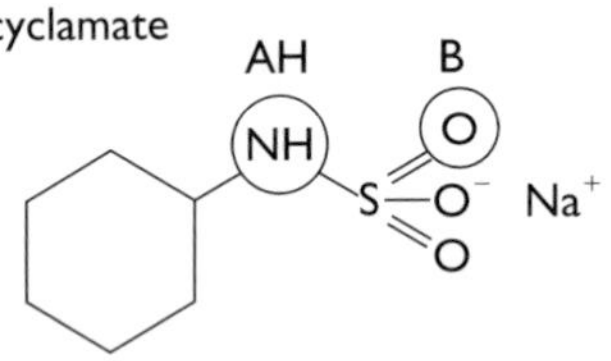

Figure 23.8 Synthetic sweeteners

persistence of the sweetness vary? In other words, why does the sweet taste last longer for some molecules than others? Is there more than one receptor? Calculations of A–B distances based on observed bond angles and lengths suggests that there are three receptors of slightly different geometry. On the other hand, the molecular geometry might alter slightly on binding to the receptor. Why does chemical modification – replacement of an ⁻OH group by ⁻Cl, for example – result in a molecule which is sometimes sweeter than the original sugar, sometimes less sweet, sometimes bitter, sometimes *both* bitter *and* sweet?

And what of beryllium and lead salts, which are very sweet? In Roman times wine was made in lead vessels so as to impart some sweetness to it, a custom that must have caused chronic, even fatal, lead poisoning among the richest men of the city and may indeed have brought about the downfall of the empire. How do we explain the sweetness of these salts? Unless we include ideas about cation hydration there are no possible candidates for the AH or B groups. If we do include the hydration sphere of the cations, and suggest that it is these water molecules which provide the AH and B groups, it is hard to explain why only lead and beryllium ions are sweet and not 20 or 30 other cations as well.

Further reading

Molecular Theory of Sweet Taste: R S Shallenberger and T E Acree, *Nature*, **216**: 481, 1967 (the original paper; 2).
Food, the Chemistry of its Components, T P Coultate, Royal Society of Chemistry, 1988 (2)

Prontosil

Paul Ehrlich was awarded the Nobel Prize for medicine in 1908 for his work on immunity. Ironically, he achieved the triumph for which he is now remembered two years later – the discovery of Salvarsan. Syphilis is very infectious, so it is readily transmitted by sex and its later complications can involve the heart or brain. Invariably fatal in those days, it is now completely curable. But almost more important was Ehrlich's enunciation of the basic principle of drug therapy: that successful drugs will achieve their effect by interaction with *a specific receptor site in the body*, and it will be *a normal chemical interaction*. Ehrlich probably assumed that interaction would be by covalent or ionic bonding, and indeed we now know that Salvarsan forms a covalent bond between the arsenic atom of the drug and the sulphur of an ⁻SH group of one or more proteins of the bacterium. Nowadays we would imagine that a drug could interact by dipole–dipole interactions, hydrogen bonds, van der Waals' forces, hydrophobic interactions and so on as well as actual covalent bonds.

This insistence that drug action was just straightforward chemistry had to wait for 25 years for another example, until the discovery of the antibiotic action of the dye prontosil by Gerhard Domagk in 1935. Domagk was head of the bacteriological and pathological laboratories of the Bayer Company in Elberfeld, working on the response of the body to streptococcus infection. Remembering that Ehrlich had managed to cure some mice of an infection by using an azo dye, he experimented with a selection of Bayer's dyes – including the recently discovered prontosil (Figure 23.9).

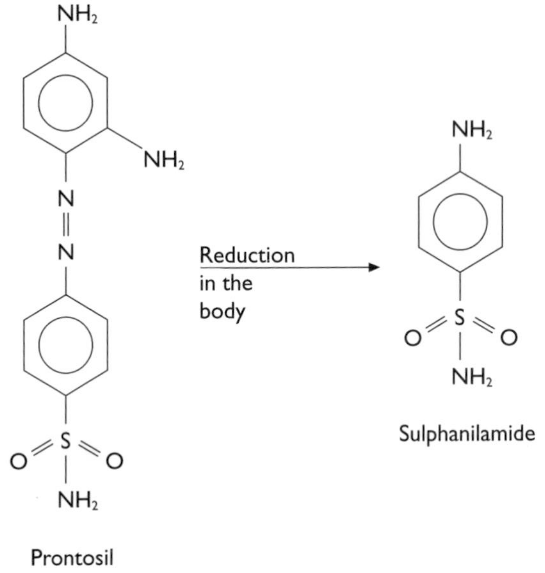

Figure 23.9 The structures of prontosil and sulphanilamide

He did this by establishing a serious streptococcus infection in the mice then injecting them with the dye. The results were dramatic: only one of 14 infected mice survived whereas all 12 of those treated with prontosil did. But azo dyes had been tried as antibiotics before, ultimately without much success, so his employers were unimpressed.

Then on 4th December 1935, Domagk's daughter was making a Christmas present, and going downstairs to get her mother to rethread a needle, she slipped and pricked her hand. Septicaemia set in and within four days she was close to death. (Such a little accident. We forget how tenuous life was in those pre-antibiotic days.) The distraught father begged her doctors to allow him to try prontosil. Her recovery was miraculous. But even then, the German medical establishment ignored him, and the first trials were carried out in London, where prontosil was used in the infections that often set in after childbirth.

Already full of irony, this story had yet another twist. Prontosil was actually totally inactive against bacteria outside the body, and it was only its reduction in the body that created the active compound sulphanilamide (Figure 23.9).

Although better antibiotics have since been developed for many conditions, sulphonamides are still the drugs of first choice for acute urinary tract infections. Their mode of action is now known. Both mammals and bacteria require folic acid as an enzyme cofactor, but whereas mammals cannot make it and must therefore consume it in the diet, bacteria synthesise it.

The enzyme which catalyses this reaction (called dihydrofolate synthetase) uses 4-aminobenzoic acid (Figure 23.10) as one of the building blocks, and it was shown

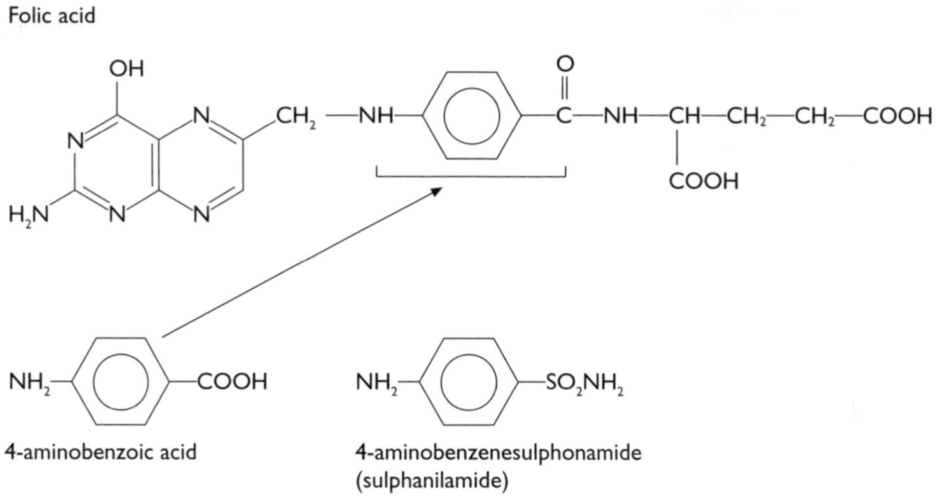

Folic acid

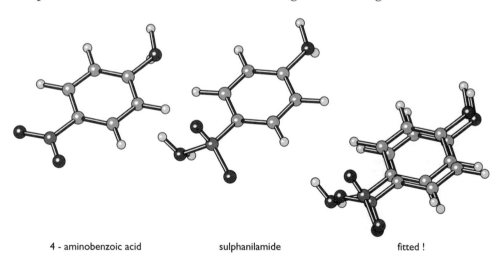

4-aminobenzoic acid

4-aminobenzenesulphonamide
(sulphanilamide)

Figure 23.10 Folic acid, 4-aminobenzoic acid and sulphanilamide

in the early 1960s that sulphanilamide takes its place in binding to the active site of the enzyme. Although the two molecules are similar enough to bind to the enzyme, sulphanilamide binding cannot lead to synthesis of folic acid, so the bacteria die.

The enzyme can accept sulphanilamide in place of the 4-aminobenzoic acid because the two molecules are very similar in most respects. This can readily be shown using models of the two molecules: Figure 23.11 shows the very good match of sulphanilamide and 4-aminobenzoic acid using the modelling software Nemesis.

4 - aminobenzoic acid   sulphanilamide   fitted !

Figure 23.11 Computer match of sulphanilamide and 4-aminobenzoic acid

This use of computer modelling to examine the match of two molecules is now central to drug design. Not only can the physical fit be examined – with calculation of parameters indicating the closeness of the fit, in much the same way as we can examine the degree of fit of data points to a straight line – but the polarities of the molecules can be used to investigate the similarity of the interactions to the active site of the enzyme.

Further reading

Selective Toxicity, Adrien Albert, Chapman and Hall, 1985 (2; a classic).

Painkillers

Almost more than death itself, perhaps, extreme pain terrifies us. Even a toothache destroys normal functioning: what of the crippling pain of surgery or of some cancers? Effective pain relief can speed recovery or make bearable the final days of life. As always, we want a drug that has no side effects: no sickness, no dizziness, no constipation, no addiction.

Unfortunately, opium does all of these things. It is obtained from the latex that oozes out from seed pods of one member of the poppy family. It has been known for at least 2500 years and probably more, and as laudanum it gained complete respectability in Victorian England. Morphine was isolated in 1803 and more than 20 other compounds have now been found in this dried latex. Thousands more related compounds have been synthesised and tested over the last 50 years. Heroin – an early variant on morphine, produced by ethanoylation (acetylation) of the –OH groups – was heralded as a non-addictive (!) alternative when it was introduced in 1898.

It has become apparent that this whole family of compounds can have at least two main effects. Some of them act to produce the same effects as morphine to greater or lesser degree. That is to say, they may act as analgesics (painkillers) and cough suppressants, and they may have many or all of the side effects of morphine itself: lowering of blood pressure, respiratory depression, nausea, dizziness and constipation. Compounds which produce the same effects as the original compound are known as agonists. On the other hand, some of these very similar molecules have quite the reverse effect. They neither act as painkillers nor show the common side effects, and if administered after morphine, they reverse its effects, often rapidly and completely. These are known as antagonists.

Because the molecules are so complex, there are many possible isomers. For example, morphine itself has five chiral carbons (see Figure 23.13), and the stereochemistry of each atom is frequently important. A particular use is made of this in propoxyphene. One stereoisomer is a painkiller, its mirror image is a cough suppressant. It may be possible, therefore, to narrow down the range of effects of any one compound by synthesising optically pure molecules, but of course the more chiral centres there are in the molecule, the more difficult and expensive this becomes.

Figure 23.13 gives the structures of a few agonists and antagonists, and shows how the activity of morphine varies as small changes are made to the molecule. Codeine is used in milder painkillers, some of which can be bought without a prescription; pethidine (also called meperidine) is a rather stronger one (carried by mountain-rescue teams, for example, and also used in childbirth) and methadone is used as a heroin replacement in the treatment of dependent users.

While many of the molecules have evident similarities of structure, some, most notably pethidine, seem to bear no relation to the others. It soon became apparent that the whole molecule was not necessary for the biological activity, but that it must possess certain key features. The crucial bits are shown in Figure 23.14: without these basic elements to the structure, a molecule usually has no opiate-like activity.

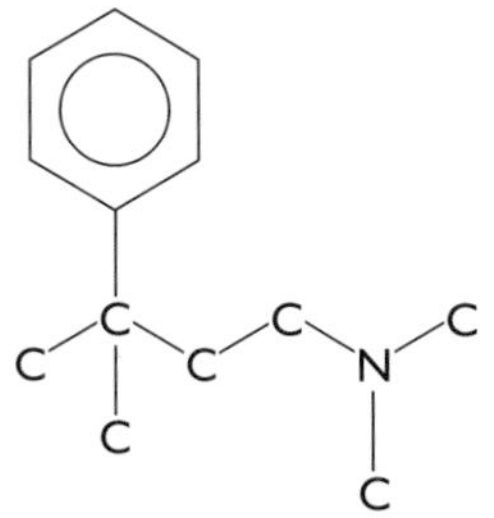

Figure 23.14 The essential bits of an opiate

It was soon observed that although some of the molecules in Figure 23.13 look very different, they can adopt shapes which are in fact very similar. This is shown in Figure 23.15.

Then in 1956, A H Beckett went further, proposing that all of these molecules interacted with a special site in the brain – a receptor – which he characterised as in Figure 23.16.

This receptor site bound the opiate, he suggested, by means of three closely associated regions. There was a flat region to the receptor; this interacted with the benzene ring of the opiate, presumably by van der Waals' forces. Every one of the opiates has a tertiary amine group: this is basic so at physiological pH of around 7.5 it will be protonated and therefore positively charged. There was thus probably a negatively charged region in the receptor (perhaps a $-COO^-$ group in the side chain of a protein) which would attract it. (Later work has made it clear that this anionic region is about 0.80 nm by 0.65 nm in area.) Thirdly, each of the opiates has an awkwardly shaped bit between these two areas of the molecule, so there would have to be a channel, a hollow in the receptor which would allow the molecule to drop into place so that the other interactions could occur. There might be further van der Waals' interactions with this non-polar region of the molecule.

If a molecule is to act as an antagonist, it must be quite similar to the original, because otherwise it will not bind to the receptor site at all. On the other hand, if it is too similar, it may bind so favourably that it triggers the receptor and produces the same effects as the original, in other words, act as an agonist. Figures 23.17 and 23.18 show how two of the opiates fit into the Beckett receptor.

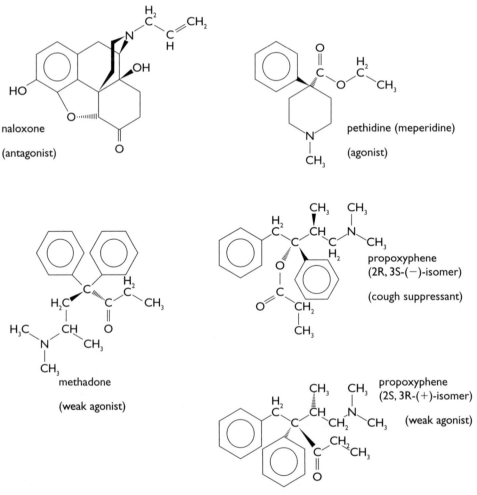

RO-	R'O-	Compound	Activity
HO–	HO–	morphine	100%
CH₃COO–	CH₃COO–	heroin	250%
CH₃O–	HO–	codeine	15%
HO–	O=	morphinone	37%

Figure 23.13 Some opioid agonists and antagonists and their relative activities

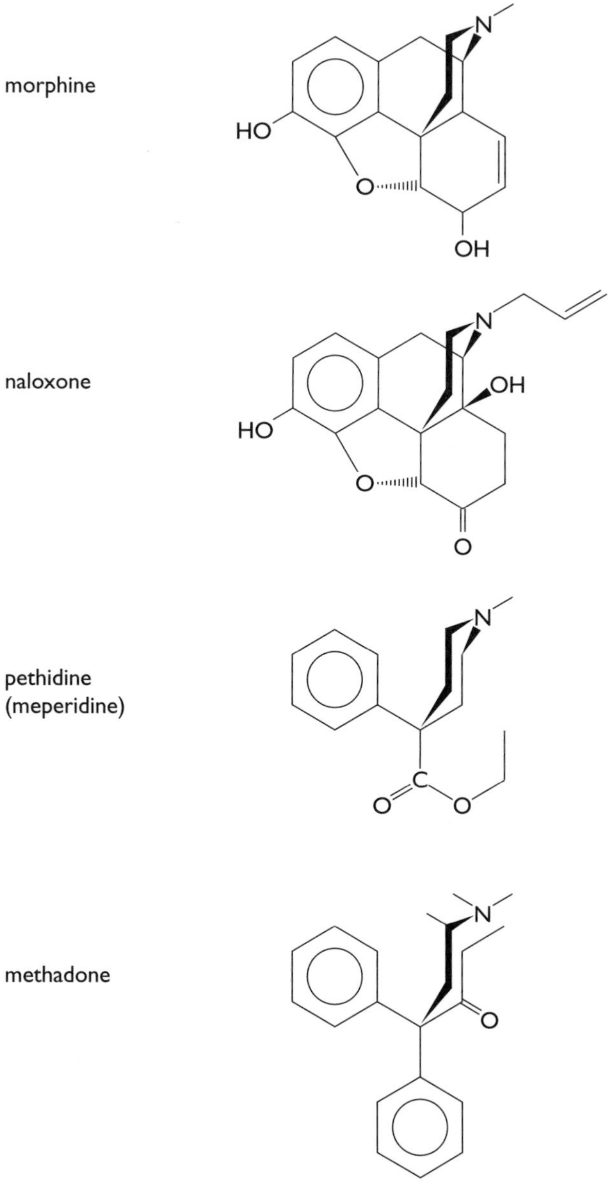

morphine

naloxone

pethidine
(meperidine)

methadone

Figure 23.15 Figure 23.13 redrawn to show similarities in shape

It must be said that although this model is a good start, it is only a start and more complex versions of it have appeared since. There has also been the fascinating discovery that there are several quite small peptides which are made in the body, interact with the same receptors and have the same effects as the opiates. β-endorphin, for example, is a 31-amino acid peptide, about 20 times more potent than morphine. What function do these naturally occurring analgesics perform in the body? What causes their release? Intriguingly, β-endorphin can produce addiction and tolerance in just the same fashion as other drugs. It has been suggested that they are produced in trauma (so a land-mine victim at first feels no

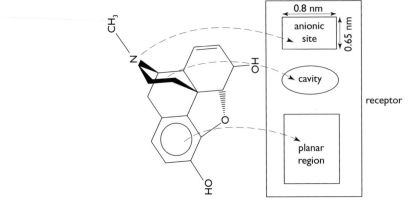

Figure 23.16 Morphine and its receptor

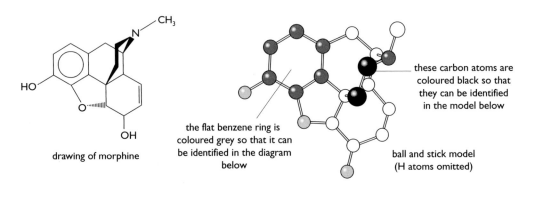

drawing of morphine

the flat benzene ring is coloured grey so that it can be identified in the diagram below

these carbon atoms are coloured black so that they can be identified in the model below

ball and stick model (H atoms omitted)

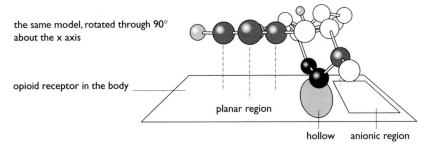

the same model, rotated through 90° about the x axis

opioid receptor in the body

planar region

hollow   anionic region

Figure 23.17 The interaction of morphine with the opioid receptor

pain when his foot is blown off) and in exercise (which may explain the exercise addiction experienced by some people). It is likely that alcohol produces intoxication by stimulating release of endorphins. Certainly naloxone, a classic opioid antagonist, is used to rouse patients who are comatose as a result of excess alcohol.

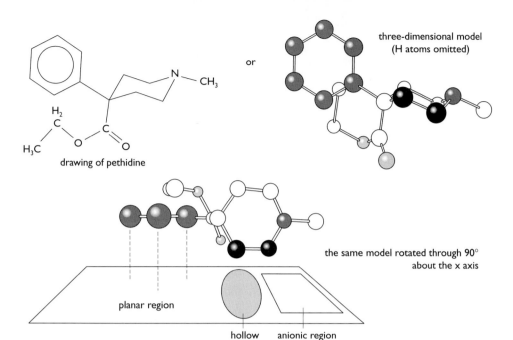

drawing of pethidine

three-dimensional model
(H atoms omitted)

or

the same model rotated through 90°
about the x axis

planar region

hollow   anionic region

Figure 23.18 The interaction of pethidine with the opioid receptor

Further reading

Drugs and the Brain, S H Snyder (one of the key research workers in this field),
Scientific American Books, 1986 (1)

Brainstorming, S H Snyder, Harvard University Press, 1989 (1)

Any modern pharmacology textbook will be useful: that by R H P Rang and M M Dale is good (2).

Internet: search on 'opiate receptor' or 'opioid receptor' (2–3)

24

SPECTROSCOPY

Spectroscopic methods are used everywhere because they often provide answers unobtainable by any other method, so the examples I have chosen are pretty arbitrary. Sampling the surface of a planet or forensic work present particular problems and I have tried to illustrate the special ingenuity needed to get results. Nuclear magnetic resonance imaging (MRI) is routine, but the theory of that is fiendish, so instead I have chosen an example to show how nmr can extend our understanding of body processes.

The atmosphere of Jupiter

Our solar system was formed as the dust and gas surrounding the developing star, our Sun, coalesced and stuck together to form the lumps we call the planets. It is now thought that the atmosphere of Earth (and probably Venus and Mars) arose from gases that escaped from volcanoes on the infant planets (see page 18), but what of the others? Did their atmospheres also arise in this way, or are they just the remnants of the gases that came together to make the Sun? We can establish its composition from the intensities of the so-called Fraunhofer lines in the spectrum of the Sun. Can we compare this with the atmosphere of one of the outer planets?

The Galileo probe was launched on its journey to Jupiter in October 1989 and went into orbit around the planet on 7 December 1995. When the landing module parachuted down, one of the instruments it carried on board was a mass spectrometer, equipped with two different sampling inlets, operating at different pressures. One opened to sample the atmosphere at between 0.52 and 3.78 bar, the other between 8.21 and about 21 bar. This ensured that the data were gathered from two distinct and fairly closely defined regions of the atmosphere at different altitudes. Some of the data are shown in Figure 24.1. Note that the scale on the y-axis is logarithmic.

The ratio of helium to hydrogen is 0.156 ± 0.006, close to the present value for the Sun, thus strongly suggesting that Jupiter's atmosphere originated there. The amount of carbon is nearly three times the solar value, and there is extra sulphur, too; presumably this arrived in meteorites after the original formation of the planet.

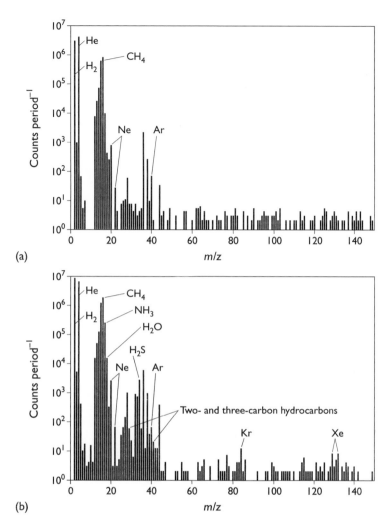

Figure 24.1 Mass spectra from the atmosphere of Jupiter; a) data obtained between 2.72 and 3.05 bar, b) data obtained between 10.6 and 11.3 bar

Further reading

H B Niemann *et al.*, *Science*, **272**, 10 May 1996, p 846 (3)

Internet: search on 'galileo'

Designer drugs

If the police arrest someone in possession of a suspicious substance, they will pass it to a forensic laboratory for identification. In the UK, the analysis will usually be done first by gas chromatography linked to a mass spectrometer (GCMS). Figure 24.2 gives the mass spectra of amphetamine and three synthetic derivatives.

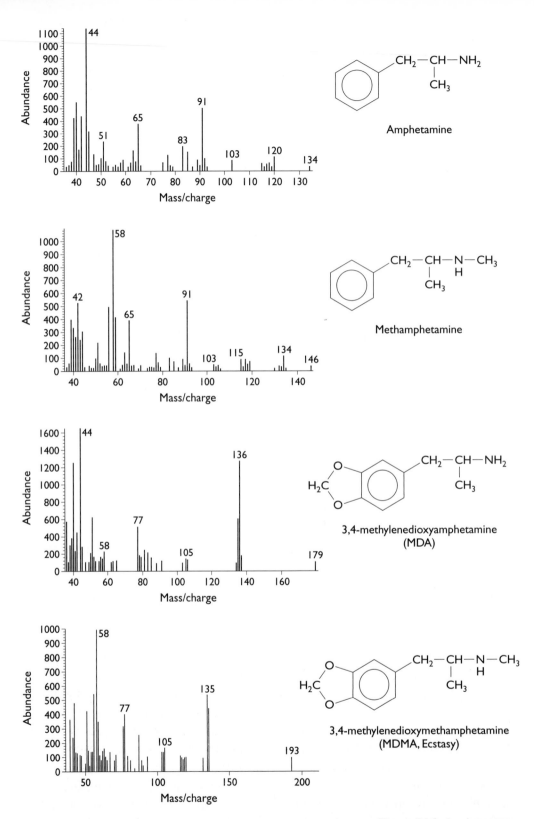

Figure 24.2 Amphetamines

Rather than matching the individual peaks, it is customary to identify a compound from the abundances of the eight most common fragments. The m/z values of the eight most abundant peaks for amphetamine are 44, 40, 91, 42, 38, 65, 45, 51. Tables of eight-peak listings of this type are consulted, and the presence of this pattern in any mass spectrum is sufficient to identify the compound as amphetamine.

But alteration of the structure of a molecule in quite a small fashion may have extraordinary effects. Figure 24.2 shows some changes which convert amphetamine (a stimulant) into the mild hallucinogen MDMA. Who knows what effect further small changes may have? And although these synthetic drugs may have been synthesised by competent chemists, the likelihood is that they have been cooked up in garages or cellars by people who have little idea of what is going on. The products may be quite different from what they expect, or they may be contaminated, or both. This can have tragic consequences. Some years ago, five students, buying what they thought was phencyclidine, PCP, sustained permanent brain damage from a contaminant.

Further reading

Modern Chemical Techniques, Ben Faust, Royal Society of Chemistry, 1992

Forensic infra red

Increasingly, science plays a major role in convicting criminals, and infra red (IR) spectroscopy is a powerful technique in this work.

Often a substance to be identified is a complex mixture. In this case, assignment of individual absorptions is inappropriate, but the whole spectrum can be compared to that of known samples. For example, Figure 24.3 shows the IR spectra of four different black inks. Similar though the spectra are, there are significant differences. For example, Waterman ink has a large peak at about $1666 \, \text{cm}^{-1}$, Mont Blanc lacks the prominent absorption at about $720 \, \text{cm}^{-1}$ and so on.

Usually very small amounts of material are available, perhaps a single fibre. Here the technique of Fourier transform infra red (FTIR) is invaluable. The original IR spectrometers irradiated the sample and measured the extent of absorption for one frequency at a time. It's like playing the piano, one note at a time. Fourier transform instruments blast the sample with the whole range of frequencies, then use a mathematical process to separate out the absorptions at each frequency. (It's a bit like flinging the piano out of a top floor window and using maths to separate out the sound of each note from the resulting crash.) The great advantage is that a Fourier transform scan can be done quickly *and repeatedly*, with each signal being added to the previous ones. The improvement in signal to noise ratio is

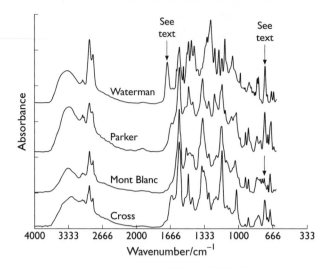

Figure 24.3 IR spectra of four different black inks

proportional to the square root of the number of scans, so 100 scans give a 10-times better spectrum. The spectra shown opposite were obtained using an FTIR spectrometer linked to a microscope. The fibres had been flattened to minimise diffraction and scattering of the light. The aperture through which measurements were taken is given on each spectrum; it may be as small as 30 *micro*metres across.

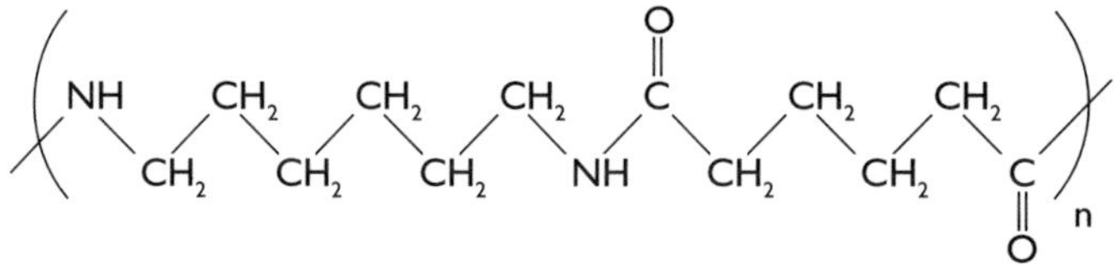

nylon 6,6

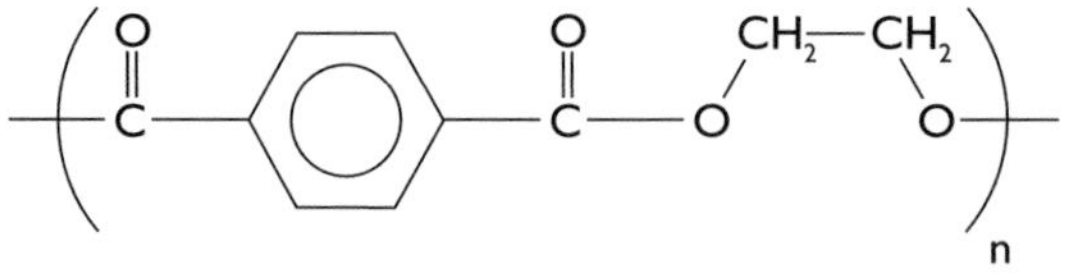

polyester (called Terylene in the UK, Dacron in the US)

Figure 24.4 Structures of nylon 6,6 and polyester

The absorptions from specific bonds can be easily identified: for example, the C=O stretch at 1650–1720 cm^{-1} or the N–H stretch at ~3150 cm^{-1}. But more important for forensic work is the fact that a *single fibre* can be identified and matched to the clothing of a suspect. That might be enough to get a conviction.

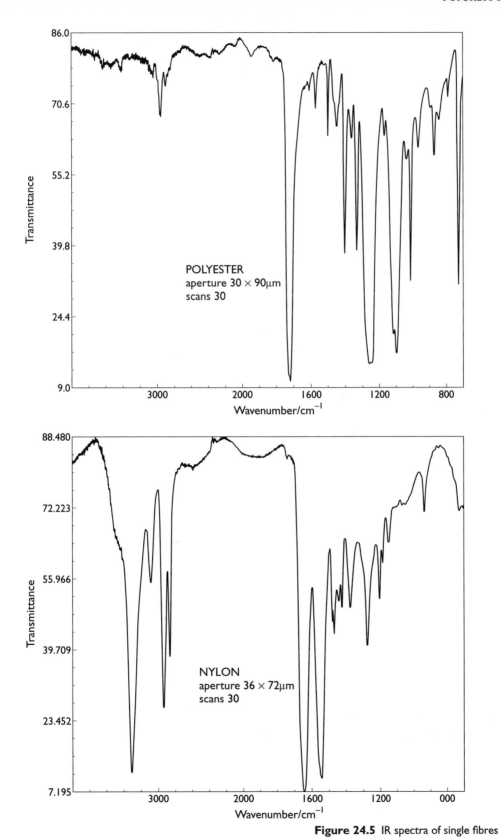

Figure 24.5 IR spectra of single fibres

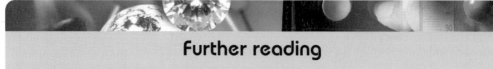

Further reading

Modern Chemical Techniques, Ben Faust, Royal Society of Chemistry, 1992

nmr of living tissue

The nmr spectra of hydrogen nuclei are complex. The spectrum of a small molecule like ethanal has two peaks, one a doublet, the other a quartet. Imagine what the spectrum of a protein or DNA would look like! (But for one use of proton nmr spectra of biological systems, see page 2.) A good alternative nucleus for biological systems is ^{31}P because phosphorus is found in many biological molecules, including ATP and DNA. The spectra are also simpler than proton spectra so the peaks are relatively easy to assign, and the range of chemical shifts is large, covering some 30 ppm, compared to around 10 ppm for ^{1}H, so the peaks are well spread out.

Unfortunately, the ^{31}P nuclei are less sensitive than ^{1}H, so the signals are smaller, but this can be dealt with by use of Fourier transform techniques (see page 197) in which repeated scans are added together to increase the intensity of the signal. As a result, small samples can be used, or insensitive nuclei, provided there is time to do a thousand or more scans.

What sort of information can we get?

Figure 24.6 gives the ^{31}P nmr spectrum of ATP, a molecule which is everywhere in biological systems and which provides energy for biological processes when it is hydrolysed. The first thing to notice is the position of the absorption, in other words, the chemical shift. This evidently depends on the environment of the phosphorus (just as with protons): the three different phosphorus atoms (labelled α, β and γ in Figure 24.6) have very different chemical shifts. Just as with protons, their resonance is split by the adjacent phosphorus atoms, with the absorption of the central phosphorus, the β, split first by one adjacent phosphorus, then each of these signals is split to the same extent by the other, so that the resonance appears to be a triplet. Complexing by Mg^{2+} ions changes all the chemical shifts.

What use can we make of this? Figure 24.7 indicates the sort of information we can get. It shows the ^{31}P signal from a muscle and from the same muscle after prolonged stimulation. (The signal is rather noisy as the concentration of phosphorus in muscle is low.)

There are seven phosphorus absorptions. Six are identified: the three signals from ATP and three from creatine phosphate, inorganic phosphate ions (predominantly $H_2PO_4^{-}$ at this pH) and sugar phosphate, respectively. The origin of the peak at a chemical shift of about zero is unknown.

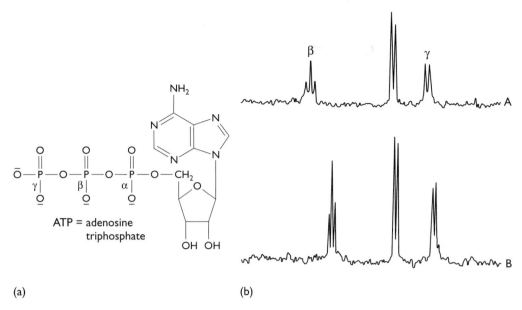

Figure 24.6 a) Structure of ATP (adenosine triphosphate),
b) ^{31}P nmr spectra of ATP (top) and its complex with magnesium
(bottom)

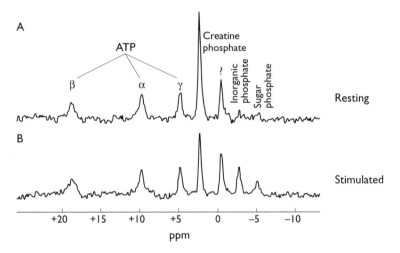

Figure 24.7 The effect of prolonged stimulation
on the ^{31}P spectrum of muscle

After the muscle had been stimulated, the signal due to creatine phosphate falls,
while those from inorganic phosphate and sugar phosphate rise; everything else is
the same. This is exactly what would be expected: as the muscle is stimulated to
contract, its energy store – the creatine phosphate – is used up and the phosphate
ions released either become bound to sugars or exist as free $H_2PO_4^-$. For the first
time, then, we have a technique that can look at *specific molecules* as bodily
changes occur, and with improving instrumentation, we can do this in living
tissues. More exciting still, we can look at signals from specific regions of a
biological sample, thus allowing us to examine phosphorus atoms in different parts
of the tissue.

25

TRANSITION ELEMENTS

Transition elements have a number of properties which differ from those of the s-block or aluminium:

- they usually have a number of oxidation states and interconversions of these are often very easy

- their ions are coloured

- they form a much greater range of complexes, and whereas aluminium and the s-block elements form complexes with oxygen ligands, nitrogen and sulphur ligands become increasingly important as the transition series is crossed from left to right

- the elements and their ions frequently act as catalysts (see page 51).

Testicular cancer

Cancer is usually a disease of age, but not in the testes: 75% of cases of testicular cancer occur in men under 50. It is, however, remarkably curable, by surgery followed by radio- and chemotherapy. The drugs of choice were discovered by accident in 1964.

Platinum forms two isomeric compounds of formula $[PtCl_2(NH_3)_2]$. Carbon doesn't, of course: CH_2Cl_2 exists only in one form, because the molecule is tetrahedral. But these platinum complexes are planar, and the chlorines can be adjacent to each other (*cis*) or on opposite sides of the molecule (*trans*) (Figure 25.1).

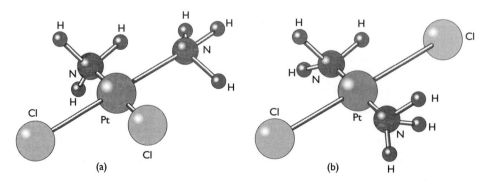

Figure 25.1 a) cisplatin and b) transplatin

The *cis* compound (cisplatin) – but not the *trans* – almost always cures the cancer, even if it has spread beyond the testes, and some 10–15 related platinum compounds are now in clinical trials for this and other cancers. The mode of action of the drug is not yet fully known, but some pointers are beginning to emerge. Because cisplatin is uncharged, it crosses cell membranes relatively easily, and once inside the cell it undergoes a ligand exchange reaction in which the chloride ions are replaced by water molecules to form $[Pt(NH_3)_2Cl(H_2O)]^+$ and $[Pt(NH_3)_2(H_2O)_2]^{2+}$, both still square planar and both still *cis*. These new Pt complexes can react with DNA to form a variety of products. Elegant evidence for this is provided by nmr spectroscopy – but looking at the ^{195}Pt nucleus rather than ^{1}H (Figure 25.2).

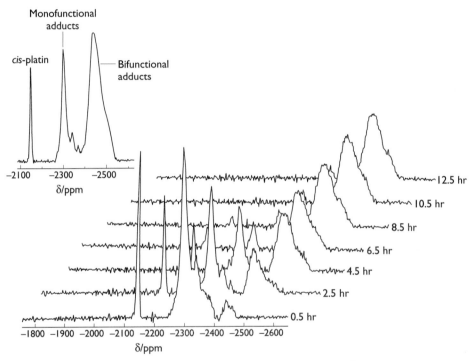

Figure 25.2 ^{195}Pt nmr signals from cisplatin at various times after injection

Within 30 minutes of injection of the drug, a strong signal (at about -2300 ppm) shows that one water molecule has been replaced by some other ligand. Even at this early stage, however, it is clear that a small amount of the bifunctional adduct has been formed in which both of the waters have undergone ligand replacement (nmr signal at about -2500 ppm). After 12 hours all the platinum is in this form.

But what are these new ligands? It is now clear that the major one is the nitrogen atom in the five-membered ring of guanine, one of the constituent bases of DNA (Figure 25.3).

It turns out that the platinum becomes bound to two guanines *adjacent* to each other in the *same* chain of the DNA. This is illustrated in the diagram, which shows the structure of the adduct formed between $[Pt(NH_3)_2(H_2O)_2]^{2+}$ and two guanine residues next to each other in one chain of the DNA. The water molecules are lost

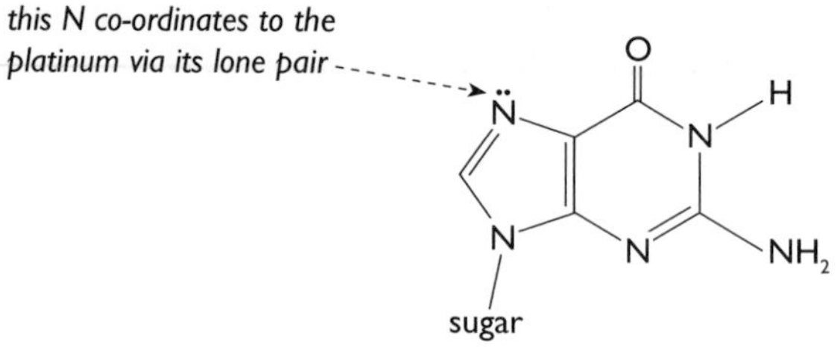

this N co-ordinates to the
platinum via its lone pair

sugar

Figure 25.3 Guanine

and replaced by the guanines. The platinum becomes covalently bonded to the nitrogens in the five-membered ring of the guanine bases. The ammonias remain bonded to the platinum and also hydrogen bond to the carbonyl group in the pyrimidine ring of the guanine (see Figure 25.4). (Although the *trans* isomer can bond to DNA, it does so differently, because the guanines have to co-ordinate in the *trans* positions.)

But what is the effect of the formation of this platinum–DNA compound? First and most obvious, the shape of the DNA molecule is changed. In normal DNA the bases are stacked on top of one another like dinner plates, with a tilt of no more than ±10°. In the platinum–DNA compound, however, the bases are tipped over to an angle of 75–90° – almost *vertical* – leading to an unwinding of the spiral and a bend in the whole DNA molecule of about 32–34° (Figure 25.5). (This is presumably because formation of the two covalent and two hydrogen bonds can only occur if the DNA chain alters shape in this way.)

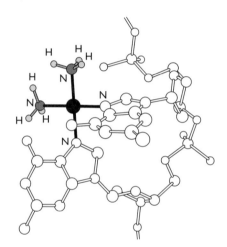

Figure 25.4 Cisplatin binding to two guanines

The change of shape has disastrous consequences: progression of both DNA and RNA polymerases is blocked, so both replication and transcription are prevented.

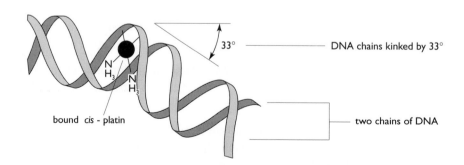

33°   DNA chains kinked by 33°

bound *cis* - platin   two chains of DNA

Figure 25.5 Platinum binding causes the DNA to kink

But there are repair mechanisms in all cells whose sole function is to cut out damaged sections of the DNA and repair it. At the time of writing it seems that there are certain proteins in the cell whose function it is to recognise DNA damage, and that the first step of the repair mechanism is the binding of these proteins to the damage site. But when they bind to the platinated DNA, they bend it even more, and repair is prevented. So the DNA of these platinated cells remains damaged, the cells cannot replicate, and growth of the cancer is stopped. (Of course, all anticancer drugs attack healthy cells as well as malignant ones, but because the cancer cells are dividing so much faster, they are more susceptible to their effects.)

Already, then, we have a drug – or rather, a family of drugs – which is extremely effective against quite a range of cancers, even in some cases when secondary growths have developed. Already other platinum compounds have been developed which are less toxic, with fewer side effects: carboplatin (Figure 25.6) is one of these. It has recently become apparent that certain tumours have developed resistance to cisplatin, and the so-called third-generation drugs have been developed to overcome this resistance. Some of these are shown in Figure 25.6.

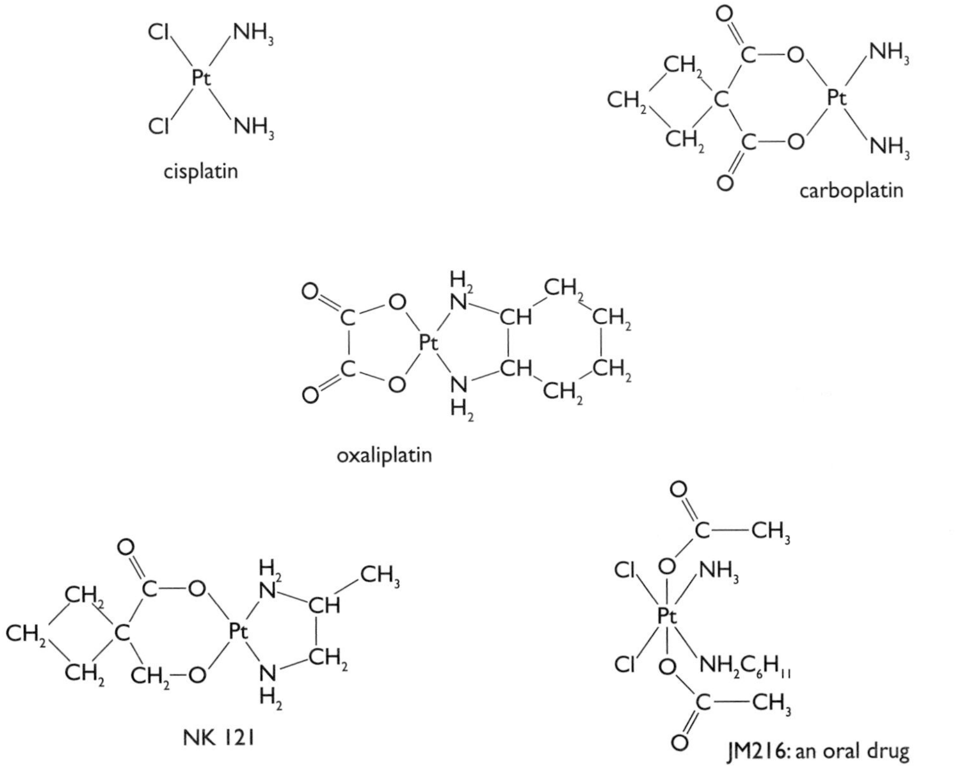

Figure 25.6 Some platinum drugs

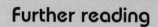

Further reading

Bioinorganic Chemistry, S J Lippard and J M Berg, University Science Books, 1994 (2)
Review article by Jan Reedijk, *Chem Commun*, 1996, p 801 (3)

Internet: search on 'cisplatin'

Haemoglobin

Haemoglobin is the red substance in mammalian red blood cells whose function is to take up oxygen in the lungs and transport it to the muscles, where the oxygen is released. It has four protein subunits. Each subunit consists of a polypeptide chain (two of which are of one type, called the α, and two of which are the so-called β chains), and each chain is attached to an iron (II)–porphyrin group (see Figure 25.7).

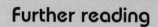

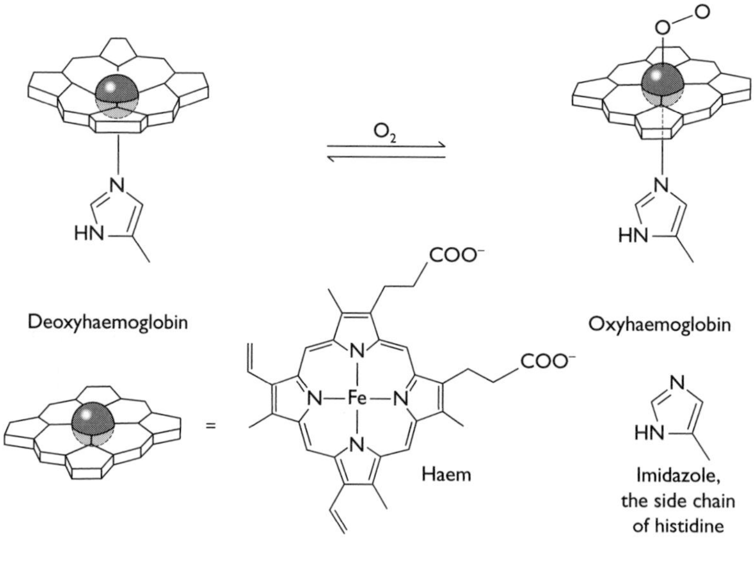

Deoxyhaemoglobin

Oxyhaemoglobin

Haem

Imidazole, the side chain of histidine

Figure 25.7 Haemoglobin

The mechanism of the transport of oxygen has been intensively studied. 'Naked' haem, in which the Fe^{2+}–porphyrin complex has no protein bound to it, is readily and irreversibly oxidised by molecular oxygen to Fe^{3+}, forming a dimer in which the two Fe^{3+} ions are linked by an $-O-O-$ group. One of the functions of the protein chain in each subunit seems to be to prevent this oxidation to the dimer. The oxygen-free form of haemoglobin contains a five-co-ordinate Fe^{2+} ion in which four of the co-ordination positions are occupied by the nitrogen atoms of the porphyrin ring and the fifth by the nitrogen atom in the side chain of a histidine, one of the amino acids of the protein.

In order to understand what happens when the haemoglobin transports oxygen, we shall have to look at some crystal field theory. This theory (see also page 146) assumes that a cation interacts with ligands electrostatically: it attracts a negative ion or the negative end of a polar ligand molecule. But the negatively charged ligand will interact differently with the various d electrons of the cation because the d orbitals are arranged differently in space. Ligands in the horizontal x–y plane (which in haemoglobin are the nitrogens of the porphyrin ring) will repel the electrons in the $d_{x^2-y^2}$ orbital more strongly because that orbital lies along the x and y axes. Similarly, the ligand along the z axis (the nitrogen of the histidine) repels electrons in the d_{z^2} orbital, but since there is just one ligand, the repulsion is less. The other d orbitals (the d_{yz}, d_{xz} and d_{xy}) lie between the axes, so they interact less with the ligands (see Figure 25.8). As a result the d orbitals are of different energy: the d_{yz}, d_{zx} and d_{xy} orbitals are of lower energy than the d_{z^2} orbital and the $d_{x^2-y^2}$ orbital is higher still (Figure 25.9).

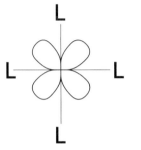

ligands on the x and y axes do not interact
very strongly with the d_{xy} orbital

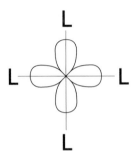

but the $d_{x^2-y^2}$ orbital is aligned along the axes,
so it interacts more strongly with the ligands

Figure 25.8 Interaction of ligands with d orbitals

The iron (II) ion in haemoglobin has electron configuration $3d^6$ and the six electrons arrange themselves as in Figure 25.9 (the so-called high spin arrangement). The diameter of a high spin Fe^{2+} ion (0.156 nm) is a little larger than the central 'hole' of the porphyrin ring, so it sits just above it (rather like an egg on an egg-cup) with the centre of the Fe^{2+} ion some 0.04 nm above the plane of the porphyrin ring (which is slightly puckered).

But then the haemoglobin takes up an oxygen molecule. How does it do this? The main piece of information comes from the stretching frequency (in the infra red region) of the O–O bond in the various systems:

Species	Stretching frequency/cm^{-1}
O_2^+	1905
O_2	1580
O_2^-	1097
O_2^{2-}	802
oxyhaemoglobin	~1105

The stretching frequency of the $O-O$ bond in oxyhaemoglobin suggests that after it has bonded it becomes an O_2^- ion. The Fe^{2+} ion has transferred one of its electrons to the O_2 molecule.

The sixth co-ordination position of the iron is now occupied by the oxygen, so we have an approximately octahedral complex, but now of *Fe^{3+}*, and the splitting of the orbitals is both altered and increased. The Fe^{3+} ion is d^5 and because the splitting of the d orbitals has increased, it has become favourable for the electrons to rearrange themselves, with all of them paired up in the lower orbitals, the so-called low spin arrangement (see Figure 25.9).

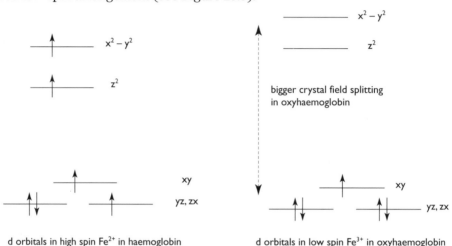

Figure 25.9 Low spin and high spin iron

This low spin Fe^{3+} ion is considerably smaller than high spin Fe^{2+} (its diameter is only 0.11 nm, compared to 0.156 nm) so that *it can now fit into the hole in the porphyrin ring*. As the Fe^{3+} ion drops into the egg-cup, it pulls the nitrogen of the histidine with it, *altering the shape* of the polypeptide chain. At first this has little effect, but when about two oxygen molecules have co-ordinated themselves to the haemoglobin, the combined effect of two Fe^{3+} ions pulling on their histidines is to switch all four subunits of the haemoglobin molecule over into a new shape (called the 'tense' or T state) which *has a higher affinity for oxygen*. Thus we see that the familiar phenomenon of haemoglobin – the first oxygen molecules to bond enhance the binding of subsequent oxygen molecules – is driven by a simple piece of transition metal chemistry.

Further reading

Inorganic Chemistry, 2nd edn, D F Shriver, P W Atkins and C H Longford, Oxford University Press, 1994 (2)

Principles of Bioinorganic Chemistry, S J Lippard and J M Berg, University Science Books, 1994 (2).

The red and the black

Clays are complicated aluminosilicates, with other elements present as impurities. When the right amount of water (about 15–30% by mass) is added, they become plastic and the potter makes whatever shape he wants. The pot is then allowed to dry slowly and much of the water evaporates. (This quite naturally produces some shrinkage and part of the skill of the potter lies in avoiding any cracking as it happens.) The pot is then heated in an oven and further changes occur, depending on the temperature reached. The remaining water is lost in two stages. First, up to about 100°C, the rest of the water added to make the clay plastic is lost. Then the structural water, part of the clay lattice, is lost: this occurs up to about 600°C. If the temperature is raised still further the chemical changes in the clay begin, changes that transform the fragile, biscuit-like material into the strong but brittle stuff familiar to us from bricks, pots, cups and saucers. Exactly what sort of material is produced will depend on the final temperature of firing. The high temperature allows the constituent atoms to break free of the existing lattice and move to new lattice sites, thus giving rise to a new material. If we fire at temperatures up to about 900°C, we end up with terracotta, a relatively soft and porous material, often a characteristic red colour because of free iron(III) oxide in the fired clay. As the temperature of firing is raised, the final substance will be less porous and stronger, presumably because processes with higher activation energies (such as migration of strongly bonded atoms or ions) can occur and the products will be those with the more stable lattices. So at 1000–1200°C we get the pottery we call earthenware, at 1300°C, stoneware, and above this, porcelain. The colour darkens as the iron(III) oxide disappears and the iron atoms migrate into the aluminosilicate structure. Even without a surface glaze being applied, the increased temperature thus makes a more glassy and more extensively cross-linked material.

When you reflect that decomposition of $CaCO_3$, requiring a temperature of about 800°C, can only just be accomplished in a bunsen, the achievement of our ancestors in firing clays to 1300°C or more is pretty impressive. Still more impressive is the chemical skill that produced the lovely Attic red and black pottery. These utterly characteristic vases originated in Greece before 600 BC (see Figure 25.10). They are among the earliest works that we can trace to individual artists: the pot in Figure 25.10 was painted by a man named Amasis and dates from about 540 BC. These vases are red with figures picked out in black. The red and black colours are produced by altering the oxidation state of the iron impurities in the clay.

Figure 25.10 Attic black vase made by Amasis in about 540 BC

209

First the clay was suspended in a large excess of water. This allowed its separation by particle size. The biggest particles settled fastest and were discarded. The slower-settling finer clay was used to make the body of the pottery and the very finest material, containing the tiniest particles of clay, was set aside to make the slip, which would be used to coat the finished pot and give it a smooth surface. The production of this slip was in itself pretty sophisticated. To the mixture of the finest clay particles with water was added plant material and wood ash. The plant material helped hold the clay in suspension, much as mustard and egg yolk keep vinegar and oil in an emulsion when you are making mayonnaise. The wood ash lowered the melting point of the slip, a crucial requirement for later in the process.

The pot was shaped and dried in air, then the design was painted onto the surface using the slip. These slip-coated areas end up black on the final article. The coating is very thin, about 50 μm in thickness.

Now the crucial firings. The first, in an excess of air, was carried out at about 850°C. The red colour of free iron (III) oxide developed over the whole pot. The air vents of the kiln were then closed and water poured over the fuel. Under these conditions, carbon monoxide and hydrogen would tend to be produced:

$$C + H_2O \rightarrow CO + H_2$$

These would reduce the iron (III) oxide to the black material, a mixture of iron (II) oxide, FeO, and the mixed oxide, magnetite, Fe_3O_4. The pot would now have changed colour and become completely black. Finally, the air supply was restored and the temperature raised rapidly to about 900°C. The slip now melted, covering those parts of the vase where it had been applied, and forming a glassy layer impervious to oxygen. The parts of the surface where slip had not been applied reoxidised and turned red once more. But since oxygen could not get through the very thin coating of sintered slip and reoxidise the iron here, these parts of the vase stayed black.

Further reading

Greek Painted Pottery, R M Cook, Routledge, 1997 (1)
Archaeological Chemistry, Zvi Goffer, John Wiley, 1980 (2)

For related material, see also **Archaeological Chemistry**, A Mark Pollard and Carl Heron, Royal Society of Chemistry, 1996 (2)

Metal poisoning

Although many of the elements of the first transition series (and some of the second) have essential roles in biology (see page 165), some are toxic and all are harmful in excess. Much effort has therefore gone into finding antidotes for metal poisoning.

A metal is retained in the human body, and has its effect, by virtue of binding to some body chemical. So the way to remove it is to find a ligand that will bind more strongly to it – and as specifically as possible – so that essential metals aren't removed as well. The stability of the complexes formed by the elements of the common divalent metals generally follows the order:

$$Ca^{2+} < Mg^{2+} < Mn^{2+} < Fe^{2+} < Co^{2+} < Ni^{2+} < Cu^{2+} > Zn^{2+}$$

Figure 25.11 plots the values of log K for formation of a 1:1 complex: in other words for the equilibrium:

$$M^{2+} + L^{n-} \rightleftharpoons ML^{(2-n)+}$$

It shows that calcium ions form the least stable complexes and copper the strongest (Figure 25.11).

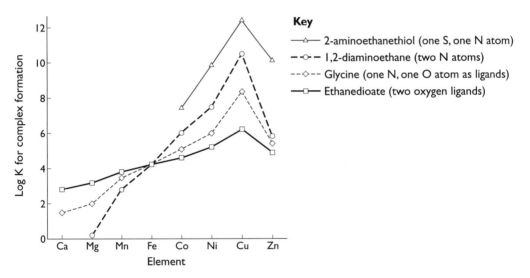

Figure 25.11 Log K plot for elements of the 1st transition series

But there is yet more information in this graph. As you go from Ca^{2+} to Cu^{2+}, the graphs get steeper as the co-ordinating atom changes from oxygen to nitrogen to sulphur. In other words, use of sulphur ligands will favour the elements at the end of the transition series – copper, zinc and nickel – more than oxygen-containing ligands will. If we wish to remove an excess of these elements from the body, therefore, we should use sulphur ligands, whereas to remove the early elements we should rely on oxygen ligands.

In general, the strongest complexes are formed by chelating agents, because not only do they interact by two, three and even up to six ligand atoms, but the entropy terms are likely to be favourable, too. When the hexadentate ligand $EDTA^{4-}$ (Figure 25.12) complexes with magnesium:

$$[Mg(H_2O)_6]^{2+} + EDTA^{4-} \rightleftharpoons [MgEDTA]^{2-} + 6H_2O$$

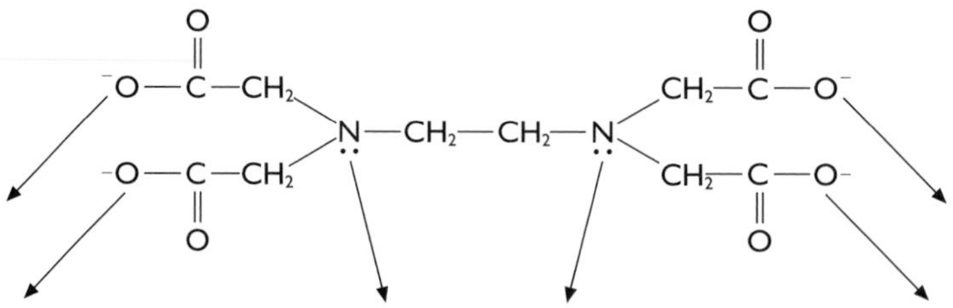

Figure 25.12 Structure of EDTA^{4-}

the free energy change, ΔG, is favourable: -48.7 kJ mol^{-1}. But this is due to the large and positive entropy change as six molecules of water are released ($+211.1$ J K^{-1} mol^{-1}). Indeed, it is generally true that the very high stability of the complexes of chelating polydentate ligands is due to a favourable entropy term. This is why most metal ions occur in the body as chelates – haemoglobin or metal-containing enzymes, for example – and why if we want to extract metals from the body, we should use chelating ligands, if possible. In addition, any ligand should be non-toxic and should result in a water-soluble complex, so that it can be excreted in the urine.

Let's see now how this can be carried out in practice. Every year some small children swallow iron tablets, mistaking them for sweets. Every year patients undergoing repeated blood transfusions for illness (such as sickle cell anaemia or thalassaemia) run into problems of iron overload. Excessive levels of iron cause diarrhoea, headache, fits, coma and death. Desferrioxamine is a hexadentate ligand which forms a very stable complex with iron. If pills have been swallowed, treatment will involve washing out the stomach with a solution of desferrioxamine, and it will be injected intravenously. The $-NH_3^+$ group at the end of the molecule and the residual C=O and N$-$OH groups make the complex rather soluble in water and it is excreted. Unfortunately, because of the $-CO-NH-$ groups, it is vulnerable to hydrolysis in the stomach and gut, so it cannot be taken orally and has to be injected.

Desferrioxamine is also effective in the treatment of workers in the nuclear industry who have ingested small amounts of plutonium.

Like iron, copper is essential for healthy growth (albeit in much smaller amounts) and is toxic in excess; cases of poisoning occur every year. As we have seen, copper shows a preference for nitrogen or sulphur ligands, and an early treatment was injection of dimercaprol, also known as BAL, British Anti-Lewisite, developed in 1917 as an antidote to war gases. However, the injection has to be deep into muscle, which is particularly painful, so although it might be acceptable in an emergency, for the (rare) sufferers of faults of copper metabolism, penicillamine (with one N and one S ligand), which can be taken by mouth, is vastly preferable.

The same sort of regime is used for cases of mercury poisoning, although there are complications. Mercury has such a high affinity for sulphur ligands that it complexes very strongly with $-SH$ groups. (Indeed, this is how it exerts its effect, by binding to enzymes.) But because the complexes are so stable, the mercury

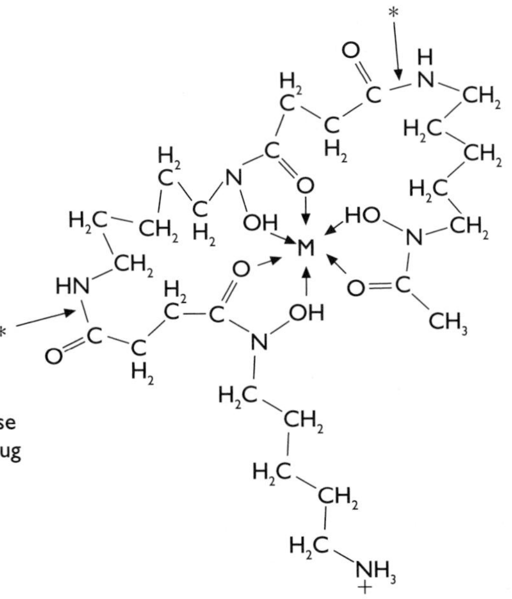

Figure 25.13 Hexadentate desferrioxamine forms an octahedral complex with a metal ion

* risk of hydrolysis at these
amide linkages if the drug
is taken orally

tends to be immobilised rather effectively, and to migrate around the body only rather slowly. Administration of chelating agents will tend to free the mercury from these stable complexes and help to mobilise it – that is their purpose, after all – and there have been suggestions that dimercaprol helps the mercury to cross into the

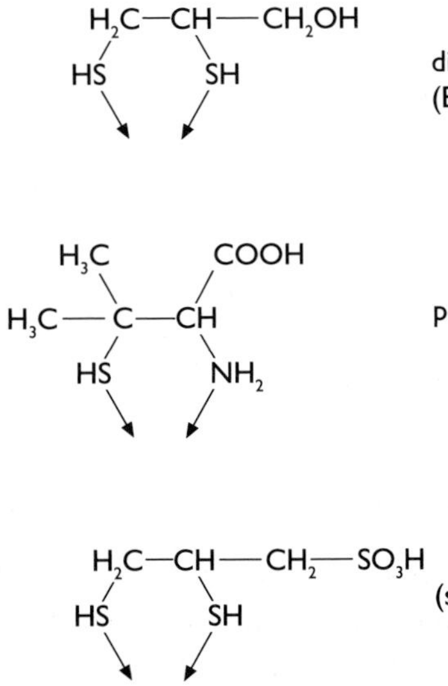

dimercaprol or BAL
(British Anti-Lewisite)

penicillamine

(see text)

Figure 25.14 BAL and penicillamine

brain, and therefore makes its effects worse. The answer is to use the corresponding sulphonic acid (see Figure 25.14). Because the $-SO_3H$ group is such a strong acid, it is almost completely ionised at pH 7.4, and the ligand and its complexes will be charged and therefore much more soluble in water. (Remember, we add $-SO_3H$ groups to dyes or detergents precisely for this reason: to make them more soluble in water.) But since the complex is charged, it is now much less lipid soluble, so will not cross the blood–brain barrier.

Further reading

Selective Toxicity, Adrien Albert, several editions, Chapman and Hall, has some material. (2)

Any pharmacology text; that by H P Rang and M M Dale, Churchill Livingstone, 1991 is good (2)

Old wives' tale 2

Rheumatoid arthritis, often popularly called rheumatism, is an inflammation of the tissue which surrounds the joints. It is *very* painful. As it progresses, it may lead to distorted and misshapen joints, and even bone destruction. It is known to be a disease of the immune system, but the cause remains a mystery. It affects 1 in 200 people between the ages of 40 and 60, so it is not uncommon: one survey suggested that only respiratory tract infections and heart diseases caused more bed disability. Although the symptoms can be helped, there is no cure and the major treatment is just aspirin or other painkillers.

My grandmother used to swear by a copper bracelet as a source of relief for rheumatism. But is this just an old wives' tale or is there any truth to it? Copper is an essential element in the human body – a 70 kg (154 pound, 11 stone) man will contain about 0.11 g of it. It has a number of roles, most notably in the enzyme which reduces harmful NO_2^- ions and in the CuZn-superoxide dismutase, responsible for destruction of the O_2^- free radical (see page 98). Some failure of copper metabolism is associated with arthritis: serum copper levels are raised in arthritis sufferers and there is a corresponding fall in the level of the element in the liver. Whether this is a cause or a consequence of the disease is not clear. Intriguingly, copper miners in Finland, who must surely absorb higher than normal amounts of the element in the course of their working lives, do not suffer from the disease. In other words, although the disease results in high blood copper levels, exposure to copper – which must surely raise the level in the blood – seems to have a beneficial effect. And indeed, studies with over 1500 patients have shown that between 30% and 90% showed some improvement on treatment with copper salts.

Which brings us back to copper bracelets. Could these act as a source of copper compounds in the blood? Certainly. In a nice little experiment done in Australia in 1976, two researchers supplied some arthritis patients with bracelets made of copper and others with bracelets made of anodised aluminium coloured to look exactly like the others but containing no copper. Many of the wearers of the copper bracelets reported an improvement in their condition, and the bracelets lost mass: an average of 13 mg per month. Not only that, analysis showed that the copper concentration in the sweat of the wearers of the bracelets was 100 times greater than normal.

How did this come about? Surely copper is an extremely unreactive metal? That's why it has wide use for water piping, car radiators and so on. And certainly, E° for the Cu^{2+}, Cu couple is +0.34 V, meaning that the reaction:

$$Cu + 2HCl \rightarrow CuCl_2 + H_2$$

is unfavourable, with a positive ΔG. (The Cu^+, Cu couple has E° + 0.52 V, which means that oxidising the metal to copper (I) ions will be even more unfavourable.) But in the presence of an oxidising agent like oxygen gas, a reaction like:

$$Cu(s) + \tfrac{1}{2}O_2(g) + 2H^+(aq) \rightarrow Cu^{2+}(aq) + H_2O(l)$$

becomes feasible. (This is why copper roofs eventually become coated with blue-green copper compounds.) If there are suitable ligands present, so that complexes could form, the reaction could be more favourable still.

Let us not forget that sweat is a positive brew of chemicals. Nineteen amino acids, 10 carboxylic acids and a huge range of other compounds – from phenol to histamine, from nicotine to morphine – have all been identified in human sweat. It is no surprise, then, that the research paper reports that when copper turnings are put into collected sweat, it turns blue.

So the bracelet could dissolve and the mass loss indicates that it does. But could the copper compounds get through the skin, into the body? As always, we must expect that it will be very difficult for an ion to cross a membrane, but in the form of a neutral complex, it may be quite easy. The radioactively labelled glycine complex $^{64}Cu^{2+}(H_2NCH_2COO^-)_2$ has been shown to cross cat skin easily. It is conceivable that the copper compounds formed when the bracelet dissolved could do likewise.

What is not yet known is the actual effect of the copper once it has entered the body. In this context it is very interesting that a number of gold (I) compounds are now in use in arthritis therapy, so it is possible that the effect of copper and gold can be identified in similarities in their chemistry. A number of enzymes are dependent on copper. The superoxide dismutase has been mentioned above; another is lysyl oxidase, an enzyme responsible for tissue repair. It may be that both copper and gold work by exerting some effect on either or both of these enzymes. The relatively easy redox change of Cu(I) to Cu(II), or Au(I) to Au(III), may be relevant here. On the other hand, both copper (I) and gold (I) are soft Lewis acids, with a high affinity for sulphur; it is possible that they exert their effect by complexing with −SH groups of enzymes.

Further reading

Rheumatoid Arthritis, *Scientific American*, **229**: 23, 1973 (1)

Copper Research, W R Walker and D M Keats, *Agents and Actions*, **6**: 454, 1976 (3)

INDEX